£2 paid

SECRET BRITAIN

Also by G. Bernard Wood

YORKSHIRE TRIBUTE (Methuen)
HISTORIC HOMES OF YORKSHIRE (Oliver & Boyd)
NORTH COUNTRY PROFILE (Country Life)
WHAT TO DO FROM SCARBOROUGH (Oliver & Boyd)
SMUGGLERS' BRITAIN (Cassell)
YORKSHIRE (Batsford)

G. Bernard Wood

SECRET BRITAIN

A Tourist's Collection of Hides, Ghosts and Stratagems

With photographs by the author

CASSELL · LONDON

CASSELL & COMPANY LTD
35 Red Lion Square, London WC1
Melbourne, Sydney, Toronto
Johannesburg, Auckland

First published 1968

S.B.N. 304 93197 7

Printed in Great Britain by
Unwin Brothers Limited
Woking and London
F. 668

To

Peter and Barbara

Contents

Illustrations

after page 46

after page 78

after page 110

after page 142

Acknowledgments

Of all the many people who have divulged some secret to me, for this book, or have made information available, I am particularly indebted to the following:

Mrs G. W. Hodgkinson, proprietor of the Wookey Hole Caves, Somerset; Father David Quinlan of Hornsea; The Reverend Mother Superior, Bar Convent, York; Marion Campbell, F.S.A., of Kilberry, Argyll; Lt.-Col. R. A. Irwin of Willingdon, Sussex; Thomas Whittaker of Littlebeck, Whitby.

Invaluable help and co-operation have also come from owners of various country houses, notably the Earl of Halifax, Garrowby, York; Sir Joslan Ingilby, Bart., Ripley Castle, Yorks.; Lt.-Col. Walter Luttrell, Dunster Castle, Somerset; Miss Daphne Du Maurier, Menabilly, Cornwall; Mr and Mrs Bagot, Levens Hall, Westmorland. Permission to take certain photographs has also been generously given by some of the above, and I am grateful to the Dean and Chapter of St David's Cathedral, Pembrokeshire, for kindly allowing me to reproduce my photograph of the *Elijah* panel recently set up there.

Librarians and curators of several museums have also entered into my exploratory scheme with zest and practical help. For securing the loan of rare, out-of-print volumes for my consultation I am especially grateful to J. B. Shackleton, M.A., A.L.A., head of the Aireborough Public Libraries.

Two others have joined in this quest for secret matter: my wife, who has eagerly followed the book through all its stages and prepared many of the illustrations; and our friend, Harold Child, whose kindness in motoring us all over the British Isles in pursuit of any whim must surely have been noted by the Recording Angel.

RAWDON, 1967.

Some Books Consulted

The Secret Valley, Nicholas Size; Warne, 1930.
Wessex Tales, Thomas Hardy; Macmillan, 1903, etc.
Brownsea Island, Bernard C. Short; Looker, 1965.
The Isle of Purbeck, Bernard C. Short; Looker, 1967.
Irregular Border Marriages, Claverhouse; Moray Press, 1934.
The Father Postgate Story, David Quinlan; Horne, 1967.
Kenneth Grahame, 1859–1932, Peter Green; John Murray, 1959.
Mid-Argyll, A Handbook of History, Marion Campbell; Nat. Hist. and Antiq. Soc'y of Mid-Argyll, 1962.
Life of Dr John Barwick, Peter Barwick; Robinson, 1903.
Honest Harry, C. W. Firebrace; John Murray, 1932.
Forgotten Shrines, Dom Bede Camm; Macdonald & Evans, 1910.
Charles Lindley, Viscount Halifax, J. G. Lockhart; Bles, 1936.
Lord Halifax's Ghost Book; Fontana, 1961.
Portrait of Barrie, Cynthia Asquith; James Barrie, 1954.
A Corner in the North, Hastings M. Neville; Reid, 1909.

Prelude

A six-year-old boy peering into the family cradle:

'Now baby brother, quick, before you forget; tell me all about God.'

'Ridin' to our dale-head,
  Lad, what shall we finnd
On this April mornin',
  Thoo, an' me an' t'wind?'

Dorothy Una Ratcliffe, *Yorkshire Lyrics*

'. . . that particular chord . . . that never fails to thrill responsive to such words as *cave, trap-door, sliding panel, bullion, ingots*, or *Spanish dollars*'.

Kenneth Grahame, *The Golden Age*

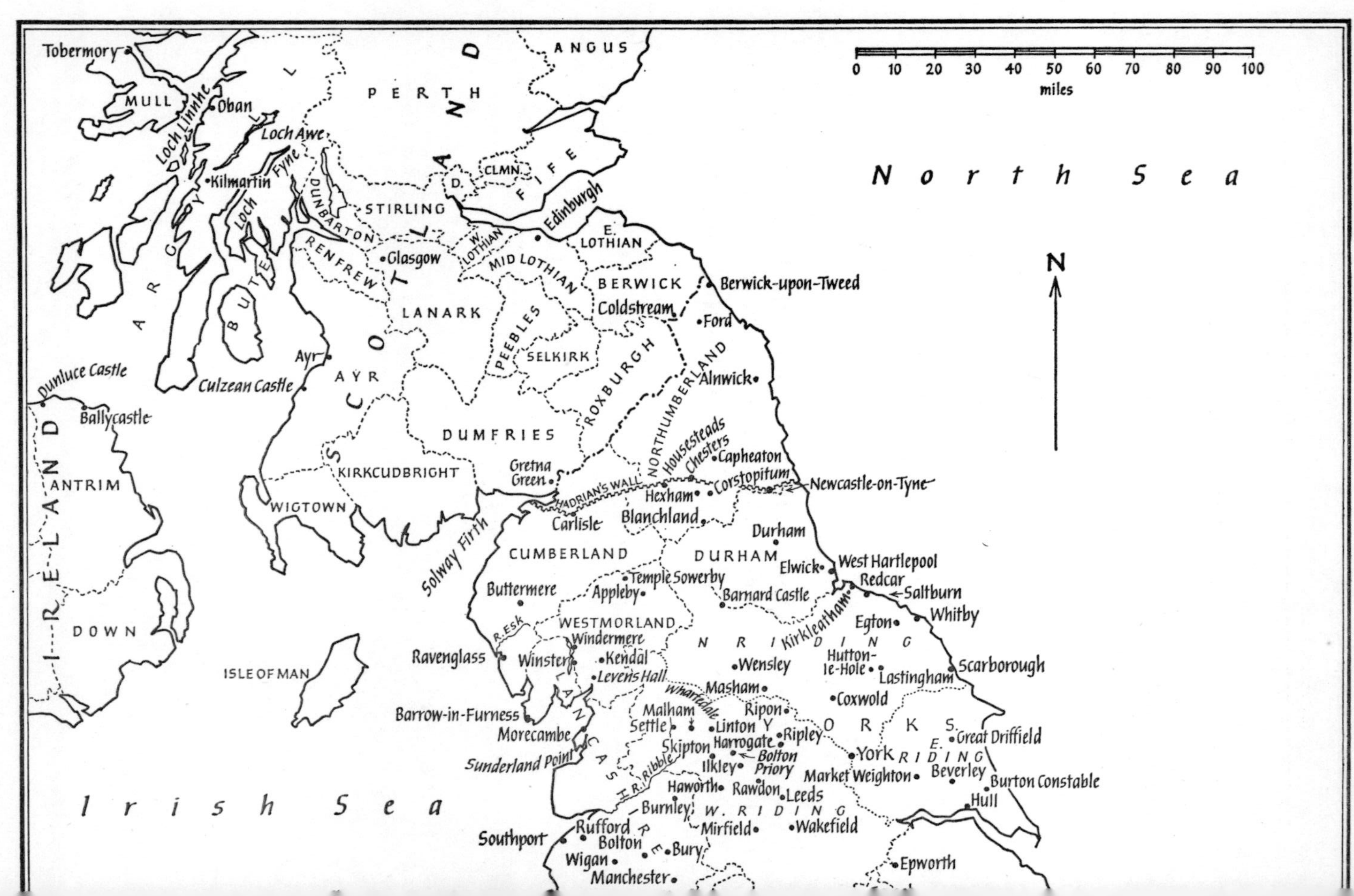

North Sea
Irish Sea
N
0 10 20 30 40 50 60 70 80 90 100
miles
SCOTLAND
IRELAND
YORKS.
LANCASHIRE
ARGYLL
ANGUS
PERTH
FIFE
CLMN.
D.
STIRLING
DUNBARTON
RENFREW
W. LOTHIAN
MID LOTHIAN
E. LOTHIAN
BERWICK
LANARK
PEEBLES
SELKIRK
ROXBURGH
AYR
DUMFRIES
KIRKCUDBRIGHT
WIGTOWN
BUTE
NORTHUMBERLAND
CUMBERLAND
DURHAM
WESTMORLAND
N. RIDING
E. RIDING
W. RIDING
ANTRIM
DOWN
MULL
ISLE OF MAN
Tobermory
Oban
Loch Linnhe
Loch Awe
Kilmartin
Loch Fyne
Glasgow
Edinburgh
Berwick-upon-Tweed
Coldstream
Ford
Alnwick
Ayr
Culzean Castle
Dunluce Castle
Ballycastle
Gretna Green
Hadrian's Wall
Housesteads
Chesters
Capheaton
Corstopitum
Newcastle-on-Tyne
Hexham
Blanchland
Carlisle
Solway Firth
Durham
West Hartlepool
Elwick
Redcar
Saltburn
Whitby
Temple Sowerby
Appleby
Barnard Castle
Kirkleatham
Buttermere
R. Esk
Egton
Windermere
Ravenglass
Winster
Kendal
Levens Hall
Wensley
Hutton-le-Hole
Lastingham
Scarborough
Masham
Wharfedale
Coxwold
Barrow-in-Furness
Malham
Ripon
Settle
Linton
Ripley
Great Driffield
Morecambe
Skipton
Harrogate
Bolton Priory
York
Sunderland Point
R. Ribble
Ilkley
Market Weighton
Beverley
Haworth
Rawdon
Leeds
Burton Constable
Hull
Burnley
Mirfield
Wakefield
Southport
Rufford
Bolton
Bury
Wigan
Manchester
Epworth

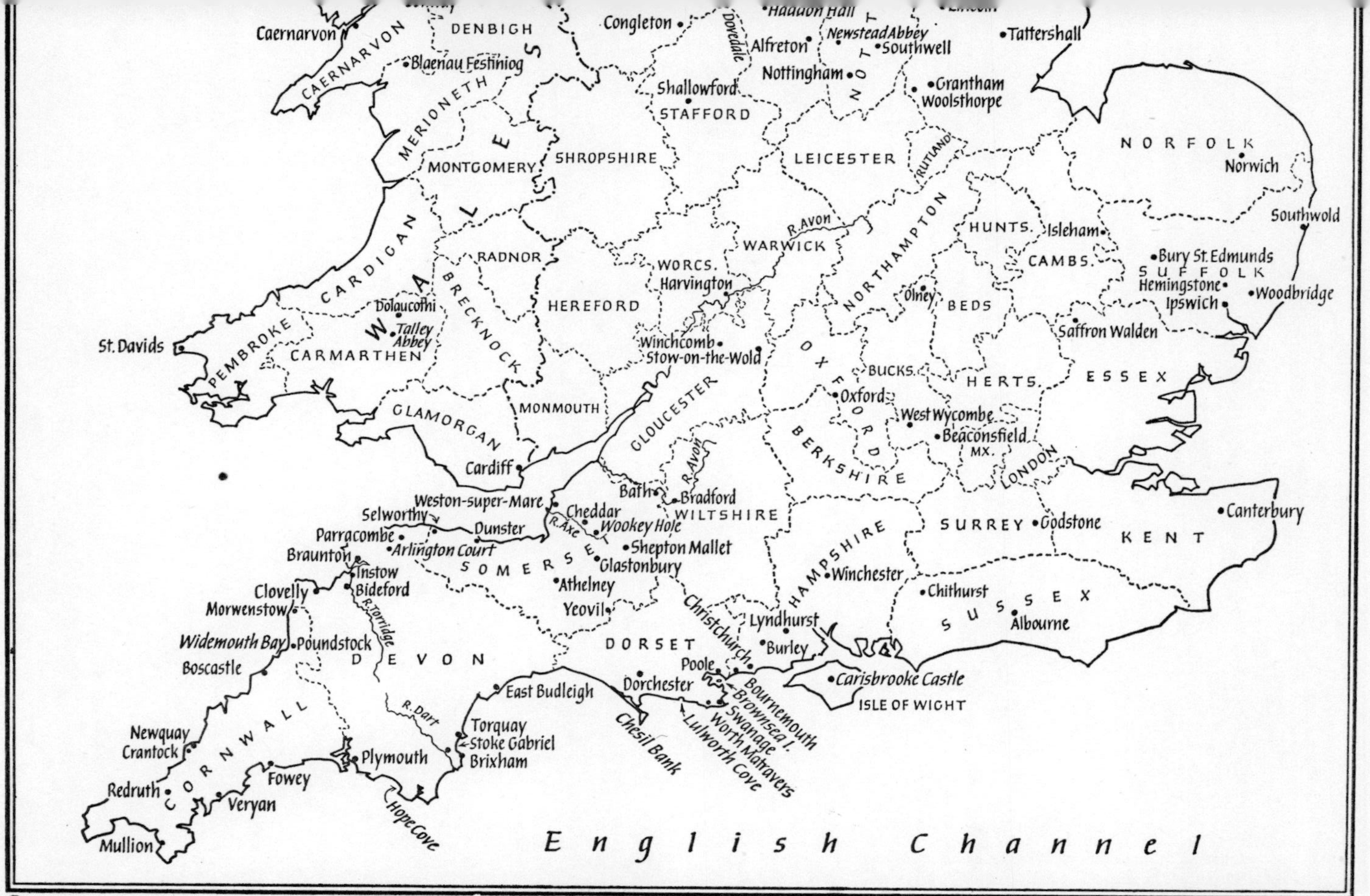

Caernarvon
CAERNARVON
DENBIGH
Blaenau Festiniog
MERIONETH
MONTGOMERY
WALES
CARDIGAN
RADNOR
BRECKNOCK
Dolaucothi
Talley Abbey
St. Davids
PEMBROKE
CARMARTHEN
GLAMORGAN
MONMOUTH
Cardiff
Congleton
SHROPSHIRE
Shallowford
STAFFORD
Dovedale
Haddon Hall
Alfreton
Newstead Abbey
Southwell
Nottingham
NOTT
Grantham
Woolsthorpe
Tattershall
LEICESTER
RUTLAND
WORCS.
Harvington
HEREFORD
R. Avon
WARWICK
NORTHAMPTON
Winchcomb
Stow-on-the-Wold
GLOUCESTER
OXFORD
Oxford
BUCKS.
West Wycombe
Beaconsfield
MX.
LONDON
BERKSHIRE
Olney
BEDS
HUNTS.
Isleham
CAMBS.
HERTS.
Saffron Walden
ESSEX
NORFOLK
Norwich
Southwold
Bury St. Edmunds
SUFFOLK
Hemingstone
Ipswich
Woodbridge
Canterbury
KENT
SURREY
Godstone
SUSSEX
Chithurst
Albourne
HAMPSHIRE
Winchester
Lyndhurst
Burley
Christchurch
Carisbrooke Castle
ISLE OF WIGHT
R. Avon
Bath
Bradford
WILTSHIRE
Weston-super-Mare
Cheddar
Wookey Hole
R. Axe
Shepton Mallet
Glastonbury
SOMERSET
Athelney
Yeovil
Selworthy
Dunster
Parracombe
Arlington Court
Braunton
Instow
Bideford
R. Torridge
Clovelly
Morwenstow
Widemouth Bay
Poundstock
Boscastle
DEVON
DORSET
Poole
Dorchester
Bournemouth
Brownsea I.
Swanage
Worth Matravers
Lulworth Cove
Chesil Bank
East Budleigh
R. Dart
Torquay
Stoke Gabriel
Brixham
Plymouth
Hope Cove
Newquay
Crantock
CORNWALL
Fowey
Redruth
Veryan
Mullion
English Channel

INTRODUCTION

A little girl of my acquaintance leads a secret life, shared only by one other person—a sympathetic, though older cousin. Within their private enclave strange little people are conjured into being; the two girls even exchange letters about their imaginary escapades. I am not privileged to peep further, yet this pattern of things is familiar to all who have much to do with children. My own daughter, I remember, often played when very young with an imaginary friend with whom she held secret converse.

At about the same age the Brontë children evolved their own countries of the mind. Northangerland and Glasstown were the private stage for all manner of wonderful adventures—the more wonderful and satisfying, at the time, because they were evoked within the rather gloomy ambience of Haworth Parsonage. It was left to the perception and diligence of such modern writers as Fannie Elizabeth Ratchford and Phyllis Bentley to plumb the secrecy of those enchanted kingdoms, hidden in microscopic runes.

It would take a wise person to explain satisfactorily this love for something hidden away beyond the common gaze. A few writers like J. M. Barrie, Kenneth Grahame and Elizabeth Goudge have the passport to that magic world. But this much can be said. Man is at heart a secretive creature. His ultimate origin and his destiny are part of the greatest mystery of all—the mystery of existence. Perhaps it is this which so often makes him—at any stage of life—partial and prone to the mysterious, to the obscure, to the 'secret that has never been told'.

But this is primarily a travel book.

My chief object, therefore, is to reveal the *locale* of many secrets which Britons have sensed, or purposely devised through the centuries. The scope of this clandestine quest is, of course, endless.

At different points of time men are hiding from some danger in a lonely cave, or priest-hole; hurriedly concealing treasure; inventing a cryptogram. Henry VIII has a passionate affair with Anne Boleyn, an affair but thinly disguised as the King's 'secret matter'.

In eighteenth-century Sheffield, Benjamin Huntsman thwarts his jealous rivals at first by casting his steel behind carefully guarded doors, but a 'harmless tramp', admitted out of pity one night, sleeps before the fire with one eye open—so Huntsman's secret methods are secret no longer! The Brontë sisters—Angrians still at heart—publish their first efforts under the cloak of rigidly preserved pen-names that keep their readers guessing. Anne Lister of Shibden Hall, near Halifax, writes her copious travel diary in a code that defies elucidation for years. A sculptor at Selby Abbey, West Yorkshire, fashions a leaf-capital which is that and nothing more, until a friendly verger lends one a torch to illuminate the head of George V ingeniously carved inside.

The common factor is *secrecy.*

Nobody can understand Irish folk unless ample allowance is made for the tenuous and unseen. Until recent times, I am told, the boys of Connemara wore red flannel petticoats up to the age of twelve. This was a disguise to cheat the bad fairies who were apt to steal young boys.

That fine writer, Seán O'Fáoláin, once recorded a conversation he had with an old Irish woman about the local fairies. 'Now Anastasia,' he began, 'do you really believe in these spirits?' 'I do not,' she laughed, but added quickly and firmly, 'But they're *there*, mind you!' The same guarded reply once greeted my own query about leprechauns. 'No, no! we don't believe in them now,' said our Bantry hostess, flashing a warning look across to her husband. The 'denial' was, I suspect, simply camouflage, for the visitors' benefit. I am convinced they took the little people completely for granted.

I have no wish to pour scorn on such beliefs. Have not some of our folklorists suggested that fairies, leprechauns, and others of that shy fraternity may have been the last people to inhabit our caves; small, vestigial types who only crept out at night, and live again in folk memory? Not far from my own home, in mid-Airedale, Yorkshire, there is a glen where, in 1917 and again in 1920, some fairies are said to have been *photographed* by two young girls. Later the photographic plates were carefully examined for possible forgery, but declared genuine. Sir Arthur Conan Doyle was so impressed that he and Edward Gardner—by whom the plates were inspected—wrote an article in the *Strand Magazine* about this amazing revelation. Nobody has ever explained, or repeated, the episode.

Scotland's best kept secret is undoubtedly 'Nessie'. What really lies behind the continuing reports of the Loch Ness Monster? This book offers no answer. The author is content to know that after years of derision, obloquy and music-hall jokes, stories of 'Nessie' are at last being treated with an open mind by zoologists. Cameras are even fixed at intervals around the fifty-mile shoreline to record anything strange that may disturb the lake surface.

Other intriguing themes, like the Fairy Flag at Dunvegan Castle, and the Ghostly Harper at Inveraray Castle, are too well known to call for more than this passing mention. Instead, we shall follow many strange trails, look on while many secrets of the past are unearthed, eavesdrop to some purpose, and peer inside a curious assortment of hiding-places.

I have been collecting this matter for nearly forty years. The effect of it all was neatly epitomized for me on a recent visit to a house at Harrogate. The tradesmen's door is fitted with a spy-hole of about $\frac{1}{8}$-in. diameter. On looking through its hardly discernible lens the owner can see any caller, though standing only a couple of feet away in the porch, in full, life-size stature. The caller waits there, completely unaware of the scrutiny he is receiving from within! In the following pages we shall peer through many spy-holes.

In this anthology of secrecy most areas of Britain are represented by at least a few stories and traditions. Yorkshire—being my own native county and by far the largest in England—comes in for a goodly share. As for London, who could hope to do justice to the fare so plentifully concealed by its old buildings and streets and customs? Here again I shall avoid the now familiar and disclose some fairly recent happenings that could so easily have passed, forgotten, into the dim chambers of history.

Part 1
COAST AND COUNTRYSIDE

CHAPTER ONE

MYSTERY IN THE CAVES

Our inborn flair for secret places has been capitalized by innumerable story-tellers. A host of eager readers, young and old alike, is assured for any narrator who can evoke the timeless appeal, say, of a dark lonely cave and its whispering echoes. How poor mankind would be without Aladdin's Cave, and the eerie cavities and tunnels invented by Jules Verne! Many a man has found relief from business or domestic troubles by exploring the underworld in this way, from his armchair. Unwittingly, perhaps, he is stirring some ancient folk memory.

Evidence that our remote ancestors did live in caves is—fortunately for the romantically-minded person as well as the scientist—abundant. Few experiences are more sobering or exciting—according to mood—than exchanging the sights and sounds of twentieth-century life for the glistening subterranean corridors and chambers used by man perhaps a hundred thousand years ago. This exchange happens every time that Kent's Cavern lures holiday-makers from the modern attractions of Torquay; or Wookey Hole and the Cheddar Caves exercise the same kind of pull.

Let us see how some of these amazing caves disclosed their secrets, after a lapse of time that makes the Bible a book of yesterday and the Pyramids a fairly recent fashion in architecture.

One of the first to gaze upon the wonders of Kent's Cavern, after its long silences, was a man who inscribed his name inside on a piece of stalagmite that happens to resemble a lion. Such inscriptions would be regarded, if done today, as vandalism, but one can excuse and even applaud Robert Hedges for thus leaving his 'signature'. The date he appended—20 February 1688—has enabled his identity to be traced with some degree of certainty. He apparently lived at a neighbouring farm and may have taken refuge in the cave during the Monmouth Rebellion. If only Hedges' propensity had also led him to make a few notes in pocket-book or diary we might have shared his stupefaction on first beholding the marvellous rock formations that surrounded him in his cave retreat.

When the archaeologists and cavers began their investigations, early in the nineteenth century, the labyrinthine passages gradually gave up their age-old secrets. Time stood aside to reveal unbelievably lovely crypts, grottoes and cascades—all now lit up by electricity. In this 'palace' which a Mogul emperor might have envied, primitive man brought up his family, sharpened his flint harpoons and awls, and occasionally took a sliver of animal bone and cut a tiny slot at one end to provide his mate with a needle. Long-extinguished charcoal fires have also been found. How odd to think of these prehistoric folk cooking their meals amongst 'living' pillars and tapestries of lime carbonate that extend far beneath the smart, residential quarter of modern Torquay, where a furnished flat with no decoration to speak of may cost upwards of £3,000 per annum.

Parts of the Great Cave at Wookey Hole, near Wells, seem to have attracted visitors for centuries. In an account of his travels through Britain in 1694, Rogers paints the following delightful picture:

> After that we had, with some difficulty, climbed up to the top of a Rock, we went along the Brow of a Hill till we came to the Mouth of the Cave, where opening a Door that gave entrance, and lighting 24 Candles of 6 in the Pound, which we provided for that purpose, we ventured in; being got within it, we found the Cave very hollow, and so dark, that the Candles there scarce burning so bright, though there were 24, as two doth ordinary in the Night in one of our largest Rooms; we thought certainly we had come into the Confines of the Infernal Regions, or some such dismal Place, and began to be affraid to visit it, viz., That although we entered in frolicksome and merry, yet we might return out of it Sad and Pensive, and never more be seen to Laugh whilst we lived in the World . . .
>
> A little farther on the right hand is another piece of the Rock that bears some resemblance of a Bell, and on the left hand a Vessel, which they term a But, in which the Beer of an old Sorceress . . . used to be worked in; 'tis a hollow Cistern of a considerable depth always filled with Water, and now and then flowing over; to which the drops of Water which continually trickle down from the top of the Rock add every moment fresh supplies; hard by stands another Vessel of hers, in which they say she made her Mault, they call it the East Hurdle, 'tis likewise hollow, and of a pretty depth. Now appears unto your view the old Witch herself, heating of her furnace which seems black and sooty; it seems Alabaster, by reason of its

> whiteness, though 'tis most probable to be the product of Nature, and not of Art, because the place is very unfit and very unsuitable for any Artist to exercise his skill in, it being oft so low, that it is impossible here and there for any one to stand upright in it; and therefore it was that we were forced frequently to stoop, and buckle almost double for fear of hiting our Heads against the Rock . . .

Regarding another chamber Rogers reports 'that it was very usual for Gentlemen and Ladies, that lived thereabouts, to bring Music and Dance here, the Music making a more sweeter Melody than ordinary . . .' His final remarks are still tinged with classical allusions:

> When we had got thus far, and almost a Mile underground, as our Guides told us, we began to think how we should return and get out safe, being afraid to find the same difficulty and trouble we had encountered with in our Entrance; for tho' the Place was somewhat resembling an Infernal Abbyss, and our Passage into it proved to be so troublesome and irksome, yet we came back without any toil . . . notwithstanding 'tis impossible to found out the way without a Guide, there being so many Turnings and Windings; nor could the Guides themselves, without a light, find the way out of this forlorn place, whereby they steer their Course; However, at last we made shift to creep up again to the top of the Rock, just as merry *Lucian* tells us old Menippus did out of a hole in *Lebadia*, after he returned from Hell, and had ended the Discourses with the Ghosts below. Thus have I given you a small Relation of this wonderful Rareity.

He had indeed!

Mrs Hodgkinson, present owner of these 'infernal regions', tells me that musical performances are still occasionally given in the Third Chamber because of its exceptional acoustics. Perhaps Clement of Alexandria was referring to Wookey Hole when he wrote this passage in *Stromata*:

> Those who have composed histories say that in Britain is a certain cave at the side of a mountain, and at the entrance a gap; then, when the wind blows into the cave and is drawn on into the bosom of the interior, a sound is heard as of the clashing of numerous cymbals.

One cannot be surprised that long before the caves were scientifically explored by Professor Boyd Dawkins and H. E. Balch, Head Postmaster at Wells, Wookey should have its witch. Wookey was a door to that underworld represented so horrifically in the medieval mystery plays, and the more lurid of our ancient stained-glass windows. Hence those dreadful subterranean rumblings that trumpeted forth. And the Devil's agent, at Wookey, was its resident witch. Did she not separate husbands from their wives, put a blight on the cattle, and cause every other kind of mischief?

At length the Abbot of Glastonbury's help was invoked. This neighbouring monastery, which guarded the Holy Grail and witnessed Joseph of Arimathea's thorn tree blossoming miraculously every year, surely had the answer to this daily menace over at Wookey. It apparently had. The Abbot sent along one of his monks, who somehow cornered the witch in her cave-lair, intoned something hot and strong from his breviary, and then sprinkled her with water from the cave floor. All this had the effect of immobilizing her for ever. Peace and plenty returned to the neighbourhood. Husbands cleaved to their wives once more.

But the witch? She retained her physical shape, yet only as a harmless piece of stalagmite. In the eighteenth century Dr Harrington of Bath versified the story. This verse refers to the resourceful monk from Glastonbury:

He chaunted out his godlie booke,
He crost the water, blest the brooke,
Then—pater noster done—
The ghastly hag he sprinkled o'er:
When lo! where stood a hag before,
Now stood a ghastly stone.

It was from the Witch's Parlour at Wookey that several stalactites were removed to decorate the grotto created by Alexander Pope as a further novelty for his freakish house at Twickenham (no longer in existence). One of Pope's own sayings could be applied to his action in stripping this cave chamber of its natural glory: 'Fools rush in where angels fear to tread.'

Fortunately, Wookey has remained largely inviolate, and it is no longer necessary—as it was at one time—to set spirit alight on nearby rocks to reveal hidden vaults and curtains of crystalline beauty. From the bank of the River Axe which flows through the cave Mrs Hodgkinson and some companions once dug out the remains of a Romano-British woman. Many other Romano-British finds have since been made, including human bones and skulls, and various pieces of pottery which those same people would have used while inhabiting the cave some 1,700 or 1,800 years ago.

Cave diving is the latest method employed here to disclose secrets almost as old as the universe.

Strange dramas are sometimes suggested in our limestone caves. What could account for the peculiar arrangement of fifty human skeletons found in the caves at Burrington Combe, Somerset, some years ago? They formed a circle, with their feet pointing to the centre. Were these cave-men holding some tribal conclave, or just sleeping, when a calamity as sudden as that at Pompeii overtook them? A fall of rock and the mouth of their cave would be irrevocably sealed. Perhaps the fumes from their charcoal fire suffocated them before they could stir? Speculation is our only recourse. Caves pose a thousand riddles that defy solution.

Another collection of human bones, this time in curious disarray, confronted some searchers at Poole's Cavern at Buxton, in Derbyshire. As the bones were found with certain animal remains beneath a floor of stalagmite, which takes aeons to form, the discovery pointed to an incredibly distant past. Professor Boyd Dawkins puzzled long over those human remains. Here was no ordered burial; nothing to indicate natural death. He therefore made a leap of the imagination, and suggested that in the depths of this cave—before history had any meaning—there had been a massacre. One can only recall the slave-massacres reported by Sir Leonard Woolley from ancient Babylon, and shudder.

Of course, nothing of this would be suspected by the outlaw called Poole who made the cave his lair during the reign of King Henry VI. He might well have stored some of his plunder on that same stalagmite floor—and one may suppose that Mary Queen of Scots, too, would step that way when being shown through the cavern many years later. She was at that time held as a state prisoner under the Earl of Shrewsbury's roof at Buxton; a woman given to scheming, using any kind of subterfuge to gain her ends. How did she react on entering this vast cavern of weird deceptions and masquerades—to which such pleasantly ridiculous names as Flitch of Bacon, Bee-hives, and Turtles have been given? All we know is that Mary halted to admire a certain pillar of gleaming limestone, and exercised her regal right by naming it as her very own. Back she went, then, into cushioned custody.

The story of discovery in the many caves of Derbyshire is far too long to be recounted here. Some of the caves are really old lead-mines, but none the less mysterious for that. As in the Mendips and the Yorkshire Pennines, wherever one treads there is the strange sense of being a *roof-walker*. A secret underworld, much of it yet to be discovered no doubt, winds beneath one's very feet.

Even the entrances to these underground chambers can be thrilling. Consider the Peak Cavern, at Castleton. I stood there with my wife and two friends not long ago, marvelling that the cottages just outside had not slithered down the final slope into the yawning abyss of the Great Cave. Are these cottages the last outposts of the small community that once thrived at this precarious spot? According to the eighteenth-century traveller, Moritz, some of the buildings seemed already to have been engulfed. Beneath this 260-ft high precipice he saw 'a whole subterranean village'. A century earlier Hobbes expressed his amazement on beholding 'Houses within and haycocks mounted high'.

One relic of that subterranean community remains. The roof of the cave is pigmented with soot from the cottage chimneys. But far beyond, in a Styx-like pool, another little community still goes about its business—a species of shrimp, blind through all the ages.

Peveril Castle stands on top of the precipice; in effect, therefore, its deepest cellars are the enormous underground crypts now known by such evocative tags as Pluto's Hall and Pluto's Dining-room.

When Queen Victoria first visited Peak Cavern, in 1834, she must have been astonished to find that the kingdom she was soon to rule contained a place of such grotesque shapes and strange imaginings.

A dose of cave-lore would cure any victim of boredom. Psychiatrists might do worse than prescribe such a remedy for some of their patients. It would restore the lost sense of wonder. Even a visit to one of Britain's cave museums could make any person realize his citizenship of an almost illimitable world still bristling with secrets, some of them as yet barely half told.

I have often gazed upon the relics displayed in the Pig Yard Club

Museum at Settle, West Yorkshire. For me, modern problems are soon put in perspective on seeing such evidence that has been 'locked' away for centuries in some neglected cave; evidence of bygone perils, humble household tasks, or perhaps domestic felicity.

The skull of a great cave bear that was twice the size of a modern grizzly helps one to visualize some of the wild life that once inhabited Victoria Cave, high among the limestone fells above Settle. A harpoon made of deer-horn and equipped with reverse barbs calls up some Izaac Walton of Mezolithic times; he would probably fish in the mere that once spread in front of this cave. A pair of bronze eyebrow tweezers also found here could have been one troglodyte's self-made means of pandering to his wife's craze for the latest fashion. Perhaps she would be one of those brunettes of old who disdained to fasten her animal-skin garments with a common-or-garden thong, and ogled her man until he produced a bronze brooch. The cave floor has yielded up several of these ornaments, each coloured with enamel and made in the likeness of a coiled dragon. In fact, Victoria Cave—like others in various parts of Britain—has proved itself to be a vade-mecum of life in remote times.

Roman coins also unearthed at Victoria Cave suggest that some Romano-British folk came here as refugees. It is known that at the two different periods represented by the coins, Romano-British villas in the Ribble Valley nearby were burned down by savage tribesmen. No friendly curtain of stalactites would greet them, however, at this cave. It has a rather grim interior, though commodious enough to shelter several hard-pressed families.

The cry 'off to the caves' must have rung out repeatedly, even in Jacobite times. William Morrison of Malham Tarn House, not far from Settle, had an amusing story about the 'Forty-Five Rebellion. When Prince Charlie's men were approaching this neighbourhood, a six-year-old boy was hurriedly despatched to Victoria Cave, with orders to hide there until given the all-clear. As it was widely believed that the Prince's troops not only ate young children but also lived on booty he took the family plate with him, too, as a precaution.

The cruel aftermath of the 'Forty-Five sent some survivors of Culloden into hiding. They lived in caves or mean huts, and despite the price put on the heads of the leaders, their secret hiding-places were rarely betrayed. It is still possible to locate some of those and other Jacobite refuges.

Earlier, during the Retreat from Derby, the disillusioned men scattered, forming small groups that could keep to the unfrequented hills without incurring suspicion. One of those hill-tracks took a group of Highlanders through the Pennines. When they reached the Malham countryside they flung themselves, exhausted, into a narrow cave which could escape notice even today. It is Calf Hole Cave, near the head of Mastiles Lane. Another refuge was Odin's Cave on the Island of Mull. This was Lord Lovat's home for nearly two years after Culloden.

The city of Nottingham rests on a thick bed of sandstone, which is honeycombed with caves, fashioned partly by nature and partly by man. Whenever foundations are laid for some modern building ancient caverns are discovered anew. One Nottingham hotel at which I have stayed straddles a series of underground rock chambers. So does the fine Council House nearby, and also the Guildhall.

These caverns have been used in the past for many purposes—as outlaws' refuges, dwellings, sanctuaries from religious persecution, and, during the last war, as air-raid shelters. During the period of Catholic persecution, several so-called 'Papist holes' were burrowed into the Castle Rock, but many of them were destroyed by Cromwell's forces in the Civil Wars.

There was a time when great numbers of the townsfolk lived in caves, and as late as 1620 one visitor to Nottingham wrote that 'cunning men like moles dwell not in houses, but were earthed in holes'. Later in the same century a local Member of Parliament strongly advocated Sunday recreation because, he declared, most of his constituents lived underground and were surely entitled to seek open-air enjoyments on the Sabbath.

The largest cave-system in the area is beneath Mansfield Road; it was here that people took refuge during the air raids. There is reason to believe that this particular place was originally used and fortified by early tribesfolk, who turned the large central cave into their council chamber. Many years ago a hermit known as Old Rouse acted as guide to this 'underground village', charging an admittance fee of sixpence per person. When he had conducted his little party of sightseers to the innermost recesses of the labyrinth, the crafty old man would demand another shilling from each person as reward for leading them safely out again.

Local records also refer to a certain Thomas Smith, whose shop in Peck Lane incorporated a two-storeyed cave below. During the troublous reign of King Charles I he used it for the storage of other people's valuables, which he accepted for a small charge—a service which ultimately led to the establishment of Smith's Bank, in due course taken over by the National Provincial Bank.

Some years ago, when I was making a study of the Nottingham caves and passages, I was introduced to Mr G. F. Campion, a local antiquary who had been engaged in similar investigations for half a century. He showed me photographs, scale-drawings and plans to illustrate his various finds. One of his chief hunting-grounds was the Castle Rock, an enormous sandstone massif some 130 feet high. Most visitors stop to admire the public gardens which clothe the slopes on one side, or to visit the Castle Museum. But for Mr Campion it was the interior of the Castle Rock that mattered. With the same zeal that took some of Jules Verne's fictitious characters into the bowels of the earth, he explored the passages and chambers that riddle the Rock. One night, in a dream, he saw an unknown cave far below the castle. The same dream recurred several times, so he took a spade and, with the help of a friend, started digging at the place revealed in his dream. At length they found what has come to be known as the Water Cave. It is 21 feet high, 36 feet long, and 15 feet wide, and is now included in the fascinating 'Subterranean Tour' made available to visitors by Nottingham Corporation.

From the Castle Yard one descends first into the mysterious cavern that is dubbed Mortimer's Hole. This penetrates the entire bulk of Castle Rock. Rough steps are cut into the steepest gradients, and nowhere do the walls cramp one's movement. The width varies from about 6 to 10 feet, and the vault soars overhead. The Minotaur's labyrinth of Greek legend could hardly wind and plunge more than this one in the heart of Nottingham. On wall and vault the crumbling texture of the tawny sandstone is wonderfully seen, with large pebbles protruding from their natural sockets and hollows, sculptured here and there, it would seem, in a mood of caprice. Every juvenile notion of what an underground passage should be here achieves reality.

It was on the night of 19 October 1330 that King Edward III and his supporters entered the castle by this secret route and surprised his mother, Queen Isabella, with her paramour Roger Mortimer, Earl of

March. Mortimer was arrested and executed one month later at Tyburn.

Mortimer's Hole was only rediscovered in 1864, and when first opened to the public it was lit by candles placed in the rock niches. Electric lighting is now installed, but apart from this innovation the passage cannot have changed much since the ill-fated meetings of Isabella and Mortimer.

Eventually the 'Subterranean Tour' reaches daylight at the base of the rock, and after a brief walk to the Water Gate and beyond, the Castle Rock is entered once more near the Water Cave for the ascent of the Western Passage. It was here that the remains of what appeared to be an oratory were discovered, suggesting that this part of the elaborate cave system was once used as a Catholic refuge. The Castle Yard is reached again after passing through the dungeons of the original Norman castle.

Castle Rock may still contain unexplored caverns. If I were younger I would investigate a passage which opens like a beaver's hole in the wall of Mortimer's Room—a cave within the ancient hostelry known as the Trip to Jerusalem Inn, which clings to the parent rock. This dark, narrow passage is supposed to connect with Mortimer's Hole.

Traditionally, the Trip to Jerusalem Inn, founded in 1189, was where Crusaders foregathered and refreshed themselves on their way to the Holy Land. Earlier still it seems to have been the castle brewhouse. More to our purpose is the fact that the greater part of the inn comprises weird caves and passages hewn out of the living rock. Where the rock roofs are sufficiently fissured, ferns and other plants send down their roots to form tasselled fringes. In one place a long, tubular shaft was deliberately cut through the rock massif at a steep angle. This may have been a speaking-tube, enabling one of the castle garrison to send down the Governor's demand for more mead.

In the Rock Bar a vertical shaft opens into the centre of the roof; long ago it would serve as chimney for a central fire. Around the orifice of the shaft there was, until fairly recently, a natural rock ledge about 2 feet wide. One day last century a man arrived at the inn and begged the owner, Susan Cresswell, to hide him at once. She directed him to the rock ledge, and there he stayed—secretly fed at intervals by the co-operative Susan—for a day and a night. It transpired later that the refugee was none other than Charles Peace, the notorious murderer.

CHAPTER TWO

DISGUISED BY NATURE

As we have seen already, Nature is often a co-conspirator with man in his varied charades and escapades. But it is not only caves that join the conspiracy. Hills and valleys, forest and fenland foster a secrecy of their own.

That forlorn band of Highlanders who found temporary respite in Calf Hole Cave during the 'Forty-Five would pass very near to a moor-top valley that is so well screened by limestone escarpments that Scotsmen of an earlier generation could never locate it. I refer to the Scottish raiders of medieval and later times. They swooped down from the north, plundering not only cattle, but 'noble matrons, chaste virgins and other women'. A trail of burned homes usually marked their progress through the countryside, and the abbeys fared no better than the wayside cottage and farm. In certain areas castles and pele towers provided some protection, but dalesmen often had to fend for themselves.

Around Malham, therefore, whenever warning came through about an imminent raid, cattle were led into this hidden valley above Malham Cove. Deserted centuries ago by its stream (which started running underground), the mile-long valley would make a splendid sanctuary. Its existence can hardly be suspected from either of the two flanking roads. Only after stepping aside for a few yards and scrambling down into the Dry Valley does the old tradition ring true.

Another hide-out occurs in neighbouring Wharfedale. The good folk of Linton and other villages would soon know when Bolton Priory, down the Wharfe valley, was being sacked by the raiders. A system of lighted cressets gave warning from their hill-tops, and as the Prior and his brother canons fled for safety to Skipton Castle, the villagers mustered all their own cattle and hurried them along, with their women and children, to the safety of Thorpe.

Thorpe occupies a cup-shaped hollow. Most tourists seem quite unaware of this hamlet. In my younger days I would sometimes 'search' for it among the enclosing fells, after pocketing my one-inch map so that I had no advantage over the marauding Scots; for it is said that—as at Malham—never once did they find where the surrounding villagers and their valuable stock had vanished! Without previous knowledge of the terrain one could wander in circles for half an hour or so—as I did once—and still be seeking.

One of Bell Scott's graphic Northumbrian paintings that decorate the Central Hall at Wallington, Northumberland, shows the landing of Danish invaders near Tynemouth Priory. The townsfolk seek hiding above the cliffs. A tonsured priest clutches a basket containing his Mass furniture—holy vessels, altar candles, and books; an old woman grabs her cat; the inevitable small boy seizes his toy windmill and boat.

There would be several places nearby which could provide refuge until the raiders left, but when their serpent-prowed galleys moved south, to storm the coast around West Hartlepool, there was a general exodus to the village of Elwick, four miles inland. Once again, Nature had foreseen human need, as it were. A hill-bound depression—now attractively carpeted by the village green—concealed the refugees and their belongings until the danger was past.

How Hereward the Wake and his men secreted themselves and their families amongst the fens is common knowledge. Just as exciting, but probably fresh to most tourists, is the story of that Secret Valley which Nicholas Size makes the subject of a remarkable and factual Lakeland romance. Hereward the Wake was eventually betrayed; the monks of Ely secured immunity for their cathedral by treacherously revealing Hereward's secret ways through fenland. But neither William of Normandy nor William Rufus, his successor, could find any fifth columnists to help breach western Lakeland.

For a long time few people—apart from those who occupied the area—knew the actual whereabouts of this half-legendary valley. Ranulf Meschin, in charge of military operations against the stubborn Lakelanders, found most of his captives adamant when questioned. Even under torture the poor fellows would only babble about some far-off place, half-hidden in the clouds. Another turn of the rack or thumbscrew might elicit equally tantalizing, and useless, scraps—like the name by which it was sometimes known, viz., Little Norway. The only real clue that came out of those forced disclosures was that the inhabitants of the remote and apparently impregnable Secret Valley gave obedience to a Norwegian jarl called Boethar.

In his search for the place Ranulf drew many blanks. At first he expected to find it near Ambleside. But this part of the Lake District did not altogether tally with the rumours of a mountain fastness where lights signalled messages through the darkness of night from every peak, and warriors emerged like spectres to engage the Norman soldiery in guerrilla combat.

Anybody familiar with the Lake District can even now understand Ranulf's sense of frustration. Eliminate the roads that today make exploration possible and one is left with a wild conglomeration of mountains, threaded by narrow tracks that seem to lead nowhere, and mirrored by eerie lakes and tarns, each as silent as death. Even the first Lake tourists, in the eighteenth century, regarded the mountains with horror.

Thwarted in every direction, and unable to report any progress, Ranulf saw his prestige at William's court evaporating. He would have been replaced—but nobody relished Ranulf's thankless mission. He was therefore left with the enigma on his hands. In desperation he and his men defied the mountain terrors and pushed their way over the Wrynose and Hardknott Passes to Eskdale. If only he had known he was now getting nearer the Secret Valley, but his grasp of this old route to the west coast soon had to be surrendered. How could anybody hold the track, let alone search amongst the enveloping crags, when—as in other places—Boethar's archers were obviously in league with demons?

To be lost in a mist in this region—as I can testify!—is to have sympathy with any person similarly trapped. The sensation is alarming, especially when voices are heard but nothing is seen. But Boethar's men used other aids besides the swirling mists. They wore 'garments of invisibility'. Nicholas Size describes them:

'These [garments] consisted of loose cloaks made of old rags of the same colour as the surrounding stones'; the wearers could slowly 'steal forward into positions which enabled them to kill their enemies in comparative safety'.

It was a spy who eventually gave Ranulf his breakthrough. Jackson the Herder had led cattle into the Secret Valley and, hoping for reward, told the baffled commander where the valley was situated and how it could be reached. The only feasible approach, said the loquacious herdsman, was via the wild, twisting pass now called Newlands.

To include a full account of the dramatic events that ensued would exceed the scope of this book. It must suffice for me to say that once again Ranulf was foiled. Boethar and his stalwarts, defending Newlands Pass like an impalpable host, created havoc among the foe; the survivors scattered, utterly demoralized. Buttermere, the Secret Valley, was still inviolate. Boethar held every card, and long continued to do so. Those 'cards' are, so to speak, the protective mountains that almost encircle Buttermere. Honister Crag, Fleetwith Pike, High Stile, Red Pike, Robinson are their modern names. Jackson the Herder had told Ranulf that the region enclosed by these mountains was 'a fearsome place, full of enchantments'. The Secret Valley of Lakeland could still be so described.

Any stretch of ancient woodland also offers sanctuary. The forests of Sherwood, Savernake, Epping, reduced in extent though they may be today, are still able to make a lone walker look back, apprehensively, over his shoulder. Even from the motoring roads that criss-cross the New Forest something can often be sensed of the old witchery of the place. I have felt it repeatedly on the outskirts of Burley. In more than one spot the forest seems to be *watching*. Shag's Heath, near Ringwood, where the Duke of Monmouth was captured, must once have been quite eerie. Macaulay, the historian, caught its spell when he came to write this page of history.

We read that Monmouth made for Hampshire 'in the hope that he might lurk in the cabins of deer-stealers among the oaks of the New Forest, till means of conveyance to the Continent could be procured . . . Monmouth and his friends procured rustic attire, disguised themselves and proceeded on foot towards the New Forest. They passed the night in the open-air, but before morning they were surrounded on every side by tails [snares]'. Soon

> dogs of quick scent were turned out among the bushes. Several times the fugitives ventured to look through the outer hedge, but everywhere they found a sentinel on the alert.
>
> At sunrise the next morning the search re-commenced. . . . At length a gaunt figure was discovered hidden in a ditch. The pursuers sprang on their prey. The prisoner's dress was that of a shepherd; his beard, prematurely grey, was of several days' growth. He trembled greatly and was unable to speak. Even those who had often seen him were at first in doubt whether this was truly the

> brilliant and graceful Monmouth . . . The prisoner was conveyed under a strong guard to Ringwood.

The New Forest had rejected him.

It is an astonishing fact that until 1849 nobody could identify the Pilgrim Fathers' country with any certainty. The veil of secrecy was cast over it by William Bradford himself. In writing the history of the Separatist Movement he referred to the region, guardedly, as 'sundry towns and villages, some in Nottinghamshire, some in Lincolnshire, and some in Yorkshire, where they border nearest together'. He had good reason for this mystification. Even though the book was written in America, after the founding of New Plymouth, his native countryside still nourished sympathizers whom he wished to protect against possible reprisals.

During the last century, through the researches of the Rev. Joseph Hunter, the veil was lifted. And for many years now, Americans of all ranks have been beating a track to the humble homesteads and farms where their forebears suffered for the sake of conscience before finding freedom overseas.

Let us follow these latter-day pilgrims—first of all to Scrooby.

This attractive village of red pantile roofs and weathered stone stands back rather furtively from the Great North Road as though it cannot even yet entirely trust those who pass along the highway. Personally, I have found Scrooby folk friendly enough, but one must never overlook the historic significance of that network of lanes which spreads between highway and village. Those crooked lanes originated as paths through the fenland. For centuries the paths spelt safety for the villagers; only people who knew them could hope to escape being bogged. It was Hereward the Wake's tangled skein all over again; not in Cambridgeshire this time, but in the northernmost tip of Nottinghamshire. Even today, a Scrooby man told me, one can easily get lost among those lanes during fog.

The swamps have been drained these many years, leaving Ryton Water to meander through the village. Past the church it flows, past Monks' Mill, past Scrooby Manor; a tiny wisp of a stream, yet marking the real start of the *Mayflower* adventure. The famous Atlantic crossing was still some years ahead, but it was down Ryton Water that Brewster, Bradford, and their friends sailed away—almost like thieves in the night, via the Trent and the Humber to initial freedom in Holland.

William Brewster lived at Scrooby Manor during the years 1588–1608. The Pilgrim Society of Plymouth, Massachusetts, has affixed to its exterior wall a plaque commemorating it as the place 'where he organized the Pilgrim Church . . .' The Anglo-American Society also erected a tablet here, in 1920, to mark the three-hundredth anniversary of the sailing of the *Mayflower* from Plymouth.

At Bawtry, two miles north of Scrooby, the Yorkshire bit of Bradford's 'maze' is entered, and then, heading away to the right as though bound for the Isle of Axholme, one suddenly comes upon Austerfield Manor. In the year that Brewster was appointed post, or official letter-carrier at Scrooby (1590), William Bradford—destined to become Second Governor of New Plymouth—was born in this modest Tudor homestead.

Since the Manor was bought by a Doncaster solicitor, in 1950, I have had the privilege of dining with him and his family in the room where young Bradford would take his meals. And I have groped my way down to the tiny, barrel-vaulted cellar where, later, Bradford and his Separatist brethren foregathered in secret.

A complete tour of the Pilgrim Fathers' country would embrace Gainsborough Old Hall, in Lincolnshire—another clandestine meeting-place; also Boston, that delightful old fenland town where Brewster and his friends were imprisoned for attempting to leave England 'on the quiet'. After release, their scheme prospered better.

But hereabouts it is the waterways I would stress. They are not particularly beautiful, except where the banks sway with rushes of gold and russet. Dykes with queer names like Pauper's Drain pattern the area, for the fens have obviously been tamed and all sense of subterfuge has vanished. Yet as they glide along several streams whisper their own earlier memories, notably of an epoch-making day in 1609 when wives, sweethearts, and children, with loads of baggage, embarked silently and alone to keep secret rendezvous with their menfolk alongside the Humber. Holland, as I have said, was their immediate lure. The *Mayflower* adventure came later.

The Scottish Covenanters furnish a corresponding page of history and one cannot go far in the Lowlands without hearing about them.

Jenny Geddes, a humble vegetable hawker, usually gets most of the limelight because it was she who 'lit the fuse'. On Sunday, 23 July 1637, Dean Hannay had only just started decanting Archbishop Laud's new liturgical manual, in St Giles's Cathedral, Edinburgh, when Jenny—outraged along with others at this attempt to force episcopacy on Scotland—folded up her stool and flung it at the Dean's head, shouting, 'Thou false thief, dost thou say Mass at my lug?'

The two Covenants later drawn up against any infliction of prelacy were confirmed by both Charles I and Charles II, but the Merry Monarch soon repented of his leniency. There followed a period of bitter struggle. At the battle of Rullion Green (November 1666) on the Pentland Hills the Covenanters' horse were routed. Their commander, Major Learmont, fortunately knew of a secret passage that ran from the banks of the South Medwin to his house, Newholm. This place evidently anticipated trouble, for it had a hidden, underground chamber. Many a preacher, and others also, owed their lives to Learmont's escape system.

Proscribed and hunted, the Covenanters took to the heather. Their gatherings were held in secret—occasionally in private houses but more often in woodland glades among the moss-hags, or at the bend of a stream where sentinels could keep watch while the others sang their psalms and prayed.

When travelling across the moors of Wigtownshire one might—if sympathetic to such minority causes—catch a lingering strain of those times. A painting by Sir George Harvey (owned by Glasgow Corporation) brings them vividly to life. In a deep cleft of the hills some thirty or forty people are grouped around the preacher. There are men in their plaids, women wearing bonnets and shawls, young children, a baby in arms. A few have evidently ridden to the conventicle on horseback; the rest will have trudged here on foot, probably in twos and threes to avoid arousing suspicion. As the Word is being expounded one worshipper cocks his ear and looks round quizzically. Has he caught the hoof-beats of Claverhouse's dragoons?

About the same period forbidden gatherings of believers were also being held in many parts of England. And kind Nature, once again, lent her aid. An overgrown hollow in Bradley Woods, near Newton Abbot, South Devon, is the so-called Pit that gave a measure of protection to early Nonconformists. If local tradition is sound, their opposite numbers around Salcombe, near Dartmouth, were only admitted to their meetings by ticket. This was their bona-fide. Spies might otherwise filter through, take note of the proceedings and then inform the authorities. In later days the wood where they met in secret was called Ticket Wood, but this has now gone the way of so many attractive bits of woodland.

I once corresponded with two scholarly Cornish clergymen who had spent several years investigating the beautiful traditions about Christ having come to Cornwall with St Joseph of Arimathea. 'Joseph was a tin man' is a phrase still occasionally heard in certain parts of the Duchy; it refers to the tin trade in which Joseph was engaged. My two informants reminded me, however, that in these sceptical days Cornish folk are very shy of their Holy Legend; it has become a kind of folk secret—to be handled with care before strangers.

The tradition is mentioned here because the miners of St Day, near Redruth—when coaxed out of their reserve—claimed that Christ had actually visited their particular mines. Now one of the abandoned workings near St Day is the Gwennap Pit in which John Wesley preached several times—the Pit where Methodists still hold a Whit-Monday service.

Antiquaries have to be very cautious where there is no reliable evidence, but it is a fascinating thought that Wesley might have felt constrained to make Gwennap Pit his open-air 'chapel' because of its traditional link with the Christ 'who once preached to the local miners'.

Not easy to find, until one reaches an inner ring of signposts, Gwennap Pit seats hundreds of people on thirteen circular tiers, cut like so many symmetrical linchets in the springy turf.

I suppose a full account of such gatherings could never be given. For obvious reasons, many would go unrecorded, save in the memories of people long dead. If any clue does survive it is often slender indeed. The religious stalwarts credited with having climbed up the stiff, rocky face of a Swaledale escarpment—in North Yorkshire—to their cave 'chapel'; who were they? Dalesfolk, one may be sure, but otherwise their identity is totally obscured—as their proscribed devotions would be—by the friendly waterfall that curtains off this well-named Swinnergill Kirk.

The worshippers who sought the refuge of a gritstone outcrop here at Rawdon, near my own West Yorkshire home, are less difficult to recall. They were the local dissenters, primed to their heroic purpose by such men as the Rev. Oliver Heywood. As we shall discover in a later chapter, Heywood had to move about circumspectly, because of his unpopular views, and I have no doubt that many of those who attended his sessions of secret worship in Rawdon Hall (see page 97) were also of the company which periodically met under the shadow of Buckstone Rock, not far away.

Buckstone Rock now supports a sports pavilion and is enclosed on three sides by a golf course. One Sunday every year, however, the golfers make way for the holding of a service beside that same gaunt, up-thrusting rock to commemorate the zeal and bravery of those seventeenth-century Nonconformists.

Looking around during a recent service here I thought of the 'scouts' who formerly kept watch at some distance lest the authorities should catch the people unawares and charge them—as they frequently did—with 'ryott and unlawful assembly'. It was a lovely July evening. A westering sun lit up the rock and bronzed the tall grasses amongst which old and young sat in small family groups. A local silver band led the hymns—but there would be neither band nor singing here in the far-off days of religious oppression. The near-silent worship then essential, in those open-air conventicles, became so ingrained that when restrictions were lifted and a proper chapel could be built nearby, singing was still taboo. Some of the early members considered it *wrong*! Alvery Jackson, a visiting minister, had to preach a special sermon on the people's *right* to sing before the old habit born of secrecy was shaken. Even then the resident minister was not convinced, though later, somebody happily recorded, hymns did come into favour because 'it pleased the Lord to give John Wilson [the local minister] light'. At last the heritage of silent praise was by-passed. The people's hosannas and hallelujahs could be given unstinted voice.

CHAPTER THREE

SMUGGLERS AND HIGHWAYMEN

If Nature conspired to help the persecuted, enough impartiality was shown to benefit others too, from the moss-troopers who long harried the northern counties, to the smugglers and highwaymen of later times.

In the Solway area of the Border country 'jinking the gauger' was a profitable if hazardous occupation. This phrase meant—outwitting the Revenue man. The same caves and hill-sanctuaries that had concealed Jacobites and other fugitives were just as likely to serve such fellows as Jack Yawkins, the smuggler who figures so prominently in Walter Scott's *Guy Mannering*.

Much of this recreant story, as it affected the whole nation (not forgetting the master hand played by the Isle of Man), is told in my book, *Smugglers' Britain*. In the eighteenth century a short-sighted, if hard-up Government imposed import duties that sent the price of many articles soaring, far beyond their actual value—and the buyer's pocket. At one time no fewer than 1,425 items were dutiable! Things like playing-cards and dice and continental pictures did not worry the man-in-the-street overmuch, but he strongly objected to having to pay through the Government nose for his rum, tobacco, and tea. And the women-folk were equally vociferous about lace and silk kerchiefs.

Ergo, the trade in these commodities went 'underground'. Smugglers and their confederates became adept at every kind of subterfuge. Never had the country experienced such clever ruses and dodges and feints. The King's ministers threatened the direst penalties. Customs men of several ranks were increased in numbers—but never sufficiently to stem the 'hush-hush' trade that involved so many. Almost every cave and bay, ditch and hollow, became suspect. A sort of whispering campaign spread over the country, and the stillness of night won many devotees.

To be a smuggler was often to live two lives; one respectable and orderly, the other mysterious, with every move calculated and carefully timed. This ulterior self also made the man as cunningly familiar with his natural terrain as were the wild creatures. The burrowing mole, or perhaps the wily fox, would have made him an apt emblem.

I do not propose to track down many of these 'free-traders' here. But since *Smugglers' Britain* was written my net has stretched much wider, making a few further revelations seem obligatory. After all, it was the smugglers who brought secrecy to a fine art. In some areas smuggling was also a synonym for villainy. When Sir John Clerk made a tour of the Scottish Border in 1739 he reported:

'We dined at Anan. . . . There are in it not above 100 houses and but a few tollerable ones, yet they have here a kind of wine trade to France and by the strength of oaths and other rogueries vend a great deal of it in England contrary to law. . . .'

A recent visit to Ayrshire has reminded me again of Robert Burns's acquaintance with these slippery gentlemen. First, however, let us see Burns in his early youth. He once confessed that his traffic with the supernatural 'owed much to an old woman who resided in the family, remarkable for her ignorance, credulity and superstition. She had, I suppose, the largest collection in the country of tales and songs concerning devils, ghosts, fairies, brownies, witches, warlocks, spunkies, kelpies, elf-candles, dead-lights, wraiths, apparitions, cantraips, giants, enchanted towers, dragons, and other trumpery. This cultivated the latent seeds of poetry . . .' Such 'trumpery' came to his aid when he wrote his poem, *Hallowe'en*, which introduces Culzean Castle—by moonlight.

Here, however, Burns was not thinking particularly of the eighteenth-century Gothic castle designed by Robert Adam, romantic though it certainly is with all manner of pleasant make-believe. What really liberated his muse were the *caves* of Culzean which honeycomb the castle's basaltic cliff. To these sea-caves came the fairies on Hallowe'en. A tradition that might have loosened Burns's sword, in later years, made these same caves the resort of some who dealt in more tangible spirits. Smugglers, in fact.

Towards the close of his all-too-short life, Bobbie Burns eked out the scanty earnings from his rhymes by becoming an Excise man. Actually, Culzean would be beyond his beat. We see him more correctly on the lonely Solway shores, searching for smugglers and their well-laden brigs—and occasionally reliving some of those boyhood terrors which caused him to 'keep a sharp look-out in suspicious places'. Being 'jinked' would have been just too humiliating for the proud author of *Tam O' Shanter* and the *Twa Dogs.*

In many of the lonelier parts of Britain smugglers' paths or 'trods' creep over hills or moorland. On the Whitby-Pickering moors, in north-east Yorkshire, such tracks tend to be hidden by heather or tall bracken; they wind inland from the coast near Robin Hood's Bay. There are places in Newtondale—behind that old-time smuggling den, Saltergate Inn—where one could walk unobserved for several miles. Sometimes the greater willow herb—great purple banks of it—preserves the secret of one's passing, and every few yards the moor is riven with hollows and crevices that could hide an outlaw, or a smuggler and his half-ankers, for hours.

Similar tracks once ran back from the Ship Inn at Saltburn, a few miles north of Whitby. Saltburn has become a well-loved resort, but its cloak of respectability was given a sharp tug, in 1966, by the discovery of a passage that formerly enabled smugglers to take contraband from the Ship Inn, beside the beach, to the once heavily wooded ravine leading inland. John Andrew, landlord of the inn during the mid-eighteenth century, was a notorious 'free-trader'.

The new-found passage appeared to be in excellent condition. From the inn cellar it led towards the ravine via Cat Nab, a well-known landmark, but further investigation was impracticable. The passage goes beneath the present road and has therefore been closed. Any smuggled goods which John Andrew and his gang might have left there are safe. The only signs of their activities were non-committal—a few broken 'church-wardens' and bits of pottery.

Tradition invests many other areas with hidden ways.

At the fifteenth-century manor house that overlooks the bay at Crantock, near Newquay in Cornwall, I was told of a passage that careered from the drawing-room to Vugga Cove, a mile distant. Only smuggling activities could explain this remarkable feature, which linked a cosy parlour where the family would enjoy their evening music and cards—with a rugged bit of the Atlantic seaboard. Unfortunately, the house end of this secret route caved in many years ago. Its entrance from the drawing-room survived longer and was only blocked up to safeguard a new owner's young children.

Another Cornish route now relegated to the realm of fable linked Penally House at Boscastle with Pentargen Seal Hole, beyond the famous harbour. The seals sometimes make their way into the harbour, but the local smugglers chose to come inland by that other route.

Moving still farther north along the Cornish coast we come to the little beach at Millock, near Widemouth Bay. Somehow, the brandy and tea and lace once landed here after nightfall had to be conveyed to Penfound Manor, the distribution centre.

Here again we cannot but marvel at the astonishing contrast. Seawards, that small pebbly beach. Then, a mile or so inland, the beautiful manor of the Penfound family, one of whom had brought home from the Third Crusade a bottle of Jordan water. This is concealed in the Great Hall fireplace to keep evil spirits away. The Crusader's eighteenth-century descendants were more concerned to keep Preventive men away. A bolt hole in the garden proceeded underground for about two hundred yards, emerging in the smugglers' lane where Penfound's mare, and other horses 'borrowed' from local farmers, would be waiting. The horses were all trained to deliver the contraband, without human aid, as and where required. If captured by the Revenue men they could be trusted to keep their own counsel!

I would like to explore all those curious lanes which tunnel through the North Devon countryside, taking advantage of any natural hollow, and arched over with conspiratorial trees and bushes. Even in early spring, before the foliage fills out, the air of secrecy is paramount.

For whose benefit were these covered ways first devised? Does anybody know? Certainly bygone smugglers would find them highly congenial, as they took their packages and barrels inland from places like Martinhoe and Lee Bay, on the Bristol Channel. From only a short distance away the lanes may be completely hidden; all that shows is a belt of greenery zigzagging its desultory way up the hillside. After a motoring trip in Devon a friend of mine expressed strong dislike for these shadowy lanes. 'We couldn't *see* anything!' he expostulated. Perhaps, in earlier days 'seeing'—in the generally accepted sense—was here sacrificed to ensure quiet, unnoticed progression.

The chines around Bournemouth nourish a clandestine story of their own. A chine is a natural chink, or fissure. Thousands of holidaymakers now walk or drive through these ravines, with senses alert only for the fragrance and beauty of the enclosing pine trees, for the heath that sometimes clothes the chines with springy turf, and for the public gardens to which they often lead. While expatiating on their healthful advantages a local M.O.H. once said, '. . . the chines also serve as channels through which the fresh sea air is carried into the heart of the town'. He might have added, *off the record*, that they had also served in former days as channels for contraband!

When local smuggling flourished hereabouts, in its eighteenth-century hey-day, the notorious Isaac Gulliver and his 'White Wigs' might well have argued that in providing such useful ravines, Nature was aiding and abetting their nocturnal activities. Nature had in fact been most bountiful. In addition to the chines that ran back from the coast towards the anonymous hollows and furze clumps of the Great Heath, was there not also a large natural harbour, indented with innumerable half-hidden creeks? And then, just beyond this harbour at Poole, there was Purbeck itself, with dozens of sea-caves and awkward rock-ledges to baffle the unwanted.

Some smugglers who once had to hide within an inner recess of the Tilly Whim Caves, near Swanage, would probably have avoided discovery altogether, but for a mischance in a million. It was not Mother Nature that failed them. And the men lacked neither fortitude nor patience. While coastguards were probing the adjoining rock chambers the smugglers simply huddled closer to their hoard and even began a leisurely, time-killing meal of bread and cheese. They felt absolutely secure.

The hunt must have continued until daylight. It might then have been called off but for one tiny clue. A small piece of bread was seen floating out from the rocks. The bobbing white lump gave the sleuths fresh heart. The search was renewed, in the area of that tell-tale fragment. So the bread fallen accidentally upon the waters gave the secret away. At last the smugglers were routed, and given fifteen days at sea in the stuffy hold of a Government cutter before being bundled over to Dorchester for trial and imprisonment.

Some of these caves are abandoned stone quarries. Mead Falkner makes great use of them in *Moonfleet*. I was reminded of this thrilling, nineteenth-century novel by the Rector's wife at Worth Matravers. After showing us through their lovely old house she pointed up to one of the dormers. 'Do you see those tiny glass panes at this near corner?' she asked. The proper dormer window faces west, but some fragmentary glass squares had been deftly inserted to give a coastward peep. 'They were put there by smugglers,' said the lady, smiling at the roguery it implied. This sly peep-hole—difficult to spot in daylight—allowed signals to be flashed at night to any waiting lugger off-shore at Winspit.

'Do read *Moonfleet* again,' was Mrs Jenkins' parting shot. 'It is all about this area.' The novel reaches farther afield, also, for its excitements and thrills, but the caves and the hidden paths of Purbeck provide the essential backcloth. Even the smugglers' secret passage beneath the church vault turns out to be a piece of truth. It is the passage leading from the Mohun family vault at East Fleet—that oddly situated village behind Chesil Bank, itself one of Nature's great puzzles.

In a smuggling story called *The Distracted Preacher*, Thomas Hardy also drew upon real places, people, and events. Lulworth Cove in Dorset is the repository of many secrets, not least the supposed landing of Napoleon, one night in 1804, to lay plans for his intended invasion. Lulworth figures in Hardy's smuggling story as the thinly disguised Lulwind Cove where contraband liquor was landed.

In smuggling lore one gets accustomed to the concealment of contraband in the local church roof, or tower, but in Hardy's tale there is an additional ruse. Some of the stuff—'turnips' to the initiated—is hidden in a garden, *beneath an apple tree*. Hardy believed this dodge to be unique; he heard of it from a Dorset smuggler—an old 'carrier of tubs' later employed as a stonemason by Hardy senior, over at Higher Bockhampton.

The apple tree grew in a large box which could be lifted—to reveal a cavity designed for the concealment of more 'turnips'. I can well imagine Hardy listening to this tale with incredulous delight, at the cottage where his father ran the family business. From the window of the upstair room where the author wrote his early stories a few of his family's apple trees would meet his gaze; perhaps they prompted a few chuckles as he recorded the smuggler's secret for posterity.

Let us now leave Hardy's excisemen to sniff for contraband spirits at every suspicious spot—apple-lofts, clock cases, cupboards, chimney-flues, haystacks, etc., and return over the mysterious Egdon Heath of his stories to Poole.

I like the way in which my friend, Bernard C. Short, opens his account of Poole's separate little 'kingdom'—Brownsea Island. His extensive knowledge of the area, garnered over many years as borough archivist, local historian, and librarian, give these words a special significance and authority:

> Because Brownsea Island has been a secret island, a forbidden territory, upon which few persons ever set foot, one tends to regard it not as part of Poole Harbour, but as an enigma, maintaining its own individuality at the harbour entrance.

A somewhat similar cloak of mystery once enveloped Derwent Isle, opposite Friars Crag, Derwentwater. In the eighteenth century a man called Pocklington took it over, established a battery of guns to send weird echoes over the lake, dubbed the place Paradise Island, and pontifically objected to somebody's scheme that threatened to lower the level of the lake as 'it would join his kingdom to England'. One is apt to think of other strange island redoubts while gazing upon Brownsea's illusory jungle from the Sandbanks car ferry, but the oddest of all—Barrie's Scottish 'island that likes to be visited': that enchanted island of *Mary Rose*—has no counterpart here. Brownsea's five hundred acres of good solid earth could hardly melt into thin air overnight, as reputedly did Mary Rose's island in the Outer Hebrides. And until the last few years brought Brownsea into the welcoming orbit of the National Trust—it did *not* like to be visited. Various owners contrived to keep the place as private as a dream.

Who were those people?

A few monks from Cerne Abbey were early on the scene. The castle built on Brownsea in the reign of King Henry VIII gave 'Mad Benson', two centuries later, his citadel of mystery, for it was commonly believed that he there practised black magic. 'In 1735,' says Bernard Short, 'a servant girl vanished from the island, and it was strongly rumoured in Poole that she had been sacrificed to some Satanic power at one of Benson's hideous ceremonies. . . . Certainly, the servant girl was never heard of again.' Soon after Benson's necromantic reign, this island which almost straddles the harbour mouth had its contingent of Revenue men, posted there to thwart the schemes and stratagems of smugglers.

One might have expected the picaresque element to disappear as time went on; actually, it *grew*.

Did Brownsea exert some strange, minatory influence? One later owner became insane and committed suicide. His successor hoped to make a fortune from the white porcelain clay his wife discovered on the island; instead, his enormous outlay on the project led to financial ruin. When he fled to Spain, in disgrace, some of the local wiseacres spread the tale that the high-grade porcelain had secretly been 'planted' so as to extract a larger purchase price for the island from the unsuspecting Colonel Waugh.

Brownsea became even more of a talking point during Mrs Christie's ownership. As Mr Short says, 'She made it a completely secret island, sealed off from the outside world.' This, in the present matter-of-fact, no-nonsense era!

Baden-Powell had camped on Brownsea with his first twenty youth-initiates in 1907; in 1932 Mrs Christie allowed five hundred Scouts to land there and celebrate the twenty-fifth anniversary of their movement. The curtain fell soon after. The lady of Brownsea became a recluse, and actually employed a Swedish physical training expert—a perfect amazon of a woman—to pitch any intruders into the harbour. This the Swedish woman effectively did! Apart from a servant or two, Mrs Christie's only companions were the island peacocks and other harmless birds.

The first decade of Brownsea's release from that thraldom has yet to be notched up. On visiting it today many people will unwittingly echo the Prince Regent's exclamation when he went there in 1818 as the guest of Sir Charles Sturt. 'I had no idea,' he said, looking round upon the island's charm, 'there had been such a delightful spot in the Kingdom.'

In a recent BBC television programme it was good to see the Boy Scouts there again, this time celebrating the jubilee of their movement. The Secret Island is secret no longer. How could it be when the public now have access, and the pine-clad shores—guarded in turn by a Tudor garrison, a madman, barriers of superstition and fear, that virago from Sweden—have at last surrendered their fabulous rôle?

Smugglers were not the only figures that moved across the face of Britain like shadows. Highwaymen had similar propensities. To them, secrecy and all manner of artifice were as vital as their blunderbusses and a swift horse.

Highwaymen provide one of the most exciting, if lurid chapters in the history of the road.

There was Claude Duval, who came to this country on the Restoration of the monarchy in 1660 and spiced his brigandry with such courtly manners that he won the hearts even of the ladies he robbed. Some of these fair dupes actually pleaded for his pardon when he was eventually captured at the Hole-in-the-Wall Inn, off the Strand, in London. The secret of his charm accompanied him to the gallows; still gay, he was executed at Tyburn.

Another seventeenth-century highwayman was Jack Shrimpton. He and his gang 'worked' the Oxford road; a hiding-place reputedly kept for his use, when hard pressed, can still be seen at the Bull Hotel at Gerrards Cross, Buckinghamshire. A certain Higgins—who achieved literary fame as The Highwayman in one of De Quincey's famous essays—lived the life of a country gentleman at Heath House, Knutsford, Cheshire. But when Lady Warburton, whose jewels he had stolen at a ball, saw through his courtly guise and recognized him as the thief, he fled with the speed of light and sought 'patrons' with less penetrating vision along the profitable Bath road.

All the duplicity of which these fellows were capable is summed up in the activities of Dick Turpin, the most famous of them all. Turpin has acquired a legendary aura, though many of the stories about him are true. The most romantic tale, concerning that celebrated ride to York on Black Bess, was, however, compounded of fiction and truth by the nineteenth-century novelist, Harrison Ainsworth. In *Rookwood* he credits Turpin with having ridden the two hundred miles from London to York in (for those days) the incredibly short time of fifteen hours. Actually, this phenomenal feat and its sequel were accomplished by a different highwayman altogether—John William Nevison, a Yorkshireman who had been dead twenty years when Turpin was born.

Unlike Turpin, Nevison seems to have had something of the traditional Robin Hood in his nature. Suitably masked, he frequently robbed the wealthy to enrich the poor. Macaulay declared that Nevison 'levied a quarterly tribute on all the northern drovers and, in return, not only spared them himself but protected them against all other thieves. . . .'

His Ride to York was sparked off by a robbery he committed before dawn at Gad's Hill, near Gravesend, Kent. When he arrived at York, fifteen hours later, he changed immediately into fresh clothes and set out for the bowling green that still exists in Marygate. Here he spoke with the Lord Mayor, thus establishing an alibi that served him well when later charged with the crime. He was acquitted, for it was contended that nobody could possibly be at Gad's Hill and York on the very same day. King Charles II was not so sure; grinning through his full-bottomed wig, he called him 'Swift Nick', then and later.

Eventually, after another audacious robbery, Nevison's barrage of deception failed him. He was tracked to one of his secret lairs—the Three Houses Inn at Sandal, near Wakefield. I once photographed the finely carved Yorkshire chair in which he was sitting when his captors pounced, on that (for him) unhappy day in 1685. The chair is not now at the inn. It was sold to the Vicar of Sandal many years ago for 'five golden guineas' which were long preserved at the inn as mementoes of this odd transaction. If Nevison's ghost ever walks it must be puzzled on finding that once favourite chair of his beside the altar in Sandal Parish Church!

As to Dick Turpin himself, his activities as a gentleman of the road have left a trail of cunning and villainy that covers many parts of Britain.

He was born on 21 September 1705 at the Rose and Crown Inn at Hempstead, Essex, where his father was landlord. At neighbouring Thaxted a building still exists that is known today as Turpin's House —reputedly the place where he sometimes changed horses to outwit his pursuers, galloping up to the stables on a black horse and departing seconds later on a white one, or vice versa.

To sketch in Turpin's career is beyond my present purpose, but a few details are necessary. From his early period as a common thief he graduated to the more exciting life of a highwayman. Danger was rarely absent, but bravado, plus skill in deploying all the subtleties of the profession, brought corresponding rewards.

'Stand and deliver!' The highwayman's rude challenge terrified many a traveller in Georgian England. Out of the tenebrous night had suddenly emerged this heavily cloaked and masked figure, with not a thing to betray his identity as he cocked his pistols and took command. . . .

One little subterfuge was sometimes left to the victims, however. Quite likely only the men of the party would be commanded to get out of the coach and deliver up their valuables. The ladies might have to surrender their rings and other visible jewellery, but so long as they could remain seated, there was a good chance that the more precious belongings would escape detection. As many museum displays of old vehicles testify (for example, at Shibden Hall Folk Museum, Halifax), family coaches often had a secret receptacle for treasure and money beneath the ladies' seat.

There was little of the gay, debonair rascal of legend in the real-life Turpin. At times he was quite ruthless. While hiding from the authorities in Essex he would rob the local smugglers by posing as a Revenue officer, and on one occasion he fatally wounded a forest keeper who had tracked him to his cave in Epping Forest. Several old inns between Epping and London cloaked the movements of Turpin and his accomplices—known as the Essex Gang—but their chief rendezvous was the White Hart in Drury Lane, London. Another haunt was the Spaniard's Inn on Hampstead Heath, where a bullet said to have been fired by Turpin during a scuffle is still shown.

Heath, woodland, forest—or the garret of some friendly inn; all subscribed to Turpin's life of crime. At length, with a price of two hundred pounds on his guilty head, he sought another kind of refuge—his wife's maiden name, Palmer. This took him to the north of England. Even earlier, however (in 1730), he had been compelled to hide himself in Yorkshire, as indicated by a letter now in Lord Halifax's possession. The letter was found in his barn by a farmer named Littlewood at Cantley, near Doncaster. I can well imagine the farmer scratching his head in bewilderment when—after the bird had flown—he first read these whimpering words:

> I William Turpin, Highwayman, was drove in here by stress of Weather and fear of being discovered, but I desire you dear friend, you who belongs to this barn, not to make any discovery of anybody being here, for I am forced to stay in this Neighbourhood for a considerable time and shall not do much more mischief than I have done you this Night to anybody hereabouts. You perhaps have heard that there is a great reward offered for taking me but let not that make you endeavour to seek my Ruin who means you no harm. Perhaps I may be forced to lye another Night.

A fake? Who can now tell? One authentic touch is the writer's use of the name *William*. For some unknown reason Turpin often called himself by that name. Another dodge, maybe.

Turpin's disguise as John Palmer served him for about two years, and it is surprising that after so elusive a career, it was a comparatively mild affair of horse-stealing that resulted in his capture—at the Green Dragon Inn, Welton, near Hull. At this inn—one of his favourite haunts—callers are sometimes shown the trap-door by which he often evaded pursuers. But none of his stratagems served him this time. He was seized and led away to imprisonment at York Castle, where his real identity was discovered by somebody who recognized his handwriting.

Just before his execution, on 7 April 1739, Turpin provided money for five men to be fitted out with black hatbands and black gloves. He was thus assured of some mourners. Then, dressed in a brand-new fustian suit as though going to meet a friend, he went unabashed to the gallows on York Knavesmire.

His long campaign of secrecy finished with this impudent swagger, in the full light of day.

CHAPTER FOUR

A TANGLED SKEIN

Today there is a grim sort of humour in the thought that while certain members of the community were hiding from a given danger, other people were hiding from something quite different. One group of persons might even try to evade two or more foes simultaneously. I think in particular of coastal smugglers who, in Nelson's day, not only had to beware of Preventive Men, but that equally insidious 'enemy'—the Press Gang.

The Bonaparte scare was very real. Sailors were badly needed to swell His Majesty's naval crews, and people at home felt compelled to hide their valuables—as well as their eligible sons. All this resulted in webs of duplicity. Nearly everybody around the coast had several things 'up their sleeve'. Secrecy thrived—on various levels.

'Boney will get you!' Even in my own boyhood days this old threat had a certain potency. Passed down through several generations it had become a half-humorous parental corrective. Some families can even recall, from inherited remarks, how their forebears had reacted when the threat was new and urgent. Around Whitby, for example, treasured belongings were hidden in places used during an earlier scare, when Paul Jones the pirate was at large. One hears of a house in Bagdale, Whitby, and another at neighbouring Sleights, both of which had a garden 'hide' reached by the owner through a secret passage. The hide was ready for any emergency.

But the whole district had long been nurtured in the arts of evasion and concealment. The groundwork had been there in Jacobite times, when people had other fears; and earlier still, when Protestant hounded Catholic.

Let us side-track the Press Gang for a few moments and look closer at this groundwork—of method, place, and (above all) mental attitude.

Here I pick up a little book, *The Father Postgate Story*, by Father David Quinlan. The main subject of this thrilling story will emerge later. Meanwhile, it raises matter that is quite relevant to our present concern.

The 'Forty-Five Rebellion had serious repercussions in and around Ugthorpe, near Whitby. This moorland district was suspected of disloyalty to the Crown. That irascible priest-hunter of Queen Elizabeth's reign—Sir Thomas Hoby of Hackness Hall—had regarded his home as 'a Protestant oasis in a Papist desert'.

In her diary Lady Hoby often refers to her husband's zeal in this respect. 'Mr Hoby that night went to search for papests' echoes through the diary as frequently as her own solemn 'praiers'. Even at this late day it is somewhat discomfiting to visualize her enjoying an evening with the alpherion, her favourite stringed instrument, while Thomas slips out to seek his prey. Particularly obnoxious to him were the Cholmleys of Whitby. The Salisbury MSS at Hatfield House contain much defamatory information about the Cholmley family and their Abbey House residence. This place, we read, 'was a receptacle to the seminary priests coming from beyond seas, and landing frequently at that port; insomuch as . . . there have been in his [Henry Cholmley's] house three or four of them together at a time, and, most coming both bare of cloaths and money, have . . . been sent away with a very great supply of both; some in scarlet and satin, with their men and horses, the better to disguise their professions.'

Dorothy Meads, who edited the published version of Lady Hoby's *Diary*, remarks truly, 'The sparsely populated moorland between Hackness and Whitby . . . together with the lonely coast, provided excellent lurking places for the priests of the old religion and their adherents.'

The above comments on Hoby versus Cholmley are a necessary prologue to Father Quinlan's own stirring account. He takes up the story about a hundred and fifty years later. Despite persecution, the 'old Faith' not only survived hereabouts; Catholic life became strongly entrenched in and around the beautiful Esk valley. And then came the Jacobite Rebellions. Catholics were once again under duress, especially during the 'Forty-Five. This is what Father Quinlan records:

> . . . the shipwrights had led a mob from Whitby, armed with their tools, to attack the Catholics of the Egton district, who probably went in fear of their lives. Fathers Hervey and Potts went back on to the moors above the Esk valley to hide, on December 10, 1745.
>
> In 1937 [continues the narrator] I thought their hiding-place should be identifiable. It would be a hollow close to the main road,

which they would have to keep under observation. After a short search I found a shallow depression from which both the road and the side road to Ugthorpe could easily be seen, while offering good shelter. As I looked at it, a voice asked what I thought I was doing. The speaker seemed to have come down out of the sky on to the bare moor—an excellent example of the concealment which is there as easy as it looks difficult. I told the man what I was about and he asked where I had heard of the two priests. When I told him I had read of them in a book (Father Hervey's Diary), he commented, "Us knows history 'fore it gets into t' books," and walked dourly off.

In a letter to me Father Quinlan says, 'I am surely the only person living who can tell you exactly where Father Hervey and Father Potts lay hid on the moors.' Had either of those priests been a 'sensitive' he would have known that the same kind of thing had happened here or hereabouts before. For these wind-swept moors and their ancient tumuli are as confidential as Dorset's Badbury Rings, to which Hardy's Mayor of Casterbridge gravitated quite naturally for his secret meeting with the wife he had previously sold.

And so it was Loose Howe that witnessed the other little drama. A pitiful drama, for after spending that winter's night in their hollow the two priests, 'doubtless defeated by the intense cold', made for Ugthorpe again and were taken into custody.

Rough justice can be seen in the fact that the next generation or so of Whitby's shipwrights and sailors had themselves to seek refuge—from the Press Gang, that iniquitous system of impressing, or seizing men for the King's navy. To avoid detection, eligible fellows would cower for days in the ruins of Whitby Abbey or in the vault of St Mary's Church nearby, or occasionally on the surrounding moors to whose secret shelter their ancestors had driven those two Catholic priests, and others before them.

The Jacobite risings challenged the ingenuity of many who wished to escape involvement. At Hackness Hall I have been shown the very cupboard into which a couple of men disappeared at that time. The oak cupboard (made in neighbouring Farndale) was then owned by a Mr Rowland of Gillamoor who let it be known, later, that when England was invaded by the Scottish rebels in 1745 his two sons lay in the cupboard for several days, to keep out of the rebels' way. Fear must have had them by the throat; the cupboard's narrow interior would force anybody save young children to fold up like clams.

Over at Mirfield, in the south-west of Yorkshire, people fled from the supposed Jacobite terror by going underground. The old, inborn instinct, of course, but as there are no caves in this area the people made use of the coalpits. They were shallow pits, however, so shallow that in places the cottagers could knock on their floors and be answered by the colliers below. When it was rumoured that Prince Charlie's 'boy-eating' troops were approaching, the good people of Mirfield gathered their children and their few belongings—and disappeared like rabbits.

When in 1875 some old coal-workings were accidentally entered at Mirfield, five stoneware jars were found—receptacles, it was believed, of the food and drink stored in this gloomy place during the 1745 scare. The Rev. J. Ismay, the Mirfield vicar of that period, left his own pithy record of those stirring times. One Sunday, according to his diary, few people attended divine service 'for want of apparel'. Their belongings were safely stowed below ground. This lack of worshippers had its compensations, however. So quiet was the singing that the few who did go to church 'were entertained with ye finest notes of a robin redbreast I have ever heard. . . .'

We can now unravel a little more of our skein and deal with the Press Gang, and the ruses they unwittingly inspired. The web of secrecy, spun so often and effectively in the past, had become a kind of heritage—a second nature, to be drawn upon as occasion dictated.

The danger of being impressed could cause unease all over the country—not only along the coast. On Tuesday, 13 July 1779, the *Leeds Mercury* published the following:

> Notwithstanding the fineness of the weather for some time past, our Fair on Saturday and Yesterday was remarkably thin, owing, as is supposed, to a report that was spread of the press having broke out here; but we can assure our readers, nothing of the kind has happened. It is imagined to have took its rise from a party of Marines parading round the streets, with colours flying, music playing, and being dressed like sailors.

A month later the *Leeds Intelligencer* issued this assurance: 'Notice to persons from West Yorkshire seeking Harvest Work in East Yorkshire, that they may safely pass as heretofore and not be liable to be pressed or molested in so doing. Sign'd, Richard Mawhood, Deputy Clerk of the Peace.'

Even so, able-bodied men were not taking any chances. There were too many tales of farmhands as well as sailors being whisked off with no by-your-leave, and no provision made for a man's wife and children. Pay for pressed men was uncertain, and the food a scandal.

Mrs Gaskell exposed the horror and injustice of Press Gang activities in her fine novel, *Sylvia's Lovers*. Much of the information woven into her story was factual and gained on the spot. It chiefly concerns a shocking 'piece o' wark i' Monkshaven [Whitby] wi' t' press-gang'. But everybody knew there was no limit to the reach of those tentacles.

At Beckwithshaw, near Harrogate—over fifty miles from the nearest stretch of coast—the local lads got fidgety one time because the Press were said to be on the prowl, even here. When things got rather too hot, the youths sought help at neighbouring Tatefield Hall. The house itself offered no effective concealment, but the friendly owner directed them to a culvert outside. The episode takes vivid shape in my mind because I have several times stood beside this culvert. Covered with flagstones, it runs the full length of the farmyard and past one end of the house. I peered through a gap left by two missing flagstones and marvelled that anybody should hide inside this long, narrow channel that directs a rather turbulent stream. Yet a thorough wetting, in cramped conditions, was a small price to pay for liberty. Such are the demands of secrecy that even a *sewer* has more than once provided a means of escape.

When home from Greenland, Captain Thomas Hawkins of the Hull whaler *Everthorpe* hit upon a novel safety device. He wore one of his wife's dresses. Thus disguised he could enjoy the air with his wife and family and treat the Press Gang with disdain.

In Ford—a Scottish border village we shall have reason to visit again—it was the village girls who came to the men's rescue. At the first sign of the 'enemy' the girls danced from house to house, singing this song:

Dance the tittery-tan, Marjorie,
Dance the tittery-tan,
Yonder is the tender,
Coming to take our men.

It was a private signal. At once the younger men ran across to the public house, climbed the wall and lay flat on its roof (probably thatched). Girls were particularly precious in early nineteenth-century Ford! Once, however, the Press Gang made a notable capture here. It was a giant of a man, who had been known to hold the generally feared King of the Yetholm gipsies over the local pit shaft to teach him better social manners. I do not suppose this Hercules even glanced at the inn, when the officers appeared. Why hide? Capture meant little to him. He just bided his time. Had he not secret reserves? When led to the waiting tender, at the nearest port, he placed his back against one gunwale and his feet against the other, and then *pushed.* The boat split down the middle—and our giant returned, unchallenged, to the comforts of home. He was too dangerous to take aboard one of His Majesty's men-of-war.

Almost every port in the country has its tales about the Press Gang and the curious methods of evasion so often employed. The Mayor's chair in the Town Hall at Southwold is flanked by the staffs and truncheons once wielded as symbols of their authority by the town's constables. These dignitaries were strongly in evidence at the periodical Beating of the Bounds, and again at the annual Trinity Fair. They accompanied the Mayor and Corporation to church. And of course they maintained law and order in this delightful little borough on the Suffolk coast. But they had yet another function. It was to hide their fellow townsmen—the hale and hearty ones—when 'wanted' by the Press Gang.

Just *where* the men were stowed out of sight I have not been able to discover. Perhaps it was in some accommodating cellar, or even the local lock-up. There are other likely places among the heath that borders the little River Blyth, and the sand dunes that smugglers often used across the ferry at Walberswick.

Even when the gang succeeded in capturing a few men, they did not necessarily have the last word. The official local rendezvous, or depot, might favour the prisoners. At Whitby the 'Randyvowse' was an old house near the harbour bridge. It has regrettably been pulled down (to make room for the Custom House Hotel), but often when I pass that way I visualize a scene that frequently happened there. The inmates are not really despondent. The chimney is tall, straight—and co-operative. Unknown to the Press Gang the flue is fitted with climbing irons. Up go the Whitby fellows, one by one, then along the roof and down the chimney of a neighbouring house—to freedom.

I wonder that the bewildered apostles of the King's 'navee' never guessed.

CHAPTER FIVE

NEGRO TRAIL

Parson Woodforde's diary contains an interesting reference to a black man who once called at his Norfolk parsonage (21 July 1787) with a dwarf travelling companion. Woodforde's dark visitor, who had formerly been in service with the Earl of Albemarle, flourished a French horn which he blew all the way up the parsonage drive to the kitchen door. After this fanfare the dwarf woman entertained the household with a few songs. At length the little concert party went off, the richer by one bright shilling.

This amusing incident at Weston Longeville reminded me of other negro horn-blowers, one of whom—Cato, the Earl of Chesterfield's 'black'—was said to blow the best French horn and trumpet in eighteenth-century England. It also prompted my resolve to seek and follow the Negro trail across our northern shires. Much of the picture so revealed is pleasant enough, though furtiveness and shame fill in the background.

The trail is easily picked up, by anybody, at Hull, thanks to the town's Wilberforce House Museum. Here, in the actual birthplace of the slave emancipator, the traffic that once disgraced humanity takes precedence over all other aspects of Wilberforce's career. And the secrecy which clothed many of the slave-traders' dealings soon becomes apparent.

Hanging in one room, for example, there is a composite series of six oil-paintings by Stuart Henry Bell (1892–3). In them he reveals the 'Life of a Slaver' at the beginning of his century. The vessel depicted is the brigantine *Orange Grove*, built at Sunderland in 1812, ostensibly for the fruit trade but actually used as a South African slave-ship. It looks perfectly innocent on leaving Sunderland harbour, but scene two declares its real objective: the *Orange Grove* is anchored off an African slave shore, by moonlight, awaiting its human cargo. At day-break the ship leaves for the West Indies but is chased, during the voyage, by an English frigate. One hopes that during the destruction of the slaver by the frigate's guns, the hidden black cargo is first rescued. But Bell's graphic pictures do not give us that assurance.

Slavery's horrifying record is taken up again in the museum's many documents relating to the sale and purchase of black cargoes. Some of the victims were sold for cash. James Wyatt pays 750 dollars at auction for a Negro named William. Some were bartered. A certain black woman called Mary is exchanged for twenty bushels of salt and a quantity of brandy and tobacco amounting in value to forty-eight dollars. 'Quamima, a good watchman but bad legs'—to quote one slave-owner's inventory—is worth only 'sixpence'.

The whole nauseous trade is brought to a point, here, by a lifesize figure of a naked Negro, who is pleading his kinship with the rest of mankind. Behind him stands a lion. Both are meant to symbolize the Dark Continent. Carved in stone, this compelling study is at the back door, facing the riverside garden.

The brighter side of the story is represented indoors by another lifesize figure, this time showing a Negro boy-attendant in late-Georgian finery. It is carved in pine and once stood inside the entrance to the Royal Pump Room at Bath, welcoming patrons with a courtly bow that completely masks the secret, jungle origin of his forebears.

During the Age of Elegance his living counterpart could be seen in many a fashionable ménage. According to contemporary portraits, however, some of the black page-boys could not have been more than nine or ten years of age.

At Newburgh Priory, in the North Riding, a painting by Andrea Soldi portrays Catherine, Countess of Fauconberg, with a small Negro page holding her coronet. At Upper Helmsley Hall, near York, Sir Thomas Herbert—friend of King Charles I—looks out from a commanding portrait in which the costume given him by the Shah of Persia (see page 154) is seen to great advantage. This portrait also includes a little black boy. Bedecked with jewelled ear-drops, the blackamoor seems to be gazing up with admiration at his master's fine turban, though he had every reason to be proud of his own sable curls, tastefully bound with a fillet.

The best evocation of a blackamoor I have seen occurs on the Staircase of Friendship at Red House, Moor Monkton, near York. This early seventeenth-century house (now a school) belonged to the Slingsby family and Sir Henry Slingsby, a well-known Royalist, describes the staircase in his diary. After referring to the carved newel posts, which still display the fascinating animal and bird emblems of Slingsby's 'especial friends and brothers-in-law', he mentions a little

The mysterious entrance to Victoria Cave,
West Yorks. Many important archaeological finds
have been made inside

Britain's 'perfect' underground passage: Mortimer's Hole, which penetrates the entire Castle Rock at Nottingham

Approach to Buttermere—Cumberland's 'Secret Valley' which the Norman invaders could never find

Gwennap Pit, Cornwall, linked in legend with Christ's visit to the local tin-miners

Two curiosities at Penfound Manor, Cornwall: the Armada timbers, and the floor recess through which a stream once ran

The chair in which Nevison the highwayman was finally captured, now in Sandal Church, Wakefield

Life-size figure of a Negro page-boy: Wilberforce House Museum, Hull

lead blackamoor provided at the 'half-pace' to hold a lamp that would illuminate the staircase. In Slingsby's day the staircase led to a 'painted chamber'; also, I suspect, at least part way towards the hall's secret room which often hid Sir Henry during the Civil Wars.

Many years ago this delightful staircase was moved to the adjacent family chapel. This transfer has, in effect, changed the blackamoor's mission. Instead of ushering Fairfaxes, Saviles, Bethels, Vavasours, and Slingsbys upstairs—that is, the families represented here with such heraldic fervour—the little fellow with the pigmentation born of hot suns in mysterious Africa now cocks a merry wink at the English schoolboys as they make for the music gallery above.

A great surprise awaited me in Dentdale, that secluded valley once favoured by persecuted dissenters, in the extreme west of Yorkshire. Nothing worse than a bit of salmon poaching had ever happened here, it seemed, but one day a chance remark disclosed something sinister from the past. A local man, I heard, had once imported a number of Negroes. Some became servants in his fine new house. Others were employed in some neighbouring marble quarries. But this was not all. Folk memory has elaborated this episode, providing several repellent sequels.

T. Wray Milnes of Lea Yeat, Dent—who has been tape-recording such tales passed down to local inhabitants—gives me a few factual details. The man in question was a Liverpool merchant called Sill; he came to Rigg End, near Dent, in the late eighteenth or early nineteenth century, bringing with him that curious black retinue. A pool in Deepdale Beck, where the Negroes were allowed to bathe, is still called Black Dub.

At this point the story becomes hazy. After building a better place for himself—the house now known as Whernside Manor—the merchant ran into some kind of trouble with his 'blacks'. Echoing their own forebears, some Dent people say that one of the Negroes, quarrelling with another man over a white sweetheart, was killed and had to be buried secretly. They also say that the black man's ghost haunts the neighbourhood. But the owner of Whernside Manor, when I called, had a different version. The Negro was accidentally suffocated. Several of them had been hastily thrust into a small room to avoid being seen by a certain visitor. When they were liberated, hours later, one poor fellow was beyond help. Hence the need for a hush-hush burial.

We now pick up the trail a few miles to the west, in the Lake District.

While William Wilberforce was at Rayrigg Hall, Windermere, he would often row out to one of the lake islands and there meditate on the slave problem. I purposely looked upon those same islands, during my quest, from the wooded grounds of Storrs Hall, near Bowness. This beautiful place was acquired, early in the nineteenth century, by John Bolton, another Liverpool merchant. Much of his trade with the West Indies was above reproach, but there can be no doubt that he also traded—on the quiet—in Negro slaves. One can discount some of the lurid tales told about him locally, and it has to be remembered that slaving—though detested by many—was not at that time illegal. For Bolton, respectability—marked by personal friendship with men like Wordsworth and Sir Walter Scott—was maintained by keeping the whole thing secret.

Storrs Hall is now an hotel. In the vestibule an attractive portrait of John Bolton is accompanied by some blunt historical notes. 'Bolton owned slavers,' I read, 'at a time when slaves were carried to the West Indies . . .' According to one tradition, 'whenever Bolton noticed any young boys among the slaves on his ships at Liverpool he would extract them and put them on a smaller boat and sail [through Morecambe Bay] to Greenodd, where a local man smuggled them up the Leven valley to Windermere . . . the boys were then taken by rowing boat to Storrs Hall.'

Servants' hall gossip at Storrs named the actual landing-place—reasonably enough—as the convenient stone causeway which juts 116 feet into the lake from a little promontory in the grounds. Later the youngsters were sold as houseboys to some of the surrounding gentry.

As if to confirm this part of the Storrs tradition, I found a house in the locality that preserves a vivid memory of those days. It is Hodge Hill, near Winster. At the top turn of the fine oak staircase there is a curious recess fitted with a tiny plank seat. Here, in a space as dark as himself, the Philipsons' page-boy sat while awaiting orders. About this time the Philipsons made their house into a distribution centre for contraband, smuggled over from Morecambe Bay by much the same route that introduced the black boys.

I have already mentioned the Fairfax family, in connection with Red House at Moor Monkton. They, too, employed one of these waifs from Africa, but doubtless treated him well. The Fairfaxes had a reputation for kindliness. He would accompany the family to their different houses, as determined by varying social seasons, but the house in which I have 'met' him is the lovely old Rectory at Newton Kyme, near Tadcaster. Here, in the seventeenth century, lived the Rev. Henry Fairfax and his wife; others of the family came into residence later.

Their black boy was not pushed out of sight in some dark hole, as at Hodge Hill. Until required for some household task, he occupied a specially prepared niche in the entrance hall. The niche is in that part of the Rectory that was rebuilt in 1725 to commemorate Admiral Fairfax's share in the capture of Gibraltar. The Admiral lived across the way, at Newton Kyme Hall. The alterations to the Rectory meant, among other things, blocking up a medieval fireplace. One end of this fireplace—the end enclosed by the Georgian entrance hall—became the black boy's cosy little arbour. From within its soft shadows he would see all the comings and goings of the family and their friends. What strange conversations and whisperings must sometimes have drifted over to him!

In some fashionable households the black boy—merged into the background and forgotten until needed—turned his enforced eavesdropping to humorous account. Few household secrets were safe from him. Listen to this passage from the *Diary of a Lady of Quality*, by Lady Frances Pennoyer of Bullingham Court, Herefordshire. It is dated 2 August 1759.

> Roused from my sleep by roars of laughter, and found my Lord and Harry in the library amusing themselves with Caesar, whom they were making imitate my Lady Yarmouth [the young King's custodian]. I could scarcely forbear joining in their mirth as I saw the boy pucker his black face into a hundred wrinkles and shake his fist at an imaginary King. The imp declares that she boxes the ears of our gracious Sovereign, and mimics the way in which he [the King] rubs his head with his august hand, and then coaxes his elderly favourite into a good temper again.
>
> I cannot have such doings under my roof. Shall our anointed King be mocked by my servants? And as for Lady Yarmouth—but enough of her in my diary . . .
>
> I took the boy to my room, calling Dearlove to help me, and I

made her give him a sound whipping. I never saw a black boy whipped before. The effects of the punishment are not so easily seen on his skin as on a white one, but, judging from his cries, it was pretty severe. I think the girl's arm ached before she had finished.

As I read this extract, in the friendly atmosphere of Newton Kyme Rectory, it was natural to feel that Lady Pennoyer's 'black' had been made the whipping-boy for the faults of others.

Yet one must admit that some Negro servants fared well. Only esteem, I suggest, would account for the inclusion of their 'black' on the Gerard family tomb at Ashley Church, Staffordshire. As in life, this worthy fellow continues to wait upon Thomas Lord Gerard, his wife and their numerous progeny; it is just as though the family would be incomplete without their man from Darkest Africa.

My final word on this theme must be about 'Poor Sambo', a Negro who, while attending his master from the West Indies, died on arrival at Sunderland Point, near Lancaster. That was in 1736. Since Sunderland Point lost its shipping to Glasson Dock, across the Lune estuary, the place has become a sanctuary for waders. And not far from the shore there is a lonely field where lichens have taken over the decoration of Sambo's simple, cairn-like grave. Thinking his master had deserted him, Sambo—it is said—died of a broken heart. Yet the merchant had only gone forward on business to Lancaster. An epitaph in verse on the Negro's grave indicates how much he was mourned. Its last few lines declare that God's approbation, at the Last Judgment, will rest 'not on a man's colour but his worth of heart'.

Who Sambo really was will never be known. It seems fitting, therefore, that he should have come to his final rest in the strange, secretive place that is Sunderland Point. From the mainland at Overton it is served by a road that is submerged at every rising tide. At full tide, Sambo's little bourne is virtually an island, as secluded as anybody could wish. With the ebb, this glistening, serpentine road over the marshes suggests a surfacing sea-monster; water slithers from its dorsal region to form swirling pools among the surrounding mud and sand.

This tenuous link with the mainland is so odd that my friends and I once went along purposely to photograph its freakish landscape. Varying in shade from soft grey to an almost inky blackness, the sandy mud is 'sculptured' by tidal fluctuations and currents in the most grotesque manner. On both sides of the tidal road there are sizeable amphitheatres, terraced into smooth galleries beloved by the curlews. There are mountains and valleys in miniature, mysterious coves and dark sinister lagoons festooned with seaweed. When swept by late afternoon sunshine, this phantasmagoria looks enchanting—a Jules Verne-ish continent of singular appeal. Yet all will be hidden again, with the flowing tide—hidden as completely as 'Poor Sambo's' early life beside some West African swamp.

CHAPTER SIX

BORDER-LINE MARRIAGE

In a previous chapter we saw something of Ford, that neat little village on the English side of the Scottish border. We saw the young men and women of the place conspiring to outwit the Press Gang. Ford now beckons again.

An introduction to our immediate theme is perhaps best obtained by stepping into Waterford Hall (formerly the village school) and admiring the scriptural wall-paintings. They were done, during the last century, by the Marchioness of Waterford, and most of the Bible characters here depicted are children—Jacob and Esau, Moses and Miriam, David as a shepherd boy, Timothy learning at his mother's knee, and Jesus himself. The Marchioness used village boys and girls as her models. It is curious to record that the parents of these children had, in some instances, been married in the secret manner then practised at several places along the Border.

Smugglers were not the only people who found the disparity between English and Scottish laws to their liking. It gave *them* a loophole for slipping contraband, unobtrusively, into England. But the same heathery fells and moorland tracks drew impetuous lovers in the *opposite* direction, Scotland being more accommodating than England in matrimonial affairs.

But let us take things in their proper order.

Among the young people of Ford, it seems, there was no open courtship; to the couple concerned their relationship was an extra beat of the heart, not a matter for public gossip. They kept company 'under hidlings'. Even when the pair became engaged, wrote the Rev. Hastings Neville, a bygone Rector of Ford, 'you hesitate to congratulate either party, lest you should give offence. You are not supposed to know . . .' This apparent unawareness that anything was in the wind even extended to those of the home circle. Silence was golden—and helped to shape the wedding ring!

Some couples resolved the secret situation at last by getting married, in normal fashion, in the beautiful little parish church. Others clung to their secret until the very last moment—by marrying eight miles away, not in some other church, but at Bridge Inn or Marriage House, on Coldstream Bridge. The swain would saunter to the rendezvous along one lane, via Branxton perhaps, and the light of his eye would take another. Only when William Dickson, the 'cobbler parson', had united them—in this quaint little building still to be seen above the River Tweed—was their myth of unconcern exploded. Hastings Neville was surprised to find, on enquiry, how very many of his aged parishioners had gone through this farrago of pretence.

Couples from farther afield usually arrived at Coldstream by coach, or on horseback, and more often than not they were runaways, with an irate parent in hot pursuit. Two other places along the Border played their part in this clandestine business. There was Lamberton Toll, near Berwick-upon-Tweed, and Gretna Green. Lamberton need not detain us. Gretna Green will be noticed later.

Meanwhile, let us look more closely at Coldstream. Beyond the middle of the long bridge that spans the Tweed one is in Scotland, where marriage was once as simple as a promise. No banns were necessary, as in England, no clergyman, no period of residence—just John's plain declaration that he and his Susan wished to wed. If the couple came as runaways the brief proceedings might well be punctuated by a speedy descent to some peculiar cellars, just above water level. And not for convivial reasons either. Wine and ale would certainly be stored down there, but it was understood that room was left among the barrels for anybody needing refuge from 'father'.

Pat Moodie was the first to start 'marrying folk' at this unorthodox place. He was a shoemaker by profession, but his illiteracy was no handicap. Registers were deemed unnecessary. Jock Armstrong, a mole-catcher, was no better equipped for recording the marriages he performed here. And the law evidently allowed these irregularities. What did cause an occasional fracas was the *garb* worn by these 'Border priests'. To give their ministrations the semblance of authority and respectability they would don clerical attire.

William Dickson, the other 'cobbler parson', was once prosecuted for this offence by the parish minister but the case was dismissed. On returning from the trial at Edinburgh, Dickson was feted and carried through Coldstream shoulder high. Business continued much as usual. He was very popular and is said to have done 'a roaring trade, charging on an average half a guinea as fee, but much more when "big gentlemen" and moneyed men required his services'.

And 'big men' there had been, if local tradition echoes the truth. On 18 November 1772 John Scott, later Lord Chancellor Eldon, eloped with Betty Surtees, the banker's daughter, and fled to Coldstream before pursuit was possible. The window through which Betty escaped from her father's house, in Sandhill, Newcastle upon Tyne, is now marked with a suitable inscription. But the marriage itself, reputedly effected in the Newcastle Arms at Coldstream, left no record—presumably because the 'priest' was our illiterate friend, Pat Moodie.

Another celebrity who sought the anonymity of Moodie's haphazard procedure was Lord Brougham. Oddly enough it was the Marriage Act introduced years later by Brougham (in 1856) which virtually put an end to these clandestine practices.

I once stayed at the Newcastle Arms here, and soon became aware of the Brougham aura. He and his Mary, daughter of John Eden, are treated as honoured, if long-departed guests. Their nuptial bedroom is probably still 'on show'. My chief object in the district, however, was to trace if possible any marriage records that *were* made. I could not find anything from the time of Jimmie Dippie (a common surname hereabouts), who was really a candlemaker, or of McEwan the tailor. Both were spare-time Border 'parsons' who tried to undercut the fees charged by others. I was more successful with William Dickson. Judging by his known records, he must have performed at least 1,446 irregular marriages.

A lady in the town had inherited some of those marriage 'registers'. Using what were obviously penny notebooks of the period, Dickson listed the different entries—some in ink, others in pencil—as though continually pulled between the claims of economy and of possible future reference. On looking through these dog-eared 'registers' I got a strange feeling. I was peering into secrets of long ago. In the earliest book, dated 1844, the first tentative entry refers to Peter Sprott of Westminster, Middlesex, and Mariah Muir of Ancram, Roxburghshire. Other entries follow, some scribbled, as if made in haste.

As I turned the flimsy pages I seemed to hear Dickson putting his stock question to each palpitating bridegroom: 'Noo, my man, what's your name, an' where div ye coom frae?' They and their brides evidently came from a great variety of places, so as to get married *sub rosa* by this homely, easy-going fellow. Jane Tait hailed from Lilburn Tower Farm, a few miles south of Wooler, Northumberland. Others gravitated from such neighbouring places as Wark, Jedburgh, Norham, Branxton and Warkworth. A one-inch map indicates the lonely moors they would have to negotiate. But Middlesbrough in North Yorkshire, and Maryport, on the Cumberland coast, are also recorded, suggesting all kinds of romantic evasions at a further remove.

Small wonder that Mrs Gray, the lady who showed me these old marriage 'registers', continually received queries from various parts of Britain. Confirmation that one's great-grandparents—who look so sedate and proper in that gilt-framed portrait—did indeed flaunt the conventions by running off to Coldstream—would cause some hilarity in the home circle.

In the *Leeds Intelligencer* for Tuesday, 16 November 1799, the following item stands out from a wearying background of auction sales and deaths:

> On Wednesday se'night set out for the Temple of Hymen (Gretna Green), Mr Cuttle, jun. of Hatheroyd, near Barnsley, with Miss E. Dicken of Knottingley; a young lady about 16, with a fortune of £3,000.

Cuttle junior and his wealthy sweetheart were among the hundreds of couples who took advantage of this other place just over the Border and its facilities for hasty marriages. Perhaps the 'priest' who tied the knot for them was the notorious Joe Paisley. In Gretna Hall he had married scores, notably John Peel to 'Bonnie Mary White', who fulfilled the best romantic traditions by having run away by moonlight. I wonder how much Paisley charged the famous huntsman; his fees varied from two shillings and sixpence to ten pounds. If any couple were obviously poor, however, he would waive his fee and accept a bottle of brandy.

Always at your service was Joe Paisley, and when haste occasionally caused confusion in 'sartifying' any marriages conducted simultaneously, so that brides might be linked to the wrong grooms, he was blandness itself. 'Aweel,' he would say, 'just sort yersel's oot!' Meanwhile, the parties so muddled had to keep an eye on the road. Either girl's father might ride up at any moment, full of sound and fury.

As one enters Gretna Green today several places where couples could marry in this furtive manner advertise their old-time rôle by displaying bundle after bundle of former marriage papers—tattered secrets of so many runaways.

Much more circumspect is the stately Gretna Hall. Long used as an inn, it stands rather aloof from the village, yet within easy reach of the busy roads that converge here. Its air of respectability is itself a disguise. Who would think that in this attractive early-Georgian house, dignified with the Johnstone coat-of-arms over the entrance, at least 1,134 marriages were once fixed up with speed, security—and guile?

Following Joe Paisley in this profitable business was John Linton. As one-time valet to Sir James Graham of Netherby Hall (the Young Lochinvar of lively fame) he had peculiar qualifications for his new profession! Then there was Robert Elliot, who imbibed the clandestine tradition by marrying Paisley's granddaughter. David Lang was another to whom subterfuge was second nature. In early life he had been seized by the Press Gang, but the naval ship on which he was planted eventually fell foul of the notorious Paul Jones. When this piratical captain turned his sloop into Solway Firth, Lang seized his chance. Under cover of darkness he swam ashore, and paths familiar to him since boyhood—paths through the Covenanters' country—facilitated his escape.

But it was Linton who lent éclat to 'Gratney Hall' and its proceedings. Such was his grandiose manner, when marrying clients, that he was dubbed *Bishop* Linton. Save for one special little service, everything he did was done with decorum. His clients had to be sober, and few parish clerks could have improved upon his marriage records. The Scottish marriage law might be simple, but it was still a law—to be administered aright.

Of course, it paid Linton to be so particular. He could collect big fees, especially from the gentry. But decorum sometimes went to the winds. Loud knocking on the door and blustering demands to be admitted were signals to complete the ceremony at once, and hurry the anxious newly-weds into the hall's secret chamber.

Then only was the enraged parent ushered within—to be assured that the couple were now legally married and had retired to their room. Dignity once more descended upon the 'Bishop', and as the secret room could only be reached through his own private apartment, the couple were nicely insulated from interference. If parental outrage should overcome the 'Bishop's' resistance (most unlikely), the couple could still escape the impending wrath—by slipping out of a well-placed window.

This hidden room, and the escape window that keeps a weather eye on whatever is happening outside, is now shown to visitors. Secrecy has therefore departed, leaving behind only a fragrance on the air, the swish of a gown, a soft whisper. And only these if one has never said goodbye to romance.

Other places once used for clandestine marriages have long been forgotten: Cuthbert Hilton's former house half-way across the County Bridge at Barnard Castle, for example; moorland dells in various districts, and one of the Tresilian caves in Glamorgan. Smugglers knew the value of these caves, but the parents of General Picton (a Waterloo hero) set a greater value on this particular one, for it had given them—and several other couples—a remote, hidden, somewhat bizarre sanctuary for their nuptials.

Gretna alone seems to capitalize the association—but the former atmosphere has vanished, along with the secrecy. Couples can still marry at Gretna—but only after a twenty-one days' residence qualification. Runaway marriages could hardly thrive in such conditions. Even so, on my last visit to Gretna, fifty couples were temporarily residing in the village, all awaiting their great day. Not for them the thrill of a mad gallop to Gretna Hall and a hasty union clinched by the ringing of the blacksmith's anvil, however; they must marry at a local church or the registry office. Shades of 'Bishop' Linton!

What, then, remains of the old set-up? Only the occasional farce of a *mock* wedding. At the one my friends and I witnessed, the kilted 'parson' opened a chest and handed out a veil for the 'bride', a fawn topper for the 'groom', and bouquets for others of the merry party. We heard strange murmurings and joined in the laughter when a huge ring was produced. The whole affair can be very funny, on the music-hall level, but tradition soon had me in its grip again. Inwardly, secretly, I longed to hear a coach dash up from Carlisle, to see the couple emerge, and then to offer myself as witness for some happy, if rather headlong union.

CHAPTER SEVEN

DIGGING FOR TREASURE

So far we have seen how, driven by a variety of compulsions, both men and women have gone into hiding, or masked some of their activities. Other examples will emerge later, but now we must pause awhile and try to find further tangible evidence of the secretive past as fostered among our hills and vales and around the coast.

The popularity of archaeology today needs no stressing from me. Never before have so many people showed such keen and intelligent interest in archaeological 'digs' and a desire to do some digging themselves. Let Egypt have its prolific Valley of Kings, and Crete its splendid Minoan ruins. Britain has a secret world of its own.

Nobody with half an ounce of imagination can walk through York or Bath or Winchester without feeling, occasionally, that beneath his feet there may be wonderful treasures—yet to be found—from past ages. The same feeling is strong in certain countryside areas. An ancient tumulus, if still intact, can quicken the pulse as much as a limestone cave. I should like to have been present when the old chieftain's ship was uncovered at Sutton Hoo, near Woodbridge in Suffolk, some thirty years ago; or the fabulous Mildenhall Treasure in the same beautiful county; or King Alfred's Jewel (of which more later) in a country gentleman's park in Somerset. Not only is each find in itself thrilling, but also the sense of unlocking the past—of penetrating the ramparts of Time to some hitherto unsuspected, or only half-known way of life.

Readers of Samuel Pepys's diary will recall how he once buried his stock of wine in his garden, also (equally precious) 'my parmazan cheese'. His gold remained a matter of real concern, for during his attendance at church one Sunday the diarist's father and his own wife buried it for him—'in open daylight, in the midst of the garden; where, for aught they knew, many eyes might see them . . .' All this was a precaution against looting during the Great Fire of London. What caused hundreds of other treasures to be hidden, at different periods of history, may never be known, though speculation can be pleasantly diverting.

That gold torque, or girdle, once found on a hill called the Billing at Rawdon in mid-Airedale; how did it get there? It was of Roman workmanship and the find-spot is only a short distance from the Roman road known as York Gate that was part of the transcoastal highway from East Yorkshire to West Lancashire. Perhaps somebody stole the torque, pushing it hastily into the ground with the idea of recovering it later. The person who *did* benefit—some eighteen centuries later—was a local artisan, whose only knowledge of metal was severely practical. This curious object, caked at first with dirt, became a useful adjunct to his hand-loom. Some time afterwards, when the gold began to show through the grime, its real nature was suspected—and the girdle that might have been worn originally by some fashionable lady of Roman York (*Eboracum*), was claimed as his perquisite by the discerning Lord of the Manor.

Such stories can be multiplied from all over Britain. One could fill a book with them. And the fascination of it is that few of those stories are really complete. There is a teasing quality about most archaeological finds—teasing and challenging.

Here is an example from the lovely country around Loch Awe in Argyll. This story 'began' in 1885 when two youths were trying to dig out a ferret. Perhaps the ferret eluded them, for something strange suddenly took their eye—a couple of bronze spearheads and a socketed gouge. One spearhead has since been lost, but the other two objects were acquired by the Scottish National Museum.

A slight discovery, some might say—but not if your name is Miss Marion Campbell, F.S.A., of Kilberry. While working on a Field Survey of Mid-Argyll in 1962 she recalled this Torran Hoard, from the Loch Awe district, and wondered if the find-spot could still be located—rather a lot to expect in such well-afforested country after nearly eighty years. Fortunately, the aged tenant of Torran Farm was able to direct her to the place—a sort of rock-shelter on a steep hillside. To her amazement, other tell-tale objects soon began to appear, below a carpet of pine needles. The boys' find, so long ago, was only a start. This is how Miss Campbell continues:

'The group of objects is best considered as a personal hoard of tools and weapons . . .' perhaps those 'of a travelling salesman carrying a sample of his wares'.

Period? The Scottish Late Bronze Age, or a few centuries B.C. How odd to think of that pedlar tramping over the ground trodden later and in such different circumstances by the Campbells and the Jacobites and others mentioned in these pages. What made him leave his spearheads, socketed axes, knife, and rings behind at Craig Beoch? Who can now tell? It would be as pertinent to ask why, two thousand years or so later, a woman of the Macdonald clan was secretly kept, with her infant, in the horrid dungeon of Ardconnel Castle, nearby, for three years. Human behaviour poses many riddles. Argyll has its full share of these, and other strange matters.

Another area vibrant with bygone memories is that spanned by Hadrian's Wall. It is no part of my purpose to attempt even a brief description of the Wall. I leave descriptions, willingly, to various competent authorities whose books bring the Roman occupation of this part of Britain vividly to life. Here, one man's desultory choice must suffice.

Up north there is a 'disease' called Wall Madness. It afflicts those who have come under the spell of this great rampart thrown across England from Tyne to Solway about A.D. 120. The madness may develop slowly. It often begins with that sensation of wonder on first beholding the Wall near Housesteads; a thing almost alive as it careers like a huge serpent over the Whin Sill crags and away into blue, incalculable distances. If such prospects, with thoughts of the chariots that once sped along that switchback wall, do not start the madness, one must be allergic indeed. The next stage is induced by watching some archaeologist at work beside a mile-castle, say, or within one of the forts. He might turn up an amulet, a vase, a gladius, or uncover more Roman masonry. His zeal is catching—especially if one looks carefully around to see what others have discovered in earlier years. Step into any of the Wall museums—at Housesteads, Chesters, or Corstopitum—and, if one is susceptible at all, the madness takes firm hold. I have seen some visitors change from their accustomed boredom with anything historic to surprise and even excitement as a Roman god peers down at them, rather questioningly, or once they realize—from the objects displayed—that the Roman garrison were human enough to enjoy games when off duty, have love affairs, or even get involved in a murder.

The 'murder house' is so called because when it was uncovered at Housesteads in 1932 a long-hidden domestic tragedy (if that is the correct explanation) lay exposed. A large civilian settlement adjoined the military quarters. It had shops, houses, and an inn. Up here on the outer fringe of the Roman Empire, among the cold winds of Northumbria, life must sometimes have been grim. Soldiers when relieved at their posts would snatch at any degree of comfort, any cheering diversion. But try as one will it is now impossible to reconstruct the events leading up to the assumed tragedy. The excavators took the first shock of it when, below the clay-covered floor, they found the skeletons of a man and a woman, side by side. The man's skeleton had a sword broken off in his ribs. Who was the culprit?

Since I was last at Housesteads the Mithraic cave below Chapel Hill has been restored, which means that the secret rites and mysteries associated with Mithraism can be the better understood. Yet many of these and other Roman features would probably have been indecipherable by now, or lost, were it not for the ruthless moss-troopers of Tudor times.

These lawless bands held the Middle Marches in complete thrall. To quote G. M. Trevelyan: 'The robber strongholds, built of oak trunks, covered with turf to prevent the application of fire, were hid in unapproachable wildernesses, among treacherous mosses, through which no stranger knew the paths.' One gang of raiders, however, hit upon an even better idea. They took over the old fort of Borcovicum (Housesteads), added a tower of their own, built a lime kiln, and feared neither man nor devil. Trevelyan points out that in Queen Elizabeth I's reign 'Camden was unable to pay an antiquarian visit to Housesteads "for fear of the moss-troopers" '. But, quite unintentionally, of course, the antiquities Camden sought, and the secrets they held from Roman days, were in safe keeping. While the robbers were in possession nobody could ransack the place!

One envies John Clayton and his helpers when, early last century, they started work on their great enterprise—as revealing of the past as anything accomplished by Howard Carter in Egypt or Leonard Woolley in Mesopotamia. Here was a wonderful monument to the once mightiest nation on earth; a crumbling monument, true, but still begging to be explored by the right sort of person. John Hodgson made the first scientific excavations at Housesteads in 1822. Eighteen years later John Clayton bought the place, and many other parts of the Roman Wall, to prevent any further despoliation. Clayton's excavation methods have since been improved upon, but this mine of history soon began to yield age-old secrets.

It is unnecessary to enumerate more than a few here, and even those few follow no particular order of merit. At Housesteads, for example, my imagination is as much stimulated by Clayton's find of a load of coal in the south guard-chamber as by the discovery of a carved relief showing three hooded deities that resemble witches. In the museum at Chesters (Cilurnum) I am pulled between the sculptured stones depicting sea-monsters, water-nymphs, and a tombstone set up 'in memory of Cornelius Victor, consular singularis . . . by his wife'; and the tiny votive offerings in the form of animals.

Our theme of secrecy is perhaps best served, in the fort itself, by a curious feature which looks like a tumulus, split open to disclose a dark, mysterious, cave-like hollow. When John Clayton began excavations here he was at length confronted by an oak door bound with iron. Originally it spelt security. When exposed to the air it crumbled to dust. Clayton was able to proceed unhindered.

His workmen were sure that the underground stable of local legend was now before them. This stable, they believed, was haunted by five hundred spectral horsemen who emerged on moonlit nights to gallop through the neighbourhood. What would the interior reveal? Neither horses nor their skeletons, of course, though it is curious that the number of those ghostly riders corresponds exactly with the strength of the Asturian cavalry who garrisoned Cilurnum. The 'underground stable' proved to be the fort's vaulted strongroom. And as if to take the place of that oak door, the stone lintel has fallen across the entry, preserving some semblance of the old privacy.

But archaeological rewards may fall to the lot of other people besides the accredited seekers. In 1915 a postman was delivering letters in the Carvoran region when he noticed what seemed to be an abandoned bucket sticking out of a boggy patch. But the 'bucket' had not been thrown aside by any moss-trooper; it was not a bucket at all. When cleaned up, strange inscriptions began to appear round the outside, showing this to have been a dry measure, a Roman modius, in fact, made about the time of Emperor Domitian, approximately A.D. 90. One of the inscriptions is puzzling. It indicates that the measure holds 17½ *sextarii*, or nearly 17 pints, whereas the actual capacity is 20 pints.

Professor Haverfield advanced this explanation: 'We may have here,' he wrote, 'a device by which Roman officials robbed provincials. The Britons . . . had to supply the Roman army with a fixed contribution of corn. Abuses clung round that system. Tacitus, in his *Life of Agricola*—written soon after the date of this vessel—notes that in Britain the officials made much money through it . . . They could easily have devised a bronze measure which enabled them to say to the natives, for every 20 pints of corn supplied, "see, you have not yet given us 17 pints".'

This bronze modius, now shown in the museum at Chesters, is therefore labelled the 'Rogue Measure'. Eighteen hundred years had to pass before the roguery was exposed!

Yet another fort serving the Roman Wall is that known as Corstopitum, three miles east of Hexham. The Wall itself sweeps across country some distance to the north, leaving the garrison and civil population at Corstopitum in close proximity to the River Tyne.

One day in 1734 a young girl was gathering driftwood on the river bank just below the fort, which was then a tangled mass of ruined masonry and debris. Seeing something bright she picked it up and had the satisfaction, later, of hearing that it was a silver lanx, or dish, used at Corstopitum during the forgotten past.

The dish was claimed by the Duke of Northumberland, as Lord of the Manor, but a replica in the fort museum lets one into the secret. On this lanx a number of Roman deities are portrayed in animated converse. Clever repoussé work gives vitality to the figures of Diana, Minerva, Juno, Vesta and Apollo, and to some strange creatures that decorate the lower border. It has been suggested that the dish—twenty inches long—might be the work of one of the famous silversmiths at Ephesus. Whatever its origin, the treasure would bring a touch of warmth and elegance to this bleak, northern outpost.

After sunny Italy the Roman prefects and their families would certainly find Corstopitum rather raw, especially in winter, but—as the museum shows—they found many pleasant diversions. The women had their cosmetics, jewellery, and needles. The children had toys, and 'baby' even its feeding bottle. Judging by numerous gaming boards also found here, the men were inveterate gamblers. One Roman workman could have no idea that his 'fed up' feeling would cause a flutter of delight so many centuries later. On the wet clay of a newly-made brick he had lazily written with his finger-tip the expressive word, *Satis*.

Archaeologists are, I think, among the world's happiest people. Always living on the edge of discovery, or gloating over its rewards.

I remember being taken through a remote part of the Yorkshire countryside, years ago, by a local gentleman. He stopped his car, suddenly, outside a long-derelict building. Cocking a wary eye at me he said, 'Are you mad, too?'—and then proceeded to tell me the 'lost' story of that heap of silent stones. There it was again—the strange kind of 'madness' that makes some people drop present-day affairs for a while and plunge deep into some forgotten era.

Poets get the feeling, too. John Masefield, in *Fragments*, expresses it through the figure of a Troy Town, long curtained off from mortal sense:

> Troy Town is covered up with weeds,
> The rabbits and the pismires brood
> On broken gold, and shards, and beads
> Where Priam's ancient palace stood.*

Gerald Gould needs only 'a little heap of golden sand' to evoke

> Turrets and domes and citadels,
> With murmuring of many bells . . .

Those who feel the 'madness' are in good company!

Yet windows on far distant time may be opened, an inch or so, by pure chance. And by quite ordinary, sane folk: a postman, a girl gathering sticks, as we have seen—or a man draining ditches.

The year is 1693, and the place Newton Park, near Athelney. Any guide book will tell us that we are now in the region of that humble cottage where King Alfred hid from the Danes, in A.D. 878. The secret of his identity was so well kept, evidently, that when he absent-mindedly scorched the cakes he was supposed to be watching (and the old story may be true!) the peasant's wife could round on him with the rebuke:

> Cas'n thee mind the ke-aks, man,
> An' doossen zee 'em burn?
> I'm boun thee's eat 'em vast enough
> Az zoon as tiz the turn.

* Reprinted by permission of The Society of Authors as literary representative of the Estate of the late John Masefield.

Alfred may have made himself as other men by removing that tell-tale object which the ditcher dug out over eight hundred years later. After cleaning, this proved to be a pear-shaped jewel, almost two and a half inches long, in gold and enamel. It is decorated with a regal figure—still something of a conundrum, and terminating with the head and snout of a boar. 'Alfred ordered me to be made', says its Saxon inscription, but as to whether it formed the head of a sceptre, an amulet, or—more probable—the central jewel of Alfred's crown, antiquaries will continue to debate until the sun goes down.

As the jewel would be known to friend and foe alike, perhaps Alfred hid it among the osier beds, hoping to recover it when the time was ripe for coming into the open. Some of these speculations appear in the finely illustrated booklet about Alfred's Jewel published by the Ashmolean Museum, in Oxford, where it now reposes. 'One of the most famous jewels in the world'—found in a lovely little backwater of Somerset. What other treasures still await the finding?

CHAPTER EIGHT

IN THE WAKE OF THE ARMADA

Another old story needing no full fanfare here tells how the Spanish Armada attacked England in the summer of 1588. But 'God blew, and they were scattered'—'they' being the Spanish galleons that were dashed by furious gales against our rockbound coasts. It is this sequel that concerns us. One could almost plan a tour based solely on Armada relics washed up by the sea, or surviving in some other way—like the New Forest ponies which some authorities believe to be descended from the 'jennets' hastily landed from some of the wrecked ships.

These ponies are always a joy to behold, whether galloping madly through some forest clearing, drinking at their water holes, or sniffing through the open windows of forest settlements like Lyndhurst and Burley. Part of their appeal is this tradition that links them to Spain through the hapless Armada. Tawny creatures and inquisitive, unless the primitive wildness is still there. Yet tame or wild, they cannot reveal their own ancestral secret. It seems a pity!

Normally, guns of any description leave me cold. But while at Bideford, in North Devon, I can join with the connoisseur of such weapons and speculate as to whether those eight guns beside the Torridge did indeed come from some foundered Spanish vessel. Some of them have been authenticated by comparison with undoubted Armada guns at Inveraray Castle, in Argyll. One cannon dredged up at Tobermory in 1740 by the second Duke of Argyll bears on its ten-foot bronze barrel the monogram of Benvenuto Cellini and the arms of Francis I of France; several cannon of this nature are recorded to have been aboard the Spanish vessel, *Florencia*.

We shall return to the *Florencia* later. Meanwhile, Bideford is not the only place in Devon with foreign guns to ponder over. Similar ones are to be seen at Westward Ho, Instow, and Clovelly; others perhaps await discovery off shore. For the local people it is all rather mysterious. If my two visits to Instow—that strange little spot near the mouth of the Torridge—had been longer, perhaps the Spanish Armada would have put up a good fight for my entertainment against the local smugglers. The place bristles with old traditions, as anybody can sense—but they need time for the telling.

It might be even more rewarding to settle down—and listen—at Clovelly, for some of the villagers here are said to have Spanish blood in their veins. Do the four Spanish cannon built as bollards into the pier ever awaken folk memories? One Devon writer suggests that Clovelly was partly created by Spanish sailors rescued from Armada wrecks. Beer in South Devon has a similar reputation.

John E. Horsley, Curator of the Brixham Museum, also in South Devon, has reminded me of Brixham's own Armada tales. The replica of Drake's *Golden Hind* moored in the fine harbour here adds piquancy to those old stories, especially that concerning *St Peter the Great*, a Spanish hospital ship.

Driven off course like the rest of the Armada fleet, this vessel made an amazing voyage. It was battered up the east coast, round the north coast of Scotland, along Ireland's treacherous western seaboard, and then limped back to Channel waters again, only to be wrecked, finally, at Hope Cove, near Bolt Tail. A letter preserved in the Record Office at London states that the inhabitants of the neighbouring village salvaged all the plate and other treasure from the wreckage. Even a hospital ship carried worth-while booty, it seems, but one would like to know which was the village to benefit: South Huish, Malborough, or Hope itself—that one-time smuggling centre? Wrecking and smuggling often went together.

Hope Cove still seems prepared for this dual rôle. It is only about thirty yards across, from cliff to cliff. A perfect receptacle for the sea's bounty! Among its jagged brown rocks my wife and I, on a recent visit, found bits of wood and cork, some old gloves, and a metal disc that made us think of doubloons until a brush of the hand removed some of its stain.

Mr Horsley tells me that attempts are being made, even now, to recover that lost plunder from the Spanish vessel. One item that has already filtered through is a dagger, of the right workmanship and period. It was given to the Curator by a local family who wanted 'to get it out of the way of the children', and is now shown in Brixham Museum.

A fascinating district, this, and thick with memories and tokens of Drake and Hawkins. Plymouth lies only a few miles to the west; Plymouth, where Drake finished that historic game of bowls before tackling the Armada. They make no secret of that game here; a modern sign alongside the bowling green on the Hoe shows him in action—on the greensward! And then, over Dartmouth way, there is the utterly charming hamlet of Stoke Gabriel, birthplace of John Davis, the navigator, who wrote a book with the intriguing title, *The Seamen's Secret.* Stoke Gabriel hides away in a little backwater of the River Dart. Perhaps it was in his mind's eye when he penned that famous treatise on navigation, which revealed unknown channels and sea routes.

But we must resume our Armada quest.

The Armada wreckage that littered our shores yielded many kinds of treasure, including beautiful furniture. Braunton Church in North Devon has a fine dower chest that rewarded some beachcomber. One Devonshire family long owned a Spanish desk that was supposed to be haunted because of the strange noises it gave forth. The spirit responsible was said to have been exorcised later, which seems a pity. A Spanish ghost would have been such a pleasant change. The desk was sold only recently.

A four-poster bed carved with Spanish motifs was thrown up on the Irish coast and acquired by Lady Limerick. This bed from a grandee's cabin is now at Penfound Manor, near Bude in Cornwall and looks quite at home, for this lovely old place harbours several Armada relics. Its main staircase is Spanish, having been contrived from some timbers salvaged from an Armada galleon wrecked in Widemouth Bay nearby. As will transpire later, Penfound Manor is a house of many secrets, but a subsidiary rôle of this impressive staircase—which still suggests the climb to some poop deck—is to *reveal* anything furtive. The polished stairs vary in height and pitch so much that any burglar who ventured thus far must certainly stumble and rouse the household.

Accredited visitors (and there are many, because the Manor is now open to public view) have to be warned of another hazard. It is an oval-shaped hollow, some nine inches deep, just beyond the Armada staircase and filling the floor space beneath an archway from the Little Hall to the Dining-room. If the Armada features—and the bottle of holy water mentioned earlier (see page 29)—exercise the imagination, what about this curious drop in the floor? Perhaps the Penfound sire who hid the Jordan water in the chimney lest it should collapse devised this other novelty?

What was its purpose? 'In medieval times', say Mr and Mrs Tucker, the present owners, 'a running stream flowed through here, the bed of which was kept covered with reeds and rushes. All scullions and house-carls entering the house had to walk through the stream, which carried away at least the worst of the mud and filth . . .' The shallow walls and bed of the oval depression were sealed up about twenty-five years ago, but when—during a recent heavy storm—two inches of water seeped up again from below, any child might have cherished the fond hope that further flood water might yet lap those old timbers from the foundered galleon.

Our next call will be on the Yorkshire coast, where a puzzle is propounded by a fine silver almsdish, now kept in Kirkleatham Church. It was washed up on the sandy shore at neighbouring Coatham about 1740 and is believed, locally, to have come from a wrecked Spanish galleon. The repoussé design comprising fruit and flowers and comic little faces is, however, typical seventeeth-century work and not characteristically Spanish. But the puzzle remains. If not Spanish, where did the dish originate, and how did it arrive on Coatham sands?

But the biggest conundrum is this. How could a dish, measuring 12½ inches across, survive any lengthy immersion in the sea with neither scratch nor other blemish? I have examined the dish for myself, and a photograph I took confirms its perfection as well as its elegance. Could the dish have been 'planted' on the beach? The Kirkleatham vicar had no answer.

Newcastle upon Tyne has its own commentary on the Armada theme. It is an anchor from one of the foundered vessels. The old sea-dogs who once foregathered in Trinity House for some nautical business, or a chapel service equally nautical, could gaze at leisure upon this huge, rusty anchor with flukes like harpoon heads, for it is fixed to the flight of steps in their attractive courtyard.

I cannot find any mention of the anchor in local guidebooks, but the Master of the House made much of it when I went along some years ago, though I was then more interested in the secret door leading from the Master's Room to the Chapel. This door is a dummy set of well-laden book-shelves.* Much of the Armada sequel remains hidden, as though beyond some baffling door. Who knows, for

* This device occurs frequently in eighteenth-century houses; for example, Nostell Priory near Wakefield, and Allerton Hall near Bradford.

example, just when and how that formidable anchor, now crusted with age, found its way up the River Tyne?

Many places offer similar challenge. I think of Dunstaffnage Bay on Loch Linnhe. All around are mountains rich in legend and story. The same little reed-strewn bay that saw Flora Macdonald brought as a state prisoner to Dunstaffnage Castle witnessed a braver sight, years before, when an Armada cannon was landed here. It had been found in Tobermory Bay, on the neighbouring island of Mull. A castle enjoying a site as romantic as its long and varied history was evidently considered the right place for such a relic. So here it is, an imposing brass cannon still proudly bearing the name of its maker, 'Asuerus Koster, Amsterdam'.

Tobermory!

For all Armada 'fans' this is the chief lure. My family doctor used to have a painting of the magic place hung in his surgery. When not probing one of us with his exploratory finger, or dispensing some remedial draught, a mystical look would come over his face and he would ruminate about Tobermory as though it was part of the Isles of the Blessed—their choicest part. Rawdon in mid-Airedale was his exile; well enough in its way. But Tobermory had ushered Harry Sproat into the world, as it was in due course to usher him into the next.

In his youth Tobermory had given him several unnerving experiences of 'second sight'. By comparison, the wrecked *Florencia* mouldering fathoms deep in the bay was an everyday matter—almost on the threshold. I never heard him speak of the Spanish princess who had sailed in that vessel, though he would certainly know the story. The princess made the voyage because a dream had shown her the man she would marry. She expected to find him somewhere in that Britain her King coveted, but alas the dream man, Duart, when he materialized, proved to have a wife already—a jealous one. Perhaps it was this lady who inadvertently started all the treasure-seeking here by blowing up the *Florencia*, including the Spanish beauty.

Fortunately some of the ship's ponies had been put ashore to graze. They are supposed to have started the island breed of nimble-footed ponies—which were the only means of transport on Mull in our good doctor's boyhood days.

No doubloons from the wreck, or any other mementoes, seem to have come his way. But it must have felt good to accompany his white-bearded father—the Procurator-Fiscal of the island—on his rounds, in a little trap drawn by one of those same ponies. The boat from the mainland at Oban disgorges its passengers on the pier, within a few yards of the sunken vessel. One may not be fortunate enough to see any treasure, but a half-Spanish pony trotting nearby can be almost as thrilling—if the old tradition is true.

But nobody is sure of this tradition, or of much else to do with the sunken galleon. Even its name veers from the *Florencia* to the *Florida.* One thing does unite the treasure seekers—a belief that the vessel carried the pay-chest of the entire Armada. Hope is also held in common. Year after year the search goes on. Divers come and go. Apart from the cannon already mentioned, and a few coins, little of real value has yet appeared. A friend of mine has a little drug jar; somebody else a scrap of rusty metal; and so on. The gold is as elusive as ever. But there is always—hope.

If I lived in that glorious part of Western Scotland (happy thought!) I should sail across from Oban repeatedly and, leaving Tobermory to the experts, concentrate on Loch Don, which indents the nearest corner of Mull. An Armada ship is said to repose here, also, beneath the limpid surface. Why should the seals that inhabit these waters have the secret all to themselves? Gold I should not expect. The ship's figurehead, its name-board, even a barnacled spar, would satisfy me.

Part II
MANSION, COTTAGE, AND INN

CHAPTER NINE

DOMESTIC CATACOMBS

The thing which triggered off this part of my quest—though unconsciously, for it happened so long ago—was seeing my own father remove a wall-panel, stealthily, and disappear into a dark space beyond. To a young boy this exciting spectacle was a visual fulfilment of what he was beginning to read, voraciously, about Catholic priests and royalists and others seeking hasty refuge.

My father was no priest—only a member of a Baptist chapel choir, but when the organ started ciphering—as it then did with satisfying frequency—it was his duty to turn round from the tenor stalls quietly, dislodge the panel behind him, and step into the gloomy organ chamber to make some adjustment. All this while the service was in progress. It gave the whole proceeding a delicious sense of the bizarre.

Many years later a booklet on priest-holes which I helped to illustrate bore on its cover an almost exact reproduction—save for the fugitive's dress—of my father's furtive exits. The artist responsible for this drawing might have plumbed my boyhood memory!

Many of the priest-hides created during penal times—when it was perilous to show any allegiance to the proscribed faith—have been swept out of existence. But the stigma of such allegiance took a long time to eradicate. The Rev. Sydney Smith, that great wit who could send earls and servants alike into gales of laughter, once wrote, with nicely barbed satire, 'I solemnly believe blue and red baboons to be more popular here than Catholics and Presbyterians . . . When a country squire hears of an ape, his first feeling is to give it nuts and apples; when he hears of a Dissenter, his immediate impulse is to commit it to the county jail, to shave its head, to alter its customary food, and to have it privately whipped. This is no caricature, but an accurate picture of national feelings, as they degrade and endanger us at this very moment.'

'This very moment' was not away back in Tudor or Stuart times, but at the dawn of the nineteenth century. And Sydney Smith, who hated all forms of religious persecution, had—for his own safety—to voice his thoughts under the pseudonym of Peter Plymley. The secret of Plymley's real self never came out, though Smith's friends made their own shrewd guesses.

The same secrecy prevailed when the dangerously outspoken *Edinburgh Review* was founded, with Smith as one of the chief contributors. Of this period Hesketh Pearson, his biographer, writes: '. . . Sydney insisted that their incognito must at all costs be preserved. It was to be a "hush-hush" enterprise . . . They would have to meet in a dark room in a dark alley, where they would arrive singly, at different times, by different lanes, through back approaches, via circuitous routes.'

That description almost exactly echoes the conditions that accounted for the priest-holes and other secretive apparatus in the homes of Catholic gentry three centuries earlier. Fortunately, sufficient of that apparatus has survived to give one a sobering sense of history, as well as a feeling of excitement and adventure.

Ripley Castle, near Harrogate, will serve admirably to whet the appetite, for a priest-hole was discovered here quite recently. This old home of the Ingilby family was long reputed to have its 'secret dennes', but when the Georgian wing was added the original tower building of 1555—where the 'dennes' would be—fell back into the shadows.

Repairs due to woodworm were being effected in the tower's topmost room, the Knight's Chamber, in 1963, when the hide was accidentally uncovered, behind the wainscoting. A small panel secured by three wooden wedges opens on to a cavity beyond that was obviously scooped out of the thick stone wall.

To get inside, Sir Joslan Ingilby, the present owner, has to crouch like a hunchback, for the barrel-shaped cavity measures no more than five feet high by three feet wide. The seat is a rough ledge six inches wide. Above, a tiny breathing-hole pierces the tower wall. There is nothing else.

A man would have to be desperate indeed to use such a refuge. No family records allude to its use, but it could well have concealed Sir William Ingilby, the royalist, when Cromwell spent a night at Ripley Castle after Marston Moor. Or, in Tudor times, Francis Ingilby who became a priest.

'Wouldn't any pursuivant detect this hide by rapping on the panelling to get that tell-tale hollow sound?' I asked, for many such places were discovered that way. 'But here,' said Sir Joslan, '*all* the panelling sounds hollow!' He is hopeful of beating the King's sleuths at their own game by locating and opening up other hides in his home. Even that already found may retain at least one secret. Why is the hide so very near the spiral stairway? This was once the only access to and exit from the Knight's Chamber. What more likely than a bolt-hole from the hide to the stairway? Of this, however, there is as yet no sign.

Another gentleman who kindly shared with me the ancient lore of his home and family was the late H. C. Haldane, a well-known antiquary of Clarke Hall, Wakefield.

His ancestors had been fugitives at the time of the 1715 Jacobite Rebellion. 'After the rebellion,' he would say, with deep emotion, as though he had been personally involved, 'we were completely burned out by the Jacobite rebels under the Earl of Mar and other Stuart adherents. We were left with nothing except the clothes we wore.' I got a vivid mental picture of the Haldanes being ejected from their Gleneagles acres during a blinding snowstorm and having to hide wherever they could—in lonely croft or obscure hollow—while making their way south; that is, the few who survived the bitter experience. The remnants of Mr Haldane's branch of the family fled over the moors to Kirkcudbrightshire, beyond Jacobite influence.

The first of the Haldanes to get a footing on the Clarke Hall estate, years later, would have no idea that this fine Elizabethan residence was fitted with its own hides, probably used (among others) by local supporters of the 'King over the Water'.

Jacobites again! But here the boot was on the other foot. Let us hear Mr Haldane speak of these hides, especially that in the Great Chamber. 'I had always suspected that the deep chimney-breast in this room might conceal a hiding-place,' he told me. 'One day I put my theory to the test.' A long-bow cupboard on the stair-landing adjoins the fireplace. After fruitlessly tapping the cupboard walls for signs of an opening, Mr Haldane found that the tiny roof—five inches thick in solid oak—actually swung round to give access to a secret chamber measuring roughly six feet each way. 'I also discovered that one of the carved overmantel panels was not a fixture, as it had always seemed; it slid upwards, revealing a small cavity connected with the hidden room.' This cavity was clearly the hatch through which food and drink would be passed, surreptitiously, to some hunted priest, cavalier, or Jacobite cringeing in the shadows beyond. Proof of this was at hand. Two wine flagons of the Civil War period were found inside. 'They could easily have served some Royalist fugitive', according to Mr Haldane, 'as the Wingfields of Clarke Hall were in favour of King Charles.'

In the Dining-room—situated beneath the Oak Lodging in the seventeenth-century Wingfield addition—another large chimney-breast provided a way of escape from the priest-hole upstairs. A door in the fireplace panelling discloses a hollow shaft that reaches up into darkness. 'When I was a boy,' my old friend would wistfully remark, 'a frayed rope still hung there'—presumably a relic of the days when a fugitive could clamber down this way after crawling from the priest-hole through the cobwebs and gloom of the underdrawing.

Some of our old houses are veritable warrens. Harvington Hall in Worcestershire is usually cited as the best surviving example in England. The secret system here runs the whole gamut of hidden trapdoors, false stairs, moveable floors, deceptive chimneys, bolt-hole, pivoted beam, etc. All of which a student of the subject might well attribute to Nicholas Owen—if Owen had not died on the rack, in 1606, while Harvington was still in Protestant hands.

Nicholas Owen—'Little John' to his intimates—was a lay-brother who served his faith with his amazing skill in carpentry and masonry. Many of the most ingenious hides ever devised were the product of his scheming mind. Priests must have felt safe indeed while behind his barrage of subtlety and deception.

It is regrettable that Hindlip Hall was demolished early last century. Also in Worcestershire, this great rambling house was thus described by one who had reason to know: 'Its every room had a recess, a passage, a trap-door, or secret stairs; the walls were in many places hollow, the ceilings false, several chimneys had double flues—one for the passage of smoke, the second for concealment of a priest; no one—except those immediately concerned, having key or clue to the whole maze of secrets.'

Hindlip must have been Owen's crowning achievement. And yet he, the servant and trusted friend of Father Garnet, was captured here, along with his master and Father Oldcorne.

A search for them in this house kept the pursuivants on their toes for eight days. But Owen had done his work well. His clever devices betrayed nothing. The thing that did beat those in hiding was—priva-

lonel John Bolton, one-time slave dealer, of Storrs Hall, Bowness, Windermere

egisters of runaway marriages kept at Coldstream by one of the old Border 'priests'

Entrance to the Roman strong-room at Chesters, Northumberland; it was once believed to be an underground stable accommodating five hundred spectral horsemen

This beautiful silver dish was washed up on the shore at Coatham, North Yorks., about 1740

Sliding panel of the food hatch linked to a priest-hole concealed behind the chimney-piece: Clarke Hall, Wakefield

The false cupboard devised last centu
at Garrowby Hall, near York, to amu
Viscount Halifax's children

Another example of
Viscount Halifax's 'playful
deceit' at Garrowby Hall—a
secret passage within the
attic wall

tion. One day, two days even, could be endured—but eight long days with little, if any food, enforced silence, and cramped conditions were worse than capture.

Picture the pursuivants at the end of that same period. Every bit of the building had been prodded and sounded; every known trick tested. Nobody could possibly be in hiding here, after all. Their suspicions had played them false. And then, down one of the corridors, two men staggered into view. Their ghost-like appearance first struck terror among the officers. Old halls were notoriously haunted . . But no, these were creatures of flesh and blood, though pale as death. Fathers Garnet and Oldcorne were giving themselves up. Owen followed.

To compensate for the loss of Hindlip Hall and its secret ramifications, some old buildings are only now beginning to show their true colours. I have mentioned Ripley Castle, to which the public are fortunately admitted. Burton Constable Hall is another shot for one's bow. It stands eight miles north-east of Hull and also welcomes visitors. There are enough secrets in this great old mansion to keep visitors' questions going for hours, but not yet is the so-called priest-hole and its astonishing network available for public viewing. It is still being explored!

Indeed, there are probably more hides at Burton Constable than have hitherto been suspected. The 'secret system' is mainly confined to Stephen's Tower, at the north-east corner, but on my last visit a young architect had his eyes—and his measuring tape—on the south tower; he was searching for hidden space. Space that cannot otherwise be accounted for, between floors, walls, staircases, etc., always excites an investigator. *Why* has that space been left? Did it serve any clandestine purpose?

Here at Burton Constable many such spaces came about when the Elizabethan building was literally enveloped by the later one. A child's building brick placed over a smaller one roughly conveys the idea. The space between the two bricks corresponds to the secret area.

The owner of Burton Constable—John Chichester-Constable, forty-sixth Lord Paramount of the Seigniory of Holderness, kindly deputed Mr W. A. Sillince to initiate my wife and me into the hall's mysteries. In another part of the house Mr Sillince has created a room devoted to Alice's Wonderland, for Lewis Carroll had East Yorkshire connections. The labyrinth with which we were soon to become acquainted is another kind of wonderland, peopled, not with fanciful creatures like White Rabbits and Griffins, but with the fleeting shadows of those who once had reason to keep out of the limelight.

Who those people really were has yet to be determined, though there is sufficient ground for conjecture. Burton Constable could well have been a mass centre—a place for harbouring priests and other Catholics. After quietly landing on the Holderness coast nearby, they could sojourn here until it was safe to disperse on their several missions in various parts of the north country.

Judging by other mass centres, and the underground movement they fostered, the priests would sometimes arrive at Burton Constable in disguise. Shortly before our visit a small, bricked-up space near the King's Bedroom was found, with some old clothing inside. The clothing awaited examination, but it set the two of us wondering. . . .

On the farther side of the French King's suite* we entered a corridor which makes me shiver every time I think of it. Our initiation really began here. Sir Walter Scott exploited the mysteries of Lyme Hall, Cheshire, in *Woodstock*; how he would have risen to this more generous bait! The very atmosphere was uncanny. And when Mr Sillince knelt down in one corner and removed a couple of short floor-boards, the centuries slipped silently away. We stood on a strange threshold.

Our guide shone his torch into an eight-foot deep vertical shaft. On edging close we could just discern another shaft, branching off laterally. Had we been better prepared (with youthful agility as well as suitable attire), nothing would have prevented our descent. According to Mr Sillince—who has been through several times—the secret passage opens into huge spaces below. 'For size, it is almost like a cathedral down there,' he said. 'Those spaces were once state rooms in the Tudor dwelling, and much of the fine old brickwork remains.' He then drew a sketch, showing how the hidden passage goes over the roof of the present family chapel (on the ground floor), and under a couple of first-floor bedrooms, before emerging at last beneath the carpet of this bedroom corridor. The secret route seems to be about seventy-five feet long, though here again current investigations may

* This fine suite was used by Louis XVIII of France during his exile after the Revolution.

well reveal further offshoots. One recent find is a Tudor latrine fitted with a chute down which it would be possible—however unpleasant—to escape. Below, a conveniently sited ditch would facilitate the getaway.

Another interesting point. This labyrinth occurs in the haunted area of the house. The 'ghost-in-chief' seems to be the nun whose portrait hangs in the Nun's Room. This room, and the Haunted Room next door, span the secret passage. I do not know whether the passage is ever traversed by the nun, or her equally transparent room-neighbour, a former nurse, but their reality is not seriously questioned here. When the late Fred Elwell, R.A., the famous Beverley artist, came over once, he was warned about the nun. She did not oblige him with her presence, he told me later. Yet his fine painting of the Long Gallery shows *two* nuns moving steadily towards the beholder. He had caught the essential feeling, anyway. Even in the kitchen quarters there is tacit acknowledgement of the supernatural, for one of the bell-ropes is marked 'Haunted Room'.

The idea of ghostly presences might have been encouraged by the family in earlier times to account for any suspicious noises in this wing and keep the inquisitive from prying where they were not wanted.

There is no telling into what strange historical byways such devious passages may lead. A hiding-place first devised for hunted priests is later used by some hard-pressed Royalist—and later still, perhaps, by the local smugglers. What would not some long confined recusant have given for just one draught of the wine stored there in such quantity, as contraband, in the eighteenth century!

The Elizabethan vicarage at East Budleigh, South Devon, could cover several of these contingencies. In fact its secret rooms proved only too convenient for a couple of eighteenth-century parsons who lived here; they actually participated in the smuggling. Their names, scratched for all to see on one of the windows—Matt Mundy and A. A. Stapleton—might have been more fittingly inscribed behind the scenes.

Tapping for the secret past at Capheaton Hall, a few miles north of Hadrian's Wall, also releases diverse echoes.

Capheaton is the ancestral home of the Swinburne family, and a letter kindly sent to me by John Browne-Swinburne provides a fascinating prologue. Referring to Sir John Swinburne, the first baronet, he writes:

> His [John's] father was murdered by a Cromwellian supporter by being run through with a rapier . . . After this, it seems, young John—presumably for his own protection—was sent to a monastery in France, and more or less forgotten.
>
> However, the story goes that some members of the Radcliffe family, who were cousins of the Swinburnes, came to this monastery by chance while travelling in France, and thought John looked like a Swinburne. On questioning him they were convinced that he was, and took him home to England. A tribunal was convened and he proved his identity by describing the markings on a cat he remembered while he was a child at Capheaton, and also the markings on a silver punch bowl.

The cat still lived, to corroborate that part of John's evidence.

The mystery of his disappearance is probably bound up with the disfavour into which the family were plunged before the Restoration. Anyhow, it was this same John who later built the present house, in 1668. His unfortunate experiences so far in life may have influenced him in so designing the house that a large empty space was left behind the principal chimneypiece. The 30-foot-long centre portion can only be entered through a ground-floor cupboard ceiling. A smaller portion is reached through a bedroom cupboard.

The walled-up space could have been a place of refuge in its own right, or simply a 'blind'—a buffer state for what once existed overhead. This was the family chapel, equipped with two more hides—one opening on to the leads, the other guarded by a picture over the altar; at need, the picture revolved on a pivot to facilitate escape. Hidden somewhere in that roof, after the 1715 Jacobite Rebellion, were some papers that would have incriminated one of the chief rebels—the ill-fated third Earl of Derwentwater.

Thirty years passed. One day a stonemason found the Derwentwater papers while repairing the roof and reported the find to Sir William Middleton. It was now the year of the 'Forty-Five, and Sir William had all the sensibilities of a violent anti-Jacobite. The papers were despatched to his own house at Belsay, and then handed over to the authorities.

For a long time it seemed as though the papers had vanished again, but they turned up not long ago at Greenwich Hospital Museum. It is astonishing how the hide-and-seek business can span the centuries.

Searching for country houses that may have a hiding-place is exhilarating, and full of surprises. The search has taken me to many parts of England, and provided many curious sidelights on human nature.

I often smile to myself about the builder of Rampside Hall, near Barrow-in-Furness. He must have been an unusual character. To start with he had twelve identical chimney-pots placed cornerwise along the full length of the roof ridge. Then he—or was it a later owner, equally eccentric?—made the house over to his offspring, stipulating, however, that on Christmas Day all twelve chimneys should be smoking in unison.

Oddity out of doors is matched by oddity indoors. All twelve fireplaces served by those chimneys are accommodated in a remarkably thick partition wall running the full width and height of the house. But the wall is largely a shell. After making every allowance for the twelve fireplaces and flues it embraces (though some are now filled in), there is much left-over space. Wasteful? Not at all. Itinerant priests had a good use for it. That hooded area must have been a godsend to them, especially if they were pursued after braving the perilous route across the Leven Sands in Morecambe Bay. The Knype family of Rampside Hall were staunch Catholics. Perhaps the name facetiously given to this house with its dozen chimneys—the Twelve Apostles—echoes those far-off days.

For centuries the sands of Morecambe Bay, together with the Kent estuary, provided the only feasible approach to Levens Hall. Roads were practically non-existent. Threaded by the shifting channels and currents of three rivers, the far-spreading sands created one more hazard for anybody hurrying for cover at Levens.

Who those fugitives really were is still largely unknown, though current research may provide an answer. It is even uncertain whether the hall's secret room is a heritage from Elizabethan days, or due to Colonel Grahame's forethought. As Grahame was an active Jacobite a hidden sanctuary for himself and his friends would be a wise precaution. Bishop George Hickes was probably one who vanished for a time here; others may have been Bishop Thomas Ken, and Grahame's brother Fergus.

It might seem a little indecent if a house of this character surrendered its mantle of secrecy too readily, if at all. But this Levens Hall is not likely to do. Several things here—besides those shadowy figures—are just beyond reach, as tenuous as the ghosts who will later materialize in the special place this book assigns to such entertaining phenomena.

Meanwhile, let us try to follow George Hickes after he has crossed the sands. He is sure to thank his Maker for safety thus far, but will have no inclination to linger in James Grahame's new garden, even though Monsieur Beaumont—gardener to King James II, whom Hickes supported even in exile—had employed all his skill to provide something novel and eye-catching. It has been called the finest topiary garden in England. I do not know whether Hickes would have appreciated yew and box masquerading as an umbrella, a Judge's wig, a lion, a maid-in-waiting, a group of little boys; there are many other striking shapes, too, and tall, narrow avenues just made for hiding.

But George Hickes must enjoy the topiary work some other time, when the troubles that have made him forswear Dutch William are past. His urgent need, now, is for sanctuary indoors. The only civility he requires is to be taken immediately to that hidden room between floor and ceiling, and to be shown how—if necessary—he may escape. For the sake of his cloth I hope the bishop was spared this further indignity; it would have meant slithering down a mock chimney to the cellar.

Rarely, however, could any degree of comfort be expected in such hideouts. Consider the building that is now the Lord Crewe Arms at Blanchland, in Northumberland. I once had lunch here, and it soon became apparent that, structurally, the place owed far more to monastic than later times. It originated, in fact, as the Abbot's Lodging. Blanchland Abbey, and the village that grew from its very sinews, had often been attacked by the Scots raiders. A hiding-place was therefore considered prudent. But the only access to the hide—a box-shaped room measuring eight feet by six feet, and six feet in height—is through the kitchen chimney flue.

On looking beyond the fire-grate one may possibly discern a flight of five or six narrow steps on the right. Normally, a fire will be burning, to provide girdle cakes, or 'singing hinnies', for visitors. Just before my own call here, however, two little boys who had listened wide-eyed to a housemaid's account of this secret room decided to investigate. Early next morning they crept from their bedroom, found the kitchen grate empty, and wriggled through to the magical place. When the imaginary Indians who were after them with tomahawks had retreated, completely baffled, the boys emerged and raced to tell their parents, still abed, where they had been. Their pyjamas lent ample, sooty corroboration.

Although this hide is usually described as a priest-hole, its best known association is with Tom Forster. He was a Jacobite—the so-called 'General' Forster who in 1715 connived with the aforementioned Earl of Derwentwater of Dilston (a few miles north of Blanchland) to raise troops in support of the Old Pretender.

The Rebellion fizzled out before it really started. Forster was captured at Preston and taken off to Newgate. His sister Dorothy contrived his escape just three days before he would have been put on trial for high treason.

Disguising herself as a servant Dorothy rode to London, pillion, behind the village blacksmith. By a clever ruse, and with the blacksmith's collaboration, a duplicate key of Tom's prison chamber was made and secretly conveyed to him.

One version states that Tom invited the Governor into his room for a drink, then dodged past, locking his 'guest' inside. A flourish worthy of Walter Scott is that 'General' Tom Forster left his dressing-gown on the steps outside as a memento of his sojourn. Another skeleton key enabled him to escape from the easy-going prison, and ride off with his 'servant'.

The best secrets have many layers, like an onion. Strip one away, and you are still little wiser. So it is with this story of the 'Fifteen. Its elusive quality has produced many variants, and tales within tales. I have heard one that gives Tom his final getaway by means of a mock funeral. More probable, to my mind, is sister Dorothy's domestic solution. Their home was the former Abbot's Lodging we have already seen at Blanchland. I can visualize her half pushing Tom into that chimney chamber, and keeping him there, until she could secure for him—as she ultimately did—a safe passage to France and the Court of the Old Pretender.

An artist using Pieter Breughel's paintings as a model could paint a fantastic picture representing Britain's long hide-and-seek period.

It would be a composite picture, showing in minuscule all manner of persons popping in and out of their various holes—almost like rabbits. A few cave-men would provide the essential background, then—wielding a lively, if delicate brush—the artist could select from the company of refugees and fugitives we have now seen, not forgetting those who had resort—not very long ago—to air-raid shelters.

What a graphic picture that could be! Yet it is such a picture that builds up in any contemplative mind, as Britain's secret history takes gradual colour and shape. I once saw such a composite scene, though the subject was different. It occupies the entire wall space of a room at a York inn, to be described later.

Meanwhile, a lot of brushwork is still necessary to fill in, even sketchily, our own mental chiaroscuro. We shall certainly have to make room for that hidden stairway at Blagroves—a curious old house (now a café) at Barnard Castle, Co. Durham. It was given to Miles Forrest as reward for his share in murdering the Princes in the Tower.

After the fall of Richard III at Bosworth Field, Forrest must have lived in constant fear that the crime would be traced to his door. I can see him making sure that every means of escape is in order—the bedside sliding panel giving access to the hidden stair that ends somewhere in the basement; the trap-door in the old banquet hall, and perhaps other devices that time has effaced. Underground passages usually belong to the mythical world of romance. Here, however, the Victorians who pored over Scott's thrilling novels would have been gleeful indeed, for such a passage really did exist; it once provided a link between the basement of Blagroves and the town's castle, not far away.

Not long before one of my own visits to this house, about thirty years ago, the then owner—Mr V. Walton, a keen antiquary—had discovered some papers stuffed into a wall-crack. They were the title deeds of the property and bore Forrest's name. He lived here, apparently, from 1483 to 1485. Mr Walton's theory was that the incriminating deeds were pushed out of sight hurriedly, while the new King's men—justifying that nagging fear—were breaking their way in. Forrest had no chance to escape. Perhaps he was wounded? Anyhow, the secret outlets had all been checked in vain.

Another hidden stairway leading to a cellar occurs at Athelhampton, near Dorchester. Mr Robert Cooke, M.P., the present owner, tells me that Thomas Hardy's father once repaired this extremely beautiful house, while Hardy himself made a watercolour of the place. I wonder whether either of them knew of this hidden stairway?

It starts beside the open fireplace in the Great Chamber and penetrates the thick wall behind the panelling. A few secret panels and a hiding-place in the attics add to the appeal of the house, built about the time when Miles Forrest was quaking in his north-country redoubt. Repeatedly in Athelhampton does one see the chained ape crest of the Martyn family. Somehow their motto seems to challenge all who might presume to probe its secrets: 'He who looks at Martyn's ape, Martyn's ape shall look at him.' The ape gets frequent audience today, for Athelhampton is fortunately open to the public.

And so one might travel, through various parts of Britain, following no set route, but guided only by a passion for riddles and things that have private, unseen existence. Our composite picture would become far too unwieldy, even for the mind to accomplish, if every place reputed to have a 'secret self' were to be included. Personal choice must depend, largely, upon the district one inhabits, or visits on holidays.

Liverpool citizens are very fortunate in having Speke Hall so handy. The mill-workers of Burnley can revel in the creepy atmosphere of Towneley Hall. And overworked Cambridge 'undergrads' might sometimes find welcome relief among the hides at Sawston Hall, not far away.

At Ipswich there is a particularly attractive combination—a first-rate bookshop in the Buttermarket, and, overhead, among the roof timbers, a room that would cause many an historical novelist to enthuse. It is a fifteenth-century chapel, completely lost to view for many years. King Charles II's coat-of-arms supplements the splendid pargeting that decorates the exterior of the building, but in this chapel—partly boarded up, perhaps, at the Reformation—the Sparrowe family hid the same royal person when he was a fugitive after the Battle of Worcester.

Sparrowe's House was therefore a link in the chain of hides that escorted him, at length, to Shoreham in Sussex, where a coaling brig took this lanky fellow who had disguised himself as servant to Jane Lane and Juliana Coningsby beyond the reach of Cromwell's spies. Trent House, near the Somerset–Dorset boundary, had a share in those escapades, but our present concern is with this grand old building where book-lovers continually browse, at Ipswich.

The proprietors of the bookshop kindly allow customers to wander up to the long-lost chapel, on request. It is an eerie experience. When I went up, alone, the silence was profound. Huge oak wall-braces curved down beside me to the floor. A finger of light came from one small lattice. I was back in Tudor times. . . .

CHAPTER TEN

CONSPIRACY AND PLOT

While in the tenebrous atmosphere of that roof-top chapel at Ipswich, transpositions become natural to the 'collector' of such scenes and places. One reaches out in imagination, especially to chapels of corresponding secrecy that are perhaps no longer in being.

My own thoughts turn first to a chapel at Myddleton Lodge, near Ilkley in mid-Wharfedale; one provided by the Myddleton family, to whom fines for recusancy were common. Undaunted, the family and others of the same faith continued to meet for Mass in their own conventicle.

Antiquaries may regret that when bigotry waned the chapel was not only superseded by a new and perfectly obvious place of worship (built in 1825), but all trace of the old dispensation was removed. Priests' hiding-places once provided here have also disappeared. There remains but one relevant feature, and that quite non-committal. It is the fine oak staircase by which the old chapel, hidden away in the top storey, would be attained. Today it leads to a corridor serving some small rooms; all innocuous.

But any disappointment on that score was banished, for me, on seeing black-robed figures pass silently up and down the gnarled old staircase—a flashback, it seemed, to penal times. Actually these Fathers are members of the Passionist Order, which acquired the premises as a retreat in 1923. At their initiation, years before, each had worn a crown of thorns—a symbol of their Order.

From the heights above Ilkley I then switch to the sylvan village of Egton Bridge, near Whitby. It is best to go along in spring, perhaps, because the daffodils of the neighbourhood—especially prolific in Farndale—are a constant reminder of Father Postgate, who cultivated them at a time when coloured flowers were few in England. The building known as his Mass House still stands, half-way down Egton Bank; the chapel inside—concealed for so long—gave up its secret early last century.

The story is told, simply, by Will Ward and William Storey in the *Life of Father Postgate (1599–1679)*:

Then one day, about 1830, a girl mounted a ladder to clean the upper part of the kitchen wall in the little house. She pressed, the plaster gave way under her hand, and she broke into the long-hidden doorway into the loft. To her amazement she found herself looking into an oratory. The altar was prepared for Mass, the vestments lay spread out upon it. The missal, crucifix, and candle-sticks were in place. Everything was ready for the Sacrifice, but the priest who was to have offered it [Father Postgate] had been hanged, drawn and quartered a century and a half ago . . .'

Father David Quinlan has kindly allowed me to expand my account by quoting from his own recent work, *The Father Postgate Story.* That Mass Chapel, it seems, was

> a small separate section of the loft. It measured only 15 ft. by 10 ft., was 5½ ft. in height, and had no window. A tunnel through the thatch . . . allowed a view of a wide area of countryside, as a precaution against pursuivants. The tabernacle was in the gable end of the house. Allowing for the steeply pitched roof, a man of normal height must have had to stand at the centre of the altar for most of the Mass. There was room for a Mass-server, but others . . . remained in the kitchen below, from which access was gained by an oak ladder. It is said that by a trapdoor in the loft floor, beside the altar, the priest could escape into a lean-to building . . . whence he could get into an underground passage from which 'he emerged very wet' nearby.

Some forty years ago the house was found to be in such bad condition that it had to be re-built—at the cost of the little chapel. During these alterations the tenant had cause to climb up into the old loft. Suddenly a number of coins showered upon him. Some were of silver, though of different dates, suggesting that Father Postgate or one of his successors had collected them for pastoral work, hiding the money in the thatch until required.

Before he retired a few years ago, Father Quinlan established at St Hedda's Church, Egton Bridge, a Postgate Centre which displayed many of the items found in that Mass Chapel. The local joiner collaborated by making a scale model of the Mass House, with part of the roof cut away to expose the oratory and its Mass furniture. The model is still on view in the church. Other mementoes are still in the district and could be located by discreet enquiry.

Discretion was Father Postgate's native air. Not for nothing had he been chaplain to old Lady Dunbar at Burton Constable—that East Riding mansion riddled with hidden passages. Later, he often masqueraded as a gardener and had a hiding-place at Ugthorpe Old Hall, a few miles north of Egton. His successors had to breathe the same furtive air. One of them, Father Hervey, referred to the Ugthorpe Mission as 'The Isle of Patmos'. It was this priest who, along with Father Luke Potts, hid on the moors near Ugthorpe during the 'Forty-Five Rebellion, as told earlier.

Potts also employed the guise of a gardener, as I found for myself once on visiting the fine East Yorkshire house called Everingham Park, near Market Weighton. The present house supplants an older one belonging to the Constable family; which means that it would almost certainly have its Mass Chapel and the usual escape paraphernalia.

Correspondence passing between Sir Marmaduke Constable and *Mr* Potts, his ostensible agent at Everingham, had to be carefully phrased, for both were suspect. Prince Charles Edward was about to make his bid for the English throne. Because of his 'dangerous' opinions and alliances, Sir Marmaduke spent much time abroad. One of his letters, dated 15 August of that fateful year 1745, and addressed to Potts, would give nothing away had it fallen into wrong hands. It runs like this: 'The Improvement and Planting in the Park must be of advantage and Pleasure to my nephew Billy who, being so young, will find them much grown if care is taken . . . Be very Tender of the old Timber. Cut nothing down that can be spared.' Instructions for a gardener, clearly, but this gardener's skill ran beyond rose culture and forestry. He could read between the lines. The secret message lay somewhere among the trees. What it was, only Father Potts knew.

Another little chapel comes readily to mind, though its present rôle is to house some friends of mine—Thomas Whittaker, the woodcarver of Littlebeck, near Whitby, and his wife. Originally the building was a hospitium chapel associated with Whitby Abbey. Monks or lay-brothers would come along here with their pannier-laden beasts, and my two friends love to tell visitors that their lounge—now finely wainscoted and furnished in typical Whittaker manner—was once the stable where the monks kept their nags. Of course, there was then no need for secrecy. This house, now known as St Hilda (after the abbey at Whitby), fits into our theme for other reasons, centring chiefly upon a Spanish monk of the present time.

One day this monk made his way to Littlebeck, and a lovely way it is, either up the tiny Littlebeck valley from Sleights, or over the heather moorlands. Nobody knew he was coming, yet he had a special mission—to order a statue of the Virgin Mary for his college, the Collegio de Inglesis at Valladolla in Spain. 'I had been chosen to carve this statue', Mr Whittaker told me, 'because an ancestor of mine, another Thomas Whittaker, had joined that college in 1638 and eventually returned to England to spread his faith. But I knew nothing of this before! The Spanish monk was surprisingly familiar with my family history and could even tell me that Thomas Whittaker, the Roman Catholic priest, had also been a *woodcarver*.'

Therefore, in the one-time domain of a great north-country abbey —that same region where Thomas Hoby had hunted priests, and Father Postgate posed as a gardener—Mr Whittaker carved this 'bit of Popery' for a Catholic college in Spain.

Later, the monk who seemed to have appeared from nowhere sent my friend a small *Book of Martyrs*. A picture of his ancestor, with the gallows in the background, occurs on the last page. Father Thomas Whittaker—who had assumed his mother's maiden name, Stark, for obvious reasons—was hanged at Lancaster Castle in 1646.

As I have said, all this came as entirely fresh news to the Littlebeck woodcarver. He had been suddenly plunged into a remote family secret. But there is an echo of the story at High Whittaker, one of the two Elizabethan halls at Padiham in Lancashire. Here, before his capture, Father Whittaker lived dangerously for his faith, and one wonders how many times he had to use the hidden passage provided at the hall as a getaway.

Equipped with a Roman Catholic chapel, High Whittaker was conveniently situated near other homes of the Catholic gentry, notably Towneley Hall, Burnley, which has a priest's room and other hiding-places. As an erstwhile craftsman in wood, perhaps Whittaker sometimes threw a professional eye over the ingenious structure of those hides. Certainly many were made by Jesuits who were also clever joiners. Nicholas Owen—whom we saw at Hindlip Hall—and Father Holtby had each a reputation for this kind of thing, in penal times, but the names of others have been lost. Could Thomas Whittaker have been one of them?

Meanwhile, the Littlebeck woodcarver is on another scent. As we have already noticed, an old house like his may have its own secrets, keeping them more or less intact for centuries. It was only when Mr Whittaker began clearing some space at the back of the building that an old stone stairway spiralled gradually into view. After uncovering about five steps and part of the centre newel shaft, Mr Whittaker thought again of that hospitium chapel of monastic times, and mentioned his find to the oldest local resident.

This man was rich in ancient lore. For instance, through traditions handed down from father to son for untold generations, he could trace the poor condition of certain farms to what he called 'a bad setback'. When pressed for details he would say, 'Mi grandfaither told me, and his grandfaither told him, that "Willy Norman burnt 'em down".' Who 'Willy Norman' was he had no idea. Yet here was a folk memory preserved in local dialect and handed down as a kind of family secret. Willy Norman? Surely this was none other than Norman William, or William the Conqueror, whose scorched-earth policy left vast areas of the northern countryside waste and useless, as Domesday Book bluntly records.

This was the oracle, then, to whom Mr Whittaker mentioned his discovery. 'Ah yes,' said the man, not really surprised. 'Those steps you've found would lead down to th' old crypt. Mi grandfaither used to tell me there were two crypts under thy house.' With the reasonable assumption that several earlier generations of the man's family had hugged this knowledge to themselves, Mr Whittaker intends to dig further and follow the staircase. I hope to get the chance of following too—right into one of the monastic crypts. These will have been lost to view, and all remembrance (save for that one long-silent family tradition) for about three hundred years. They were probably filled in when the house was reconstructed in 1638.

Ever since I went to take photographic records of the Bar Convent in Blossom Street, York, during the Second World War, a charming little memory has remained with me. While busy with my camera in the convent's chapel I caught a seraphic smile from one of the nuns as she glided past. I am not a Catholic, but that flash of Heaven kindled again, recently, when Sister Loyola kindly sent me some details of this same chapel. Once more I saw that beautiful little eighteenth-century oratory, with its frieze depicting the Lamb of God stepping repeatedly among palm trees. But Sister Loyola's letter stirred another scene—a grim one, concerning a raid on the convent soon after its establishment here in 1686.

'We are told', she writes, 'that the officiating priest had barely time to hide, as the event took place just after Mass and there was no time to put away the vestments, which were carried off.' The Mother Superior, Frances Bedingfield (alias Long), and her assistant and niece, Dorothy Bedingfield, were also carried off, and later imprisoned in the loathsome 'Ousbridge Gaile'. I have been given a copy of the letter addressed by this old lady of nigh eighty years to the Archbishop of York, begging for mercy. It is a pathetic document and a nauseating commentary on contemporary affairs. Fortunately, her plea for 'releasement' was eventually granted.

But how did the priest escape in that raid? Presumably by resorting to a certain hiding-place, whose exact position was probably lost when the floor of the present chapel was laid in 1767. Some years ago, while the building was being wired by electricians, a curious hollow was found beneath the chapel floor. In all likelihood this hole was the lost hiding-place, though the original entrance has not survived.

A lid has been fixed into the floor, enabling one to peer within. In the room immediately below there is a housemaid's cupboard which could have provided an exit. But at this point conjecture is now virtually the sole guide—conjecture based in part on the tradition that escape was further facilitated by an underground passage leading to the River Ouse nearby.

One cannot leave York without calling to see Margaret Clitherow's House, in the Shambles. In front, the projecting upper storey rests on a low, slanting beam, and at one side a mere wisp of an alley runs back, furtively, from the narrow pavement. A small wooden oriel window beside the entrance is obviously new. It illuminates a shrine, indoors, erected not long ago to the memory of Margaret Clitherow, the Catholic martyr and so-called 'Pearl of York'.

In 1586, though still a young woman, she was literally pressed to death. Her 'offence'? Harbouring priests in this old house and enabling them to escape. One priest was Francis Ingilby of Ripley Castle. The house had been searched by the local sheriffs. At first they could find nothing irregular. A small boy who looked on was then questioned, but it took a whipping to break down his silence. Reluctantly he showed them the secret room, and the place where Margaret concealed vestments and books. These the sheriffs carried away, but Ingilby they could not find.

To the left of the altar in the new shrine a few original timbers have been preserved. They are part of the large, open fireplace which somehow conjured the priests out of sight and danger. In a fine life-size statue of Margaret Clitherow—made by an Hungarian refugee—the Pearl of York seems to embrace with her youthful smile those of all faiths who assemble here, also a few figures from the past—priestly figures lurking in the soft, fireplace shadows.

These hiding-places associated with private chapels must not deflect us from the domestic orbit, which is our present theme. Secret ways pertaining to a few cathedrals and churches will come to light in the final section of this book.

The best evocation of chapel and house combined which I have seen in the North is at Hazlewood Castle, near York, once the home of the Vavasour family. For a brief period about ten years ago the castle was open to the public. New ownership has unfortunately brought the curtain down again.

The Vavasours were never forced to worship here in secret. In return for various important services rendered, including Sir Thomas Vavasour's command of the *Foresight* against the Spanish Armada, Queen Elizabeth overcame her Protestant scruples and allowed the family to observe the rites of their Catholic faith unmolested. A fuller account of this strange immunity is given in my book, *Yorkshire*.

All the same, on looking round this chapel I could sense the clandestine atmosphere that prevailed during Elizabeth's reign. Sir Walter Vavasour did his best to banish this atmosphere early in the eighteenth century by introducing an imposing Georgian reredos, and some altar rails from York Minster. But the entrance door is still fitted with the iron grille that gave some warning of those who approached, and I should not be surprised if there was once some quicker way into the adjoining castle-home than walking along there—as now—via the main drive.

I was assured that the *carte blanche* given to the family by the Queen was not foolproof. One or two members had been apprehended and fined. The chapel also bears witness to those less fortunate, for a carved stone receptacle conceals the skulls of two recusants executed at York. One was probably Edmund Catterick, whose head had first been spiked, as a warning to others, on Micklegate Bar at York.

Sir Walter's Georgian refinements appear in the main building, too, but they do not altogether mask what existed before. Behind an old disused door I saw part of the original stairway. It spirals through the thickness of the wall to the battlements above, and down to a warren of passages that suggest their own tale of subterfuge. The section of stairway I saw had crumbled alarmingly, making any investigation impossible. Another wall, in the north tower, sheaths a priest-hole, but again I was thwarted. An enormous cupboard stood sentinel immediately in front. My young hostess—a Vavasour by birth—could only tell me that the hide connects with roof and cellars. It would be interesting to know who had the cupboard placed just there, and when, rather than seal up what lay behind. But nobody was able to tell me.

Hazlewood's tenuous link with James I* reminds me obliquely of Huddington Court in Worcestershire—home of the Winter family whom Robert Catesby involved in the Gunpowder Plot. This plot to rid the country of its King and his Parliament involved many. Guy Fawkes, of course, was its best-known victim. His Yorkshire birthplace comes into our story later. Meanwhile it is interesting to learn that the Winter family's ancestral home in Worcestershire was one of 'Little John' Owen's masterpieces.

The plotters who foregathered here on 6 November 1605, after the failure of their plans and the capture of my fellow Yorkshireman, were in surroundings that might have been designed for them. One cleverly made hide adjoins the family chapel and is entered by moving a panel in the wainscot. Another hide, discovered fairly recently, is reached through a bedroom wall.

Catesby and his friends were not the only ones who had fondly thought that the accession of James would bring to an end all the hide-and-seek business that had bedevilled life in England for so long. Instead, the penal laws against Popery were reinforced. One should remember this when burning Guy Fawkes' effigy on Bonfire Night.

* The north wing was specially built to welcome James while on his way south to ascend the throne as Elizabeth's successor, but he changed his plans and sent his portrait to Hazlewood instead, which so enraged Vavasour that he took his sword and slashed the picture to ribbons.

At his old school, St Peter's at York, 5 November is never celebrated as in other places. Fireworks and bonfires are taboo. His 'secret matter' might have been treasonable—but, after all, Guy Fawkes was an 'old boy'!

Several counties still preserve family chapels or associated features from that testing period. Rufford Hall, near Southport in Lancashire, may have lost several of its hides, but not very long ago, during repairs, part of the large timbered canopy in the Great Hall was found to be hollow, and lined with clay and rushes—a sound-proofing device. Little Moreton Hall—that much photographed house near Congleton, in Cheshire, with a moat to reflect its splendid 'magpie' architecture—retains sufficient of the right atmosphere to justify all one's romantic expectations. Above the chapel there is a prayer room, and not far away—beyond the Guests' Hall—a parlour which unfortunately suffered damage when a farmer once used the room for storage.

People who have little sensibility of the past sometimes thoughtlessly commit acts of vandalism. In my own district the beautifully panelled room at Rawdon Hall where that pioneer Nonconformist, the Rev. Oliver Heywood, held his secret gatherings, was actually whitewashed for the supposed benefit of the pigs one farming tenant kept there! At Little Moreton Hall some of the parlour panelling vanished altogether, including a sliding panel that led to a little chamber marked on the house plan as a secret room. Many visitors get this room into their photographs without realizing they have done so. The room inevitably associated with harassed priests and Jesuits occupies a first-floor projection, thus affecting the outline of the building.

Near Kendal in Westmorland the village of Skelsmergh has its own memories of persecution, but I only have these on hearsay. All my efforts to pierce the time barrier here have so far been in vain. One hears of many cupboards that have 'swallowed up' fugitive priests. Other tales have leaked out, with tantalizing brevity, but the house chiefly concerned, Dodding Green, prefers to keep silent, as though pursuivants were still in vogue. It is very sad. If only Father Gerard had been lodged here we might have had a thrilling story to relate, for he boldly recorded his experiences in some private diaries.

One of those experiences takes us along to Essex. The stage-setting is Broadoaks, near Saffron Walden. Because a servant treacherously revealed his presence in the house Father John Gerard, the Jesuit priest, had to be bundled quickly out of sight—into a small hide near the family chapel. There was just time to hand him a few biscuits and some jelly before the search party entered the house. His confinement lasted four days.

But let us hear Gerard himself.

'They made a thorough search', he wrote, 'in every part, not forgetting to look under the tiles of the roof. Finding nothing whatever they began to break down certain places they suspected . . . they measured and sounded the walls and all the floors to find out and break into any hollow place there might be.'

That was on the first day. Next day the search was intensified.

'They had gone into the room above and tried the fireplace through which I had got into my hole. Then they got into the chimney to sound by means of their hammers. One said to another, within my hearing, "Might there not be a place here for a person to get down into the well of the chimney below by lifting up this hearth?" "No," said the other, "but there might easily be an entrance at the back of this chimney." So saying, he gave the place a kick! I was afraid he would hear the hollow sound of the place where I was.'

The third day dawned, and one wonders whether a single biscuit yet remained. A fire was now kindled on the false hearth that gave Gerard his entry. Hot ashes and sparks reach him where he crouches. But the trial by smoke and heat is somehow halted, for, as Gerard recalls later, 'the guards noticed the loose bricks and . . . remarked that this was something curious. I thought that they were there and then going to break open the place and enter, but they . . . put off further examination until the next day.'

No prisoner on a medieval rack suffered worse torture than this long-drawn-out agony, now surely nearing its hateful climax. Yet reprieve is at hand. For some inexplicable reason the searchers abandon their task and withdraw. On the fourth day Gerard emerges —not as captive, but still a pitiable sight: 'I was all wasted and weakened with hunger as with want of sleep, and with having to sit in such a narrow place.'

In that sentence Gerard speaks for countless priests and other hunted persons. His horrifying experience occurred in the Saffron Walden countryside, only forty miles or so north of London, but it must have been typical of many all over England.

*

Wales, too, had its own secret assignments. Owain Glyndwr set the pace with those caves and secret valleys that gave him ambush or refuge. One of the caves is on the north shore of the beautiful Tal-y-llyn; so lonely is this place, beneath the southern flank of Cader Idris, that even today a man could enjoy the life of a hermit among the lakeside rocks without much fear of being tracked. A piece of harness decoration from Glyndwr's horse turned up at Harlech Castle in 1923. It is a gilt bronze boss bearing his arms—four lions rampant.

Centuries pass. Wales comes to terms with her ancient English foe. But there is still unrest, religious as well as political. That is why two priests had to take over the Cross Keys Inn at Holywell, on the Dee estuary, one acting as landlord, the other as ostler. When any Catholics called they could be served with wine at the bar, and Mass somewhere in the back quarters.

As this chapter strikes the domestic phase of our subject I have chosen one house which characterizes much Welsh history, and keeps a few of its best secrets for some future time. The house is Plas Mawr, in Conway, and if anybody can pass this imposing, step-gabled building without being drawn inside, he would make a poor companion for me.

Plas Mawr was long the home of the Wynne family. One of them—Sir Richard, the second baronet—adds a certain piquancy to the story of the house by having accompanied Prince Charles (later Charles I) and Buckingham on the venture known as 'the Spanish match'. It was supposed to be a secret venture, Charles and his favourite, Buckingham, travelling incognito as Tom and John Smith. Yet on their return they were publicly acclaimed with hundreds of bonfires. The people of England had guessed what was in the wind, and really rejoiced because the Infanta had not come too! They did not relish having her as future Queen. I fancy Sir Richard's part in this mission that failed would provide much back-stairs gossip at Plas Mawr.

An Elizabethan house like this—tall, commodious, and full of odd corners—is always exciting. Now the Georgians were so symmetrically minded, so sure of themselves, that their houses offer nothing more secretive than an occasional dummy door, born of the same whimsy that produced garden follies. The mock-bookshelf door and the hidden fountain that squirted the unwary were a bit of harmless play-acting.

But Plas Mawr was not designed for fun. The nearest approach to humour is the amazing variety of heraldic emblems contrived in plaster on walls and fireplaces. Wynnes, Griffiths, Lathoms, and Fitzalans all proudly display their eagles, Englishmen's heads (very forlorn, these), storks, boars, unicorns, and suns, etc. But I cannot help wondering how many of these people had inside knowledge of a certain little space sandwiched beyond sight between the reception room and the lantern room?

Wales was slow to renounce the 'Old Faith'. Romish priests would be *persona grata* in some of its mansions and halls long after other parts of Britain had—outwardly, at least—conformed. One of the Wynne family by marriage was executed for his complicity in the Babington Plot to murder Queen Elizabeth I and put that devout Catholic, Mary Stuart, on the throne. The district was then thick with plotters. Local Catholics included a certain 'Mr Pew who keeps a pinnace and dwells on a fortified rock'—a neat ambiguity for Pugh of Penrhyn Hall at the foot of the Little Orme at Llandudno. Then there was the Mistress Holland of Conway who, folk whispered, 'prays daily for the safe and prosperous success of Irish and Popish recusants'.

The influential Wynne family had their fingers in many a Welsh pie, and doubtless their secret room was a ready stand-by in case of need—others' need, perhaps, as well as their own. It would have been interesting to know the mechanics of the hide. As it is, there is just that significant space—and a haunted room at one side!

On the house plan this room is designated the Lantern Room; a reference to the charming little oriel window which once threw a light into the courtyard below. But a fascinating ghost story recovered by J. R. Furness, the first curator here, quickens the tempo considerably.

> The lady of the house—evidently Mistress Robert Wynne—was expecting her husband to return and, accompanied by her three-year-old child, had been watching from the tower. In descending she slipped and fell down the stairs, stunning the child. The result was serious as she was expecting another child. The housekeeper put her to bed in the Lantern Room.
>
> As the Mistress's condition grew worse the family doctor was sent for but as he was not at home his young assistant, Dr Dick, came in his place. He wished to fetch the more experienced practitioner, but the housekeeper asserted that her mistress must not be left, and

locked Dr Dick in the Lantern Room. A man-servant was dispatched for the family doctor but the man *never returned.*

The husband came home that night. Finding the Lantern Room door locked, he burst it open. The three-year-old child lay dead on a couch. The mistress lay dead on the bed, and an infant, prematurely born, lay dead in the window on the right of the fireplace. Such was the knight's reception on his return from the wars. He could only ask, 'Who has been here?' The poor old housekeeper could only reply, 'Dr Dick is somewhere in the room.' The knight quickly drew his sword but Dr Dick was nowhere to be found. Too excited to listen to words of comfort he pushed the housekeeper away, saying, 'I'll never leave this room until I have been revenged on Dr Dick. Daylight will tell the story.' He shut the door and paced the room heavily for hours until at last, with one last cry of bitter anguish, he expired at the foot of the bed on which his dead wife lay.

Dr Dick was never seen again, the surmise being that, although perfectly innocent and blameless, he sought to escape from his gruesome surroundings by means of the chimney. It is said that passages from the chimneys communicated with the various hiding-places, and in this labyrinth of gloom he got lost, and, overcome with the fumes of charcoal smoke, he slept the sleep of death. One of the passages can be seen high up in the chimney from the Small Kitchen fireplace. With certain superstitious folk the belief is that the knight still walks the room to be revenged on Dr Dick, whose bones, they affirm, are still somewhere in the chimney, and until they are found and put to rest with his forefathers in the churchyard, the ghost of Plas Mawr will never be laid.

Mr Furness, our narrator, seems to have been steeped in the romantic prose of an earlier day, but one mystery beyond the first remained unsolved. What happened to that retainer who had been sent for the older doctor? He had barely left the house when he was seized by the Press Gang and put aboard a vessel in the harbour that was ready to sail. This only became known when, after many compulsory years at sea, he returned to Conway and heard of the multiple tragedy.

The above story is here given by permission of the Royal Cambrian Academy of Art, who have their headquarters at Plas Mawr. It is based on the old housekeeper's version of events and adds a touch of the macabre to this old mansion. On my visit the haunted room was bare, except for a solitary chair beside the fireplace. This chair was the one concession to mundane needs. The room seemed to be *listening*, but the knight was evidently wary of me and kept out of sight.

Mention of this family ghost should really have waited for its congenial sphere in this book; its premature 'appearance' here is due to the secret passages at Plas Mawr. Similar intrusions may occur in our next chapter, for ghosts are notoriously difficult to control. We shall see.

CHAPTER ELEVEN

PARODIES AND PRANKS

It was inevitable, I suppose, that priest-holes and their aura of mystery should at length become the subject of parody. Kenneth Grahame was a brilliant exponent of this playful art.

Here was a man with two divergent selves—one, august enough to hold a senior position at the Bank of England; the other, elfin, fanciful and still at home with childhood delights and the rich world of make-believe.

To enter his 'secret world of imagination' one has to see him first as a boy in Argyll, messing about with boats beside Loch Fyne, and listening, perhaps, for the Ghostly Piper of Inveraray Castle. Later, the Berkshire Downs enfold him, with the River Thames around Cookham and Marlow filling his dreams. Cornwall, especially Fowey and the Lizard, adds its spell. The River Fowey, in fact, tinctured by a Thames that obligingly shifts its course somewhat, gave us *The Wind in the Willows*.

When my wife and I sailed towards the 'little grey sea town' of the fable in a coastal vessel, many years ago, we were unwittingly following in the wake of Grahame's Sea Rat. The cold breezes which made us all huddle together on deck would have been mitigated in their effect had we also known that the cliffs on our port side witnessed the scene in which Sea Rat shares with Water Rat his visions of 'violet seas, tawny sands, and lizard-haunted walls'.

Every Kenneth Grahame fan will recall Toad Hall and its hidden passage. In the story it is Badger who divulges the secret of its existence and whereabouts. To his incredulous companions he says, impressively, 'That very useful tunnel leads right up under the butler's pantry, next to the dining hall.'

In a piece of imaginative writing, such as *The Wind in the Willows*, there is no need to seek or expect topographical leanings, but in his charming biography of Grahame, Peter Green does suggest a few possible derivations. Badger's subterranean home may reflect the underworld created for himself last century by the fifth Duke of Portland at Welbeck, in the Dukeries. Toad Hall itself 'contains elements from

Harleyfield Manor, Mapledurham House, and Cliveden'. At Mapledurham, near Reading, the secret element is a priest-hole entered by means of a rope. But we may be sure that the whole ethos of the secret passage—of which I have given so many examples—influenced the author when he projected Toad and his friends into Toad Hall by its hidden route to evict the weasel interlopers.

Another entertaining parody is Eden Phillpotts' play, *The Purple Bedroom*. Here we have the entire apparatus of Tudor intrigue, mystery and deception: a secret chamber opening from the guest bedroom, three ghosts, a blood-curdling tradition, and a long-lost heirloom. I have just re-read this play, for about the fiftieth time, and find it as funny as ever. Yet there is that substratum of reality.

In this play the ghosts try to find one mortal with enough nerve to look on as they re-enact their old quarrel as it actually did happen, not as tradition made out. At Penfound Manor in Cornwall we hear of three ghosts who, because of similar confusion, might welcome Phillpott's solution to their own tangled story. . . .

It is known that Kate Penfound was about to elope with John Trebarfoot when her father, Nicholas Penfound, intervened. He rushed into the courtyard, saw Kate descending a ladder from the solar and John waiting with his horse below. Out came Father's sword and there ensued some kind of scuffle. Curiously, all three soon lay dead. What really happened nobody knows. Perhaps that is why on the night of 26 April—the anniversary of the tragedy—Nicholas and Kate and John are supposed to reappear.

It would be no hardship to watch this little drama from the Civil War period re-enacted, for the courtyard is a lovely spot and one could peep out from the medieval porch. But nobody seems to have had enough courage. Only Kate has been seen—'a pretty girl in a white dress'—wandering through the house towards the top of the Armada staircase. Could she be trying to lure some brave soul into the courtyard for another rendering of that midnight scuffle?

But we must return to our parodies.

Not long ago I stumbled upon the perfect simulacrum—the quintessence of the hue and cry period of English history, yet all done simply 'to amuse the children'. This was at Garrowby Hall, near York, home of the Earl and Countess of Halifax.

It is first necessary to get the instigator of this fantasy into focus. He was Charles Lindley, Viscount Halifax and grandfather of the present Earl. For many years he played an important part in High Church affairs, and strove valiantly for reunion with Rome. He was a well-known figure in Court circles. And yet there was that in his nature which made him—all his long life—not only delight in the world of make-believe but give it continual expression.

At Hickleton Hall, Lord Halifax's south Yorkshire home, he usually had some of the family in disguise to startle the others; or in hiding, or playing charades. And the telling of ghost tales—the more hair-raising the better—was part of the ritual. It was the same when the family went on holiday. The pranks went with them. Of one trip to the Moult in Devon, Halifax made this note: 'After luncheon draped Mary up in Agnes's [his sister] old fancy gown and told Edward [his son, later Viceroy of India] she was a fairy.' On this occasion the ghosts had been invoked a little earlier, as dessert.

Christmas spent at another house produced some tableaux, 'Francis and Edward impersonating the Princes in the Tower, and Mary looking "very pretty as Lady Jane Grey".'

But of all the houses Halifax frequented he most enjoyed Temple Newsam, near Leeds—the home of another sister, Emily Meynell Ingram. It was 'full of ghosts' and had a history to match. Agnes once told her brother, 'Temple Newsam is the place where I am always most frightened, especially if I have the Blue Room.' 'Why,' said Halifax, 'in the Blue Room you are close to Emily and her maid.' 'I know,' she answered, 'but you have to go into the passage to get to them, and I always think that *they*, or whatever *they* are, are always near the door.'

Temple Newsam and its ghosts must not divert us from our immediate frolic. *They* are almost certainly *there* and have been seen fairly recently, one being the Blue Lady whose portrait graces one of the many rooms. *They* flit around the *Book of Ghosts* compiled by Lord Halifax. (They also materialize in our next chapter.) But with all his flair for the supernatural, Halifax could hardly endow Garrowby Hall with a reputation for being haunted—except through one of his invented 'hair-raisers'. The house was only built in 1892–3, in a hidden valley of the Yorkshire Wolds, ringed by some ancient barrows.

What Lord Halifax did achieve in this house, brilliantly, was a gallery of playful deceit. Through the kindness of the present Earl, my wife and I recently went along with a friend to see for ourselves this astonishing throw-back to Tudor times. Lord Halifax seems to have assured his architect that its period oddities were only intended to amuse his children—but, says the Earl, 'he got a lot of fun out of them himself'. If the old gentleman had here needed any boon companion for his imaginary escapades, other than family and close friends, E. V. Lucas would have been his man. I wish Lucas had known of Garrowby Hall and its pleasantries when he wrote that delightful essay, *On Secret Passages*.

Lucas invokes the perennial glamour of 'secret drawers, secret cupboards, secret chambers', citing such episodes as the Abbé Faria excavating the secret passage from his cell to that of Edmond Dantes, in *Monte Cristo*; and—nearer home and reality—the Prince Regent enjoying his nocturnes with Mrs Fitzherbert by means of an underground passage at Brighton Pavilion. The attic storey at Garrowby Hall would have led 'E. V.' into cleaner pastures of joy, where guile and trickery were as innocent as a game of charades or hide-the-thimble.

At Garrowby the game really begins in an elegant ground-floor room called the Hall. In style it is Georgian. But wait. The Earl steps towards the portrait of an ancestor (Edward Courtenay, Earl of Devon) and lays hold of the wall-panel on which it hangs. Suddenly it swings out like a door, revealing a narrow space dimly lit by one narrow slot window. This is distinctly Elizabethan, and just big enough to hide a tallish man. A spy-hole (closed when desired by a wooden peg) pierces the panel just below the portrait and affords a glimpse into the main room.

'When we were children,' the Earl told us, 'my brother would often hide in there and make ghostly noises, which always succeeded in frightening a cricket "pro" who used to stay here. To make the noises more convincing, the "pro" was always plentifully served by me with ghost tales.'

Formerly, when the walls of this Hall were painted dark, it would be almost impossible to detect the trick, and as bewildering as that 'speaking portrait' with which Sir Walter Scott mystifies Colonel Everard in *Woodstock*. Was Lord Halifax familiar with that novel, I wonder, or—even better—had he seen the device that inspired Scott—at Lyme Park in Cheshire?

The Earl and Countess then led the way to the garret via some narrow stairs with a rope as handrail. Their dogs swarmed excitedly round us, and were as keen as ourselves to explore this unknown territory.

First we peered into a carved oak chest, uncomfortably reminiscent of the Mistletoe Bough. No grisly remains were inside, however; in fact the chest was empty. Its secret is the back panel which shifts to one side, enabling anybody with sufficient agility—and a slender figure—to crawl through to a crooked passage that emerges a few feet away in the main attic. The passage is about ten inches wide and six feet high. One exactly like it, though straight, continues along the attic wall for about nine yards. Each passage can be closed with doors having hidden catches, and further concealed among thick folds of tapestry. When this top storey was divided off into bedrooms, those cryptic passages must have been places of particular allure to the Halifax youngsters!

The *pièce de résistance* here is a built-in cupboard. It stands in a corner, near the chest, and looks at first like scores of other cupboards. When the doors are opened one simply sees a set of box-shelves—just waiting, it would seem, for a few old books and documents. But the dogs sensed something odd. They pranced around the Earl as he reached down to release a hidden catch; when the whole set of shelves tilted aside, crazily, on one edge, the alcove took on a new dimension. It was no longer a storage place, but the vestibule to a secret chamber.

This lay beyond, or rather *through* the cupboard. After squeezing my way beneath the tilted shelves I stood in a small, square space lit by one window—a window hidden from outside, I discovered later, by a convenient gable. This, then, was the family 'priest-hole', which Lord Halifax once impishly offered to his friend Canon Wylde, 'in the event of the Church Association breaking into a new and violent persecution'. His biographer, J. G. Lockhart, goes on to say that 'behind the fun there may have been a lurking hope that some day, perhaps, with great good fortune, he [Halifax] might find himself playing hide-and-seek in the house with the emissaries of Scotland Yard pursuing him for some high ecclesiastical offence'.

A frequent guest at Garrowby was Robert Hugh Benson, the priest and novelist, who later joined the church of Rome. Having seen these secret devices I can well understand why Stanfield Place in Benson's story, *By What Authority*, bears such a resemblance to Garrowby!

One thing I half expected in that hidden room was a Missal or some other tell-tale book. To leave such a book about was an old dodge.

It was meant to divert attention from the possible existence of an *inner* hide. Of this possibility here, however, there seemed to be no sign—until the Earl pulled the arras aside. There, in the shadow, was a small door; it led into a tiny room not much bigger than a watchman's hut. And beyond, again, a bolt hole led through another friendly cupboard into the main attic.

Nicholas Owen, I think, would have fully approved of it all, though the masks would have him guessing.

One of these masks grinned down at me in the 'priest-hole', momentarily suggesting the skull of some hapless recusant. Other masks and skulls are arranged beneath a black cloth over the entrance cupboard. 'My father,' said the Earl, 'often contrived to pull this cloth away, unseen, to alarm visitors. For he, too [that is, the Viceroy to be] enjoyed the old jokes and secrets as much as anybody.' Indeed, they seem to be part of the Garrowby inheritance. During their boyhood the present Earl and his brother put one of the hideous masks (second from the left in my photograph) in the bed of a visitor, pulling the sheets right up to its bearded chin. When at the day's close this French abbé sleepily entered, he gave one glance at the frightful creature that had materialized from space, and struck it with his stick. How grandfather Halifax would have chuckled!

Actually, the French abbé was—to this extent—sampling the horrors which Halifax loaded upon 'Colonel P.' in his own fabricated story of Garrowby. The skull which startled both of them recalls one of those unearthed in the neighbouring, prehistoric barrows—mysterious places, remarked Halifax, supposed to be 're-visited by the spirits of the departed in the shadowy resemblance of the bodies they once animated' and haunted, at times, by 'curious lights and sounds'.

This garret at Garrowby, with all its roguish subterfuge, is the *mise en scène* for *Colonel P.'s Ghost Story*. Heavy footfalls, creaking boards, slow lifting of the tapestry, and 'a dark figure crossing the patch of moonlight'; familiar ingredients to any student of historical byways, but here Lord Halifax's wish fulfilment.

Before we left the attic the dogs had to be carefully rounded up. This was their initiation—as well as ours—into the secret places of the house. It would never do to leave one behind in the 'priest-hole'. A dog might whine there for hours and never be heard. The garret is rarely used in these days. It really awaits more children.

CHAPTER TWELVE

A GALLERY OF GHOSTS

I wish I could have eavesdropped at one of the ghost sessions held by Lord Halifax at Hickleton Hall (now a Sue Ryder Home for Iron Curtain victims) or Garrowby. They must have been a little unnerving at times, however, for he really believed in ghosts. To him 'the seen was so trivial, the unseen so tremendous'. And with all his flair for 'dressing up', spooky stories could so easily be 'authenticated'.

One memorable Christmas evening at Hickleton in 1918, for instance, the ghost of Mrs Box—'a housekeeper who had hanged herself, in the remote past'—walked the corridors again. The younger guests showed some alarm, until they discovered that the ghost was a clever impersonation by the 79-year-old Viscount.

Sir W. Richmond's painting of the Viscount, at Garrowby, portrays an austere, almost monastic figure. His contemplative glance rested upon us during our visit. And yet there is a warm humanity in that face; a smile, one feels, is about to emerge and release his *alter ego*—the self that revelled in wizardry and all things occult.

His sister's palatial residence, Temple Newsam, gave him abundant fodder for his fireside tales. He often spoke of having seen an elderly woman of great beauty gliding through the Blue Damask Room in her silk gown and lace shawl. 'She paused at a dressing-table,' he would recall, 'searched for something and then passed into the Miss Ingram room.' This at three in the morning. Others of the family have heard deep sighs issuing from nothing but the space around them. A tutor who once lived in the mansion confided to the family that 'every day he was awakened between three and four in the morning by a tremendous noise, as of furniture being moved overhead—when the only room directly above his was the Long Gallery'. Many guests were similarly disturbed and asked for a different room. One lady described the commotion as a 'phantom ball'.

The underground passage beneath the Clock Court must have gratified this connoisseur of secrecy. It is not open to the public like the rest of the mansion (now an art gallery), but I have been through the passage from end to end. Its original purpose had nothing to do with the plotters and schemers who once lived here, however. Those who took this way were the servants. It was a short cut to the dining-room and helped to keep the meals reasonably hot. Yet it is a ghostly sort of place. Down there anybody could imagine things. All the traditional phantoms of the house become credible, including those which members of the staff claim to have seen in recent years.

Lord Halifax's Ghost Book, a collection of stories made by him, was first published in 1936 and is now available in paperback form. As the present Earl of Halifax says in his Foreword, 'the true secret of the appeal made to his [Lord Halifax's] thought by the mysterious, or so-called uncanny, was the glimpse that such narratives or events might seem to afford of the hidden realities of the unseen world'.

By good fortune I have been able to visit many of the haunted houses that figure in Lord Halifax's book. One of them is Burton Agnes Hall, near Driffield. This glorious Elizabethan house is now open to the public, but when I first went there the conditions were still those which prevailed while Mrs Wickham-Boynton, the owner, enjoyed uninterrupted privacy—if one excepts the shadowy visitors. She recounted the following experience for Lord Halifax's benefit:

> We were having tea in the hall when I looked up suddenly and saw a small thin woman dressed in fawn colour come out of the garden, walk very quickly up the steps, and disappear through the front door, which I thought was open, into the house. I imagined it must be the parson's wife and remarked to my husband, who had seen nothing, 'There is Mrs Coutts. Go and bring her in.' But he could find nobody.
>
> Then I remembered the old story of a *fawn* lady who had been seen about the place . . . she is probably the Griffith ancestress whose skull is still in the house here, though no one knows exactly where it is walled up.

Much has been written about the Burton Agnes skull and the pandemonium that ensued when a maidservant once threw it out of doors as useless lumber. Only when the skull came back was calm restored. To prevent further interference it was hidden somewhere in this large, many-roomed mansion, and the secret of its actual whereabouts has since been lost.

The household kindly resumed their speculations for my benefit

A modern statue of Margaret Clitherow, who was martyred for hiding Catholic priests in her home in the Shambles, York

'Miss Ingram', as portrayed here, is the Blue Lady whose ghost flits through Temple Newsam House, Leeds

In the Silver Room at Rawdon Hall, W. Yorks., Priscilla Rawdon—whose father sponsored secret religious gatherings here two hundred and fifty years ago—still carries on a 'subdued conversation' after nightfall

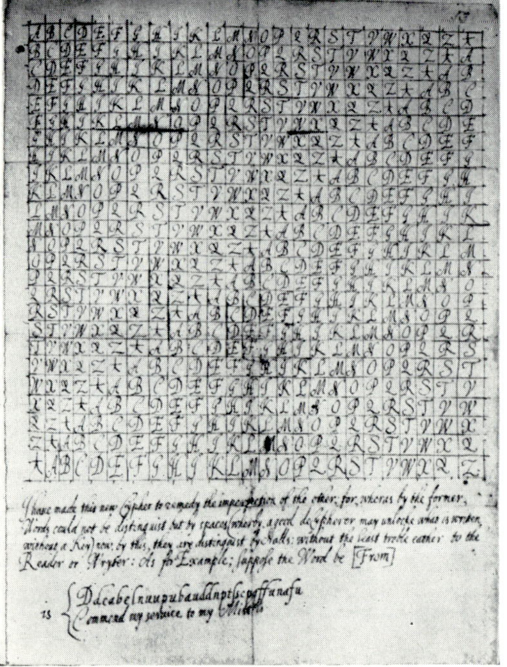

I have made this new Cipher to remedy the imperfection of the other; for, whereas by the former, Words could not be distinguist but by spaces (whereby a good decipherer may unlocke what is writen, without a Key) now, by this, they are distinguist by Nulls: without the least trouble either to the Reader or Wryter: As for Example; suppose the Word be [From]

Ddcabelnuupubauddnpthscpffunafu
Command my service to my Mistris

One of the ciphers used by the imprisoned Charles I, at Carisbrooke Castle, Isle of Wight, to keep in secret touch with his accomplices

The 'escape' staircase, used by Henry VI while in hiding at Waddington Hall, near Clitheroe

Two of the Round Houses built by a former parson at Veryan, Cornwall, to keep the Devil at bay

The Round Towe
Ardmore, Co. Cork:
of Ireland's eighty s
towers, which
puzzle antiqua

when I went along. The Haunted Bedroom was surprisingly out of favour as the skull's resting-place. Other spots then suggested themselves—the famous honeysuckle ceiling, the large heraldic overmantel, the dining-room wainscoting. Or what about the Dance of Death fireplace in the ground-floor drawing-room; surely its macabre display would provide congenial cover for that too-potent skull?

There is reason to believe, however, that the skull reposes somewhere above the majestic screen of stone and alabaster in the Great Hall. If this surmise is correct St John, writing his Gospel under the watchful Eye of God—the subject of the nearest carving—has an additional responsibility! It is this part of the house that the Fawn Lady attempts to enter.

Another house mentioned in the Halifax collection is the old Rectory at Bolton Priory, in Wharfedale. One could have understood its being haunted by a white-robed canon from the neighbouring Augustinian monastery, but in the experience of several observers the resident ghost wears a long, dark garment 'like a dressing-gown'. After seeing the apparition on the stairs, Lord Hartington once said, 'There was no question of his being transparent; he was as solid as any actual man.' This led the Duchess of Devonshire to suspect the existence of a secret hide into which the rather too-too-solid figure could vanish. But no such retreat has ever been found here, to my knowledge. Perhaps the local children had an inkling who the man really was? At any rate they always referred to him with affection as Punch.

When very young my two elder children loved these surroundings. There was the ruined Priory, with the rectory close by, bounded by the most idyllic river scenery in Yorkshire. I never heard my youngsters talk about Punch. More in their line was Emily Norton's little white doe that still flits among the tombstones, if one has eyes to see. One of these stones gave them special pleasure. It was a table-tomb near the old choir. They would sit happily at one side and pretend it was a piano.

Oh, blissful childhood that can conjure celestial music from such an instrument! Oddly enough, two adult visitors had a strange 'musical' experience nearby about twelve years ago. While approaching the priory church (still used for services) they distinctly heard a choir singing to the accompaniment of an organ. When they stepped eagerly inside, the place was empty! What is the secret of such attunement?

If I was asked to name the most uncanny house known to me, there would be no hesitation. I must have visited scores of historic halls all over Britain, but for eeriness, and a sense of the past breaking its sinister way into the present, few places can hold a candle to Newburgh Priory.

My first introduction to this place was through the lively imagination of a youth—a pupil at Newburgh Priory over twenty years ago when this was being used as a school. He was a French boy and the tales he had to tell gave full play to the renowned eloquence of his countrymen.

Alexandre Dumas shone in his eyes and directed his gestures as he described for his mother and me the door that one schoolmaster could never keep shut, lock it as often as he liked. There was another cupboard which everybody was solemnly warned to keep tight closed at night, lest the malicious wraith lurking inside should be liberated. The youth excelled himself when describing what happened, once, when this precaution was overlooked. The darkening inn parlour where the three of us were sitting, during this narration, gave him all the atmosphere he needed. We could *see* the smoke-like shape which emerged from that cupboard, and *feel* its stranglehold upon the negligent master. Still miming the man's supposed experience, the youth then wrestled with the spectre and finally managed to force it back to its lair—this time remembering to turn the key.

That recital at the Fauconberg Arms, in Coxwold village, would, I thought, reflect as little truth as many another chance effort. The lad might well have been romancing, as lads will before a fond mother. But now—after several visits of my own to Newburgh Priory—I feel as though I am romancing too when I set down what my notebooks record.

One's first impression is of a grand old house in a painter's paradise, with the Hambleton Hills over to the north. Adapted from a twelfth-century Augustinian priory, the house is approached from the Coxwold–York road along a drive flanked by two enormous yews, each in its contrived shape rather like a cardinal's biretta.

Monastic memories are still pervasive here, yet the last Prior so far forgot his calling as to leave a curse on the place. When the order for its dissolution came, in 1539, a new apartment in the upper storey was still unfinished. The Prior vowed that if anybody in future times should presume to complete the room, there would be a sudden death in the family. Early this century Sir George Wombwell ignored the tradition and started making the room habitable by plastering the walls. The work ceased abruptly when he heard that his heir had been killed in the South African War. Another son had died just before. The room is still in that unfinished state, as some of those schoolboys found when it became their temporary dormitory.

The present owner, Captain V. M. Wombwell, once saw a man's ghost issuing from that same room. It was a strange figure wearing silk breeches and a powdered wig. Afterwards the Captain said, 'I have seen some evil things in my time, but nothing so vile as the look on that fellow's face!'

This is the creepy part of the house. Even the owner's dogs notice it. Mrs Wombwell told me that her poodle would never venture beyond a certain point; at that point, near the staircase landing, its hair bristles as though it is terrified. I thought the sensitive creature had done well to come upstairs at all, but as it was being soothed in Mrs Wombwell's arms perhaps the 'presence' of the woman who was long ago murdered here and now kicks her own head down the stairs could for once be tolerated.

We were standing, just then, at the head of another staircase. To the left, between us and the unfinished room, stood Cromwell's vault. To the right, down a lonely, empty passage, was the bedroom where a box, affixed to the mantelpiece, contains a missal. One of the Augustinian canons left it thereabouts at the Dissolution, saying that it must never be moved. A housemaid who once took it to her own room became violently ill. Captain Wombwell takes no chances with those outraged monks; the holy book is now securely padlocked in its receptacle.

Other ghosts that haunt Newburgh Priory are mentioned in my *North Country Profile*. But Cromwell's tomb, also described in that book, demands its own place here.

The tomb occupies one end of a narrow chamber. That evil-looking ghost seen by Captain Wombwell must have passed within a few inches of the inscription which states: 'In this vault, it is believed, are Oliver Cromwell's bones, brought here by his daughter, Mary, Countess of Fauconberg, at the Restoration, when his remains were disinterred from Westminster Abbey.' The family tradition is that when Cromwell's remains were dug up at the Restoration, Mary bribed somebody to substitute another corpse for the intended desecration and had her father's remains conveyed secretly to this specially prepared vault at Newburgh.

There has always been an element of doubt concerning the tomb and its contents. For some obscure reason which it would be fascinating to unravel, certain Catholic families in York used to say that the one interred here was not the Lord Protector, but Margaret Clitherow—the sixteenth-century martyr. Like his forebears, Captain Wombwell resolutely refuses to have the tomb opened. Cromwell—if it is he—seems assured of his repose. The only one who knows the secret is Mary, Countess of Fauconberg; she smiles cryptically from her life-size portrait in the dining-room below.

Equal mystery now surrounds Cromwell's severed head. My sister-in-law once saw this grisly relic at the Woodbridge (Suffolk) home of the late Canon Wilkinson. When he removed its silk wrapping she beheld the teeth and hair of the man whose thunderings once reverberated throughout Britain. Even the famous mole had left its mark.

I expect she was then told the remarkable history of this head, since it parted from the rest of the corpse. For long years it was hidden away, and then—when secrecy was no longer necessary—it changed ownership several times. One impecunious actor exhibited the head to raise funds for himself. Later, a lady became its owner, but she soon gave it into the custody of her doctor, and he—wise man—conducted a kind of autopsy on it, an historical one, discovering much that had happened to this lonely head since it had been ignominiously spiked, for twenty-five years, above Westminster Hall. Canon Wilkinson inherited the head from his medical ancestor.

When the canon died in 1957 antiquaries fondly hoped that the tomb at Newburgh Priory might now be opened and the head restored to its rightful owner—if, indeed, Cromwell does rest here. Instead of that, Old Noll's head has gone to earth again. It is interred in the grounds of Cromwell's old college—Sidney Sussex, Cambridge. The actual spot is a secret, known to only two or three personnel of the college.

Many books have been written about ghosts and the buildings they are supposed to haunt. I have no pressing desire to add to the number of such books, but the subject being compounded of mystery, it warrants some attention here.

It is easy to explain ghosts away—if you have never met one. Ghosts seem to shun me, but I respect (and almost envy) those people of my acquaintance who claim to have 'seen and heard strange things'.

Once, on a visit to the charming Lancashire hamlet of Wycoller, my wife and I called at Wycoller House. While waiting for tea, our young boy played with the little girl of the house. We heard, later, that she had recently made an exceptional friendship. The family had come to live here about eighteen months before. At first, little Mary slept upstairs in a long-disused room. She surprised her mother by asking, several mornings in succession, 'Mummy, who is that lady who comes to see me every night?' Mary's mother was the only woman in the house, but the girl had evidently 'seen' another.

There was no fright in her, only childish curiosity. One morning before breakfast she confided, 'The lady says "It's all right you playing here if you don't make too much noise".' And so the odd little friendship grew, between the child of three and the woman of some bygone time—until Mary was given a more suitable bedroom. But the other room held the secret. Only a young child, perhaps, has the right key.

Within a one-mile radius of my own home in mid-Airedale there are two old halls of some ghostly renown. Low Hall at Nether Yeadon has such a timeless attraction for Lady Julia Barwick that a slate slab had to be inserted in one bedroom window to prevent her flitting in and out by that embarrassing route, though she sometimes emerged from the family priest-hole. Mr and Mrs Pickard, the comparatively new owners here, are disappointed not to have seen the ghost yet, but they are still hopeful. Meanwhile, their golden retriever willingly responds to the name, Julia.

Rawdon Hall has an equally shy guest. Its Grey Lady is the kindly Priscilla Rawdon, lingering from the seventeenth century. Judge Nevin, who now lives here, says that she 'moves happily about the house at night with an occasional tinkling of bells and a rustling tranquillity. On a windy night she can be heard near the priest-hole by the chimney in the Silver Room, carrying on a subdued conversation. We sleep right above and often hear these strange sounds.'

It is not only the traditions that interest me, but their great variety. What secret happenings account for the Negro page-boy whose ghost steals into a certain bedroom at Hawksworth Hall and leaves his imprint on the pillows? The last private owner of this hall—also within my home orbit—often told me about him. Who he was, nobody knows.

It may seem 'reasonable' for Anne Boleyn and Guy Fawkes to revisit their former homes, one at Blickling Hall in Norfolk, the other at Scotton, near Knaresborough in Yorkshire. And where else would the priest whose remains were found in the secret chamber at Lyme Park, Cheshire, wander, but in this home of the family he served? It is the 'unusual' ghosts that puzzle most.

Who was 'Jeffrey', who plagued the Wesley household at Epworth Rectory so much that Susannah Wesley could write to her brother Sam, 'send me some news, for we are secluded from the sight or hearing of any versal thing except Jeffrey'? Outwardly, this Lincolnshire homestead looks the very embodiment of eighteenth-century rectitude and piety, but indoors something strange was at work. Robin Brown, servant-man to this clerical household, was once grinding corn in the attic when—according to the family annals—the ghost took over, turning the handle with unwonted vigour.

Where is the secret spring that unfolds such mysteries? Surely human invention, or hallucination, is too facile an answer in some instances. If, as Sir George Sitwell once remarked, the 'ghosts' that people see are not really ghosts, what are they? What dim recesses of the mind do they inhabit? And how can one fairly explain the experience which Colonel Lane Fox had in his own grounds at Bramham Park?

I first heard about the Ghost Horses during my visit to this lovely estate near York. They are supposed to be galloping from the Battle of Bramham Moor, fought two miles away in the year 1408. The tradition once fructified for the Colonel, for he *heard* the horses. While near the cricket ground, one day, this keen huntsman told me, he noticed the noise as of many hooves approaching; he actually opened a gate to let the horses through—but none appeared!

The Colonel has since suggested that these ghostly sounds 'may well be but the echo of the countless hunters' hooves that have thundered on the turf of the Park through hundreds of years'. Age-old echoes? We are still in the realm of riddles.

The North Bailey, in Durham City, might seem too hallowed an area to harbour any ghosts. Yet the proximity of the cathedral and two churches has apparently done nothing to exorcise the spirits that are said to haunt the Bailey and some of its old houses. I have heard of a 'little twisted nameless man' who, clad in black breeches, white ruffled shirt and a nightcap, occasionally steps from the cellar of a house formerly owned by a chief constable of the city. I have also heard of a grey-haired lady whose usually invisible, though pervasive, presence used to leave one householder quite calm. He was the late Canon Greenwell, a renowned antiquary.

The ghost that really disturbs the serenity of the North Bailey—if one is alive to this sort of thing—was himself an eighteenth-century churchman, during the privileged times of the Prince Bishops. When his annual month's duty as canon at the cathedral drew near he would linger on at his beloved Weardale estate, then dash over to Durham at the last possible moment to qualify for residence. His four-in-hand lurching along the Bailey and then swinging through the college gateway at the last stroke of midnight, with a couple of Dalmatian hounds panting at the rear, is the canon's legacy to posterity.

Phantom clergymen may be rare birds, but I came across one in Cornwall only a few months ago. At Crantock Manor, near Newquay, Dr Pusey offsets the smugglers mentioned earlier who made such profitable use of this fifteenth-century building. Theology, not contraband, was Dr Pusey's speciality; when he wandered down to the beach by the steps that still bear his name he was doubtless cogitating holier thoughts and speculations. Perhaps these matters are still unresolved, else why should he pace about the old manor at dusk, mystifying visitors of our day?

The manor is now a guest house, and one old lady's experience here is worth recording. She walked into the drawing-room one evening and noticed a strangely dressed man looking out of the window. She spoke to him, but got no reply. The lady complained to the owner of the guest house about his rudeness to her, a newcomer, to be told that she was the only guest! Other people have apparently met this same 'rude' man. Pusey is still deep in his theological abstractions.

Equally entertaining stories come from all parts of Britain. Even if there is no discernible element of truth or credibility in them, there is still a wide margin for enjoyment. But occasionally the most hard-boiled person may be silenced. Take the story told to me in all good faith by our old doctor. It concerns a youthful experience of his on the Scottish island of Mull.

While he and an older man were walking down a quiet lane two men in front suddenly stood respectfully to one side and doffed their caps. When the other two caught up with them and asked the reason for this strange behaviour they got a strange answer. The front couple claimed to have just seen the cortège of a certain neighbour pass by. When this neighbour died, *two days later*, the doctor admitted to a queer sensation—which no medicine could touch.

My final word on this tenuous theme will again bring Levens Hall to the fore. Tourists often say that such and such a house *ought* to have a ghost; it may look receptive in that peculiar way. They would certainly regard Levens Hall in this appraising manner—and would not be disappointed.

This house on the banks of the River Kent, in Westmorland, has had seven centuries in which to build up its fascinating history—and a shadow history besides.

Grey ladies seem to distribute their favours in many places, but the Grey Lady at Levens is of a different vintage from most. In life she is supposed to have been an eighteenth-century gipsy who was refused admittance to the house when begging for refreshment. Her vengeance was terrible. She vowed that there would be no male heir in the family 'until the River Kent ceased to flow and a *white* fawn was born in the park'. The curse presumably expired in 1895 when the River Kent was frozen solid. Later in the same year a white fawn was born in the neighbouring parkland. Soon after there were great rejoicings at Levens over the birth of Alan Desmond Bagot.

The present owners of Levens—Robin and Annette Bagot—rather discredit the curse tradition, but are in no doubt concerning the Grey Lady herself. Mrs Bagot assures me that her own daughter, Lisa, when a child of seven, saw the gipsy outside and was able to describe her appearance convincingly.

Other 'presences' have also been noticed here, among them being the Pink Lady, wearing a mob cap; the Black Dog which scampers about one's feet; and a concourse of people who are *felt* rather than seen. Perhaps these latter are or were some of those who once assembled here for the annual Radish Feast, at which Morocco beer 'brewed from a secret recipe and very potent' was used for the traditional toast, 'Luck to Levens whilst t' Kent flows'.

But I am most intrigued by what Mrs Bagot says about the supernatural influences at work today. Her husband has the unusual hobby of making harpsichords. He plays one of them in a fine old room here that is emblazoned with family coats-of-arms. This instrument has been heard on B.B.C. and I.T.V. programmes. Yet it seems to have undertones, or overtones, beyond normal hearing. This is how his wife puts the matter in the official guidebook for visitors:

'Mr Bagot has been seen and heard playing his harpsichord here when he was, in fact, in Keswick. He denied that he was thinking hard of his music at the time, and there seems to be no reason at all for his unexpected appearance.'

On seeking further details about the above episode I was given the following strange account:

> One tea-time Mrs Bagot and some friends were in the Library having tea. There was a prolonged power-cut (it being winter) and candles had been lit in the Library and were being carried about. The late Father Julian Stonor came down the stairs—after visiting someone who was ill in bed—and in the Hall he saw a harpsichord in what was, in fact, its usual position. Someone was playing it, by the light of an *electric lamp* by the fireplace. Father Stonor waited for the (unidentified) tune to stop, but when it did, the player went on to something else, so (not knowing Mr Bagot just then) Father Stonor took him for a tuner . . . and went back to the Library, joining the other guests.
>
> At the door Father Stonor said how glad he was that the power-cut had ended; this caused surprise as it had not. So he explained that the light by the harpsichord was on, and Mrs Bagot then said the harpsichord was not even there—which, when they all went in, indeed it was not. Father Stonor was very disturbed by this incident, especially when he later met and identified Mr Bagot as the player he had seen.
>
> Mrs Bagot at the time was afraid that her husband had been killed, whereas in fact he was just arriving in Keswick, in his car, to see to the instrument before a concert there.

She now rounds off the experience with courtly charm: 'If Mr Bagot continues, after his death, to appear at Levens in this way he will be a delightful addition to our gallery of pointless ghosts.'

CHAPTER THIRTEEN

MISCELLANY

'The time has come', the Walrus said,
'To talk of many things:
Of shoes—and ships—and sealing-wax—
Of cabbages—and kings—'

LEWIS CARROLL

Earlier in this book I referred to the countryside secrets that creep into some of Thomas Hardy's stories. The theme could have been expanded considerably, as anybody will realize who has explored Hardy's beloved Dorset, preferably with one or two of the Wessex novels in hand. Even the village maidens' secrets were open to him, for he—one of the few educated persons in an illiterate area—was often asked to write their love letters!

It is fitting, therefore, to open this new chapter in the garden of that thatched cottage at Higher Bockhampton, near Dorchester, where Hardy was born and later wrote some of his revealing stories. The cottage is hidden away, at the woodland end of a narrow country lane. There are a few deer in this woodland; they sometimes steal down into Hardy's old garden for a quiet forage.

In after years Hardy once took James Barrie, creator of *Peter Pan*, to see the old place. The episode is best described in the words of Lady Cynthia Asquith, Barrie's secretary, who witnessed the whole proceeding. A furtive element was introduced when they found the cottage door locked.

> Barrie, refusing to be thwarted in his intention to enter the hallowed precincts, made me hold together two decayed ladders while, treading on my fingers, he precariously clambered up to the window and contrived to open it. He scrambled through and shortly afterwards, with a bow, opened the door to Hardy, who, returning the bow, re-entered the home in which, eighty-one years ago, he had first cried because—to quote words so much after his own heart—he had 'come to this great stage of fools'.

To me this episode has an added piquancy, by bringing together—in this amusing manner—two such writers, each in his different way a master at breaking into the secret places of the human heart. Hardy made this cottage the home of Tranter Dewy in *Under the Greenwood Tree*. But, with that brooding curtain of trees so near, what a fine setting it could also have made for Lob and his magic wood in Barrie's *Dear Brutus*.

It is not difficult to find a factual counterpart for such fictional disportings of the human spirit. We have seen how religious intolerance, fear, and a sense of the supernatural have endowed many old houses with an aura of subterfuge or mystery. Barrie knew how to strike that note. Again according to Cynthia Asquith, Francis Lister once said, 'I acted the Australian soldier throughout scores of performances of *Mary Rose*, yet every single time that door into the empty room opened *from the inside* my stomach turned to water'.

But what remains to be considered from the world of fact? Over what strange thresholds have we yet to step?

Manchester provides one such place, and that in the very centre of its daily tumult. Even the war-time bombing raids left Dr Dee's old sanctum at Chetham's School inviolate, although other parts of the school were badly damaged. This is the so-called Audit Room. Although this room was never haunted in the ordinary sense, it certainly witnessed strange happenings after Dr John Dee was appointed Warden of the then College in 1595. Here he dabbled in the occult. If one wishes for details there are no livelier expositors than the Chetham boys!

Some years ago four of the boys donned their traditional Tudor dress and met me, by appointment, in the Audit Room. The stage seemed to be properly set, but although the lads did their best it needed old John Dee himself to put on the main act and summon his familiar spirits from the shades.

Beneath this oak ceiling carved with such diverse subjects as an angel, and the famous Giant of Notting Hill swallowing one of his youthful victims, the wizard would experiment with his magic glass, causing weird lights to flash from the windows after dark. He kept a 'great many stilles' going, and produced curious brews or 'collations' for inquisitive visitors.

One angel, called Uriel, gave him a crystal that revealed 'all secrets'. With great glee the Chetham boys described for me how the old fellow, his long beard 'white as milk', once attempted to summon his favourite angel but, using the wrong formula, called up the Devil instead. 'That is the mark Satan left', said one of the boys, pointing to a bit of charred wood.

Dr Dee's diary is most entertaining. While at the College he began to have strange dreams. Under the date 6 August 1600 he recorded, 'I had a dream after midnight of my enjoying and working of the philosopher's stone . . .' Despite all his unique privileges and insights, however, he does not seem to have found the secret of good health. He awakes one morning with an aching head and 'some wombling in my stomach'. For a severe kidney attack he resorts to crabs' eyes and carp's head crushed to powder and mixed with white wine. One might have expected Uriel to tell him of a better cordial!

Dee adds to our gallery of men with strangely compounded personalities. He lent support to the scientific survey of Britain then being undertaken by Christopher Saxton, the mapmaker, and was a renowned mathematician—and yet, there was all that voodooism. His large library contained many books on witchcraft. The amazing secrets of the black art these particular books contained subsequently influenced many Lancashire magistrates when handling cases of supposed witchcraft and demonic possession.

One breathes a very different air—despite the same pall of industry—a few miles away at Bolton. Dr Dee's dream of turning base metal into gold remained a dream, but in the splendid black-and-white Tudor house known as Hall-i'-the-Wood, Samuel Crompton made a dream come true which had a cash value far beyond immediate computation. He invented the spinning mule.

With this machine—produced in secrecy and poverty—he could make the most delicate yarn and fabrics. To shield his invention from prying neighbours, he had to hide the mule when it was not in use. The shallow box he made for the purpose is sunk into one of the attic floors. But if only he had known, this fine old residence was already provided with hides that would have served admirably.

He was a devout man, writing hymns which he sang to his fiddle or the organ he built. How would he have felt on pushing his mule into that priest-hole since discovered in the kitchen wall? Or, if this was placed too high for convenience, into that corner closet now uncovered in the Norris bedroom? A heritage of penal times serving the Industrial Revolution might have brought a wry smile to his face. But it was not to be. He had to make his own secret place; and while walking through the house today one hardly knows which to admire most—that hole in the attic floor, with all it implies, or his organ and fiddle that cheered the family when the mule was 'a-bed'.

These industrial pioneers were sometimes in as great peril as any Catholic priest of Elizabeth's day. John Kay, another Lancashireman, had revolutionized the wool trade by his invention of the fly-shuttle. As this dispensed with the need for several workers who had always thrown the shuttle by hand, Kay was a marked man. When the rioters broke into his house at Bury his wife had to conjure him away. This she did, resourceful woman, by rolling him in a woollen sheet, so that he must have resembled an Egyptian mummy when the hired cart led him off. He is shown thus 'embalmed' in one of Ford Madox Brown's fine murals at Manchester Town Hall.

What unexpected twists there are to the recurring need for subterfuge!

Some sixty miles north-west of Manchester one can pick up another, though earlier, thread of secrecy. Two of Madox Brown's murals evoke the period, approximately, by showing the founder of Chetham's School, upon whom Charles I thrust the expensive honour of collecting the notorious 'ship money', and Bradshaw's defence of Manchester against King Charles's troops in 1642.

The next few years were to weave a web of secrecy that spread over most of England. One of the men chiefly responsible was born at Witherslack, a Westmorland hamlet so secluded, even today, that it seems destined by nature for some clandestine mission. A friend and I motored through the Winster valley, near the Kent estuary, several times before locating this charming little backwater.

Having arrived at last we found 'our man', Dr John Barwick, without difficulty, for he provided both church and school here, as some inscriptions testify. From one of the leafy lanes nearby, as we looked around, a young girl emerged to post a letter. It was rather jolly to realize that when she, or any other 'local mayd', marries, there will be a wedding gift of money for her from that reverend gentleman who—on behalf of Charles I—dispatched hundreds of letters, secretly though, and in cipher.

The whole story would make a good thriller. It really began with Barwick—then at Cambridge University—helping to outwit Cromwell and his minions by conveying money and plate to Charles through quiet English byways, rather than the main route between Cambridge and Huntingdon where the enemy were waiting to pounce. He was a born schemer. Several Biblical episodes involving hiding which he expounded on Sundays must have popped into mind and coloured his own escapades as he hid in the London home of the Bishop of Durham, using this as a base for espionage.

He acted as a spy in the Parliamentarian army. 'His Majesty', we are told, 'commanded Barwick to put himself into a lay habit, and, with a sword by his side, to join that expedition which Cromwell's party were making towards London, with a pretence of fighting under their banners; but in reality, that from a careful observation of their behaviour and acclamations, he might inform himself how both the common soldiers and their officers stood affected towards the King . . . and give an account thereof to his Majesty.'

Infiltration of messages to these soldiers was often accomplished by hiding them among the wares of wandering pedlars. In the biography of Dr Barwick written by his younger brother Peter, there is an exciting, if somewhat diffuse, reference to other persons Barwick employed to distribute literature that defended the royal cause. He speaks of 'certain adventurous women' who 'used frequently to travel on foot, like strowlers begging from house to house, and loitering at places agreed upon to take up books . . . which Mr Royston [one of the conspirators] had conveyed by stealth among other merchandize into the western barges on the Thames . . . Now it was easy to sew letters privately within the cover of any book, and then give the book a secret mark, to notify the insertion of such letters therein.'

We hear little about Witherslack in the biography. Barwick must often have longed for the quiet of its woods and lanes, and a sight of the peaceful cottage where he was born. This countryside is especially lovely in springtime, when the damson blossom is out. But for John Barwick there was even further embroilment in national affairs, and increasing danger, when Charles was made a prisoner in Carisbrooke Castle, on the Isle of Wight. Charles here communicated with the ever-faithful Barwick by letters 'written with the King's own hand in secret characters', and kept a copy of the cipher in a crack of the wall in his chamber.

As this part of the castle underwent drastic rebuilding in Victorian times, there is no chance of seeing that odd little 'post box' today. But some of the ciphers have survived. They were published in the biography of another of the King's accomplices—Sir Henry Firebrace, known to his friends as Honest Harry.

According to this biography, written in 1932 by Captain C. W. Firebrace, the ciphers were mostly of the 'same character—rows of numerals, each denoting a letter, syllable or word, while blank numerals, or "nulls", are inserted at intervals to make the deciphering more difficult. Charles kept a different cipher for each correspondent, so that discovery of a key to one letter was no help to the decoding of another, if addressed to another person'. The King, we are told, 'had implicit faith in the secrecy of his ciphers, but Parliament succeeded in decoding all his letters that fell into their hands. The correspondence taken at Naseby is said to have been deciphered for them by Dr John Wallis of Oxford, a famous mathematician.'

Here is an extract from one of Charles' code letters to Henry Firebrace concerning plans for the royal escape from Carisbrooke:

> D; [code letter for Firebrace]
>
> I desyre you first to remember to leave perfect Instructions with L: and F: [Osborne and Dowcett] how to send my letters to London & to receave answers from thence without suspition . . .
>
> Now as to my maine Business; be careful to make L: rightly to understand the Desygne of the Backestairs Window, as lykewais that other of my Window . . . also you must rememb.[er] W: [Titus] to lay Horses, one the othersyde of the Water, & let me know, when & where; nor let that be long a doeing; for it wer a wofull thing to loose an opportunitie heere, for falt of preparations there. As for those other Desygnes, you towled me of, I leave those to your managing, only promising you exact Secresie therein . . .'

We are not here concerned with the plot itself (which failed) but with Carisbrooke as a nest of intrigue. This, the Firebrace letters—transcribed by Peter Barwick—make only too clear. Among this correspondence (now kept at the British Museum) there is a list of the persons mainly involved, with their respective code signs. L signifies Richard Osborne, a gentleman usher; W is Captain Silius Titus, equerry; N is Jane Whorwood—the King's 'sweete Jane Whorwood'—whom he entrusts with a casket of jewels; F is Abraham Dowcett, Clerk of the Royal Kitchen; A is Francis Cressett, Steward and Treasurer, through whom John Barwick despatched a weekly missive to the King.

Another of Firebrace's code lists reaches much higher in the social scale. Here, both the King and his Queen have their appropriate letters—J and M; G stands for Prince Charles and S for the Duke of York. Then follow Lady Aubigny, Lady Wheeler, Lady Carlisle, Colonel William Legg, Groom of the Bedchamber, and Mr Low, a merchant in London—each hidden behind some letter of the alphabet, though for Lady Carlisle and Mr Low there is an additional sign, devised by Firebrace to indicate they were 'faulty', or unreliable. In a code message to Titus, the King—using numerals this time—refers to some of this wambling:

'I think 457 [Lady Carlisle] wishes now well to me but I believe she loves 546, 493 above all things.' The 493 is one of the King's 'nulls'. The significance of 546 is now lost, but may suggest *Scotland*.

Firebrace's private 'letter box' when conveying written messages to the King is best described by himself: 'I made a slit or chink through the wall, behind the Hanging; which served as well as the opening of the Dore [into the King's private chamber] and was more safe; for upon the least noyse, by letting fall the Hanging all was well.' This chink, one presumes, was the one also mentioned by Dr Barwick.

When not bending over his ciphers during that trying period between November 1647 and September 1648, Charles would take a little exercise by walking on the ramparts, or playing bowls on the castle green. He is supposed to have written his *Eikon Basilike* here, and to have done a fair amount of reading. Yet I cannot help wondering how many times his perusal of Fairfax's *Tasso* or Spenser's *Faerie Queene* was interrupted by the arrival of yet another message through that hole in the wall.

And did he sometimes think of Mary Stuart, his own grandmother, and the ruses *she* devised when a state prisoner like himself? She too had conducted a secret correspondence, partly in cipher—not from an island fortress like Carisbrooke, however, with only a strip of the English Channel between her and friendly France, but from various places up and down the English mainland.

Mary's first 'prison' on English soil was Bolton Castle in Wensleydale, North Yorkshire. I have been shown some of the needlework she did while waiting here at cousin Elizabeth's pleasure. Lovely creations they are, in coloured silks and trimmed with gold lace. You could not buy such materials in a place like Castle Bolton, the enclosing village. Milk, cheese, eggs, and a fat duck for roasting—yes, but if you wanted materials for the embroidery frame they had to be sent for.

That is what Mary Stuart did. She wrote frequently to the French Ambassador asking him to secure for her so many 'ells of crimson satin', or a few 'ells of gold lace, ornamented with silver spangles'. Woven among the 'ells', no doubt, were a few carefully spun pleas of a nature likely to be better understood by an ambassador of state. There were many secret glances, too, here at Bolton Castle. Knollys, her ostensible 'gaoler', once intercepted some of these—and ordered that Kit Norton, one of the guard, should keep watch 'no more'. Kit Norton was the susceptible youth—one of many—who fell a victim to Mary's charm and contrived her (short-lived) escape from Bolton.

When the charmer was 'moved on' the plotting increased. At Tutbury Castle in Staffordshire her custodian was the sixth Earl of Shrewsbury. His wife, the renowned 'Bess of Hardwick', suspected a love intrigue between the two of them, but Miss Bridget Talbot of Kiplin Hall, North Yorkshire, a descendant of the Earl, once showed me a portrait of him and declared he was one of the few men in England who were impervious alike to Mary's schemes and her glamour. The man of her heart (and political ambition) just then was the Duke of Norfolk. They were secretly engaged and wrote to each other in cipher. This correspondence continued after his arrest, but now Mary had to conceal her messages in beer bottles. Their corks were marked to distinguish them from those of the other bottles delivered to the Duke's cell in the Tower of London.

Mary Queen of Scots took another step along that tragic road to Fotheringhay, and liquidation, on arriving at Chartley Castle, also in Staffordshire. Here she soon became entangled in her own web. There were more letters in cipher. Mary entrusted them to Gilbert Gifford, unaware that he was a secret agent, acting for the two opposing factions—the Catholics *and* Elizabeth. He seemed genuine enough, supplying Mary with a box which could safely be hidden in the false bottom of the barrel that contained her supplies of wine. That box held the letters, 'in' and 'out'. But it was easy for such a man as Gifford to make fair copies of her letters and send them to Elizabeth's advisers.

One item of this 'barrel correspondence' was Babington's letter acquainting Mary of his scheme to murder Elizabeth, put Mary on the throne, and hire a Spanish army to back full Catholic support. Another, outgoing item was Mary's approval of the plan. It was the beginning of the end. The barrel 'leaked' once again. Walsingham acted swiftly. Babington and his fellow-conspirators were rounded up and executed. Mary must have felt strangely bereft.

Staffordshire has certainly been one of England's chief whispering galleries. Most country lovers will associate the county with places like Dovedale (at its lower end), the folk dancers of Abbots Bromley, and the Roaches that rear their goblin shapes above the fine road from Leak to Buxton. It is the county that gave birth to Izaak Walton and many who are not anglers by inclination would willingly 'loiter long days by Shawford brook' with him, watching 'a blackbird feed her young' or 'see sweet dewdrops kiss these flowers'.

Yet dear old Izaak was not always as innocent as he might look, when at his cottage at Shallowford, or fishing for timorous trout. In this cottage, then as secluded as Nature and man could contrive, he is said to have hidden Bishop Morley from the Parliamentarians for a whole year. And it may have been from this same thatched cottage that the author of *The Compleat Angler* set out for London with one of the Crown Jewels.

The story is briefly told. Perhaps Walton and his neighbour, George Barlow of Blore Pipe House, had sometimes fished the same waters. Some little time earlier, Barlow gave refuge to Colonel Blague, a royalist who secreted on his person one of the Crown Jewels known as the Lesser George. Blague was captured, but not before the jewel changed hands. It was first conveyed to Robert Milward, then imprisoned at Stafford. Izaak Walton's mission was to restore the jewel to Blague, who had meanwhile escaped from the Tower of London. This transfer was effected, though how many wayside perils it cost Walton, how many feints and evasions, only an imagination steeped in this turbulent period of history can properly conceive.

What chiefly matters is that Blague gets hold of the jewel again and delivers it in person to Charles in France. That is about all we know of the episode. Breathing a sigh of relief, doubtless, the inimitable Izaak takes up his rod once more and casts a careful line. He had done what he could for the King, whose flight after the Battle of Worcester had been aided by Jane Lane; the same King who had hidden for a time within Moseley Old Hall, at Bushbury, his hair cropped short and his face stained with walnut juice. A strange baptism for the one who, after the Restoration, was to be called the Merry Monarch.

Two garden stories may well conclude this chapter.

We saw earlier how Fathers Postgate and Potts masqueraded as gardeners, away there in Yorkshire. It was an old dodge, dating back at least to the Wars of the Roses.

After the Battle of Hexham (1464) Henry VI became a fugitive. He sojourned for a time at Bolton Hall, in Bolton-by-Bowland, and then at Waddington Old Hall in the same lovely countryside between Yorkshire and Lancashire. Another hide-out was Crackenthorpe Hall in the Eden Valley. The King's Bedroom, here, has its own memories of that time, but the King's Garden gives a keener edge to the story for it was among these flowerbeds that the scholarly King worked in gardener's humble attire, spattered with dirt, when Yorkist troops were scouring the countryside for him.

This is a lovely corner of the Eden Valley, with Appleby Castle not far away and the Lakeland hills over to the west. Henry's secret was well kept at Crackenthorpe. Waddington Hall cloaked his presence effectively, too, until twelve months later he was betrayed by a 'black monk of Abington' and handed over to the Yorkist party. From the garden at Waddington Hall one can visualize the place from which Henry escaped by spiral stair and ladder, only to be seized a mile away while crossing Brungerley Hipping, or Stepping, Stones on the River Ribble.

Bishop Juxon, who attended Charles I on the scaffold and thus became thoroughly unpopular with many people, was luckier in his enforced retreat. His brother John owned a quiet manor in Sussex. Albourne Place is quiet today, half lost in that fine country to the north of Devil's Dyke. The Bishop composed himself here for a season; whenever the search for him came too close, he picked up a trowel and pretended to be a bricklayer. It is easy to believe the story on noticing that one of the manor chimneys is of such remarkable size and shape! The Bishop had put more concentrated labour into it, apparently, than ever his sermons were likely to receive.

Gardens still have their secret uses. The lady who lives at Chithurst Abbey, over in West Sussex, has made it known that in a hollow walnut tree in her garden she hid forty bottles of wine when invasion seemed imminent during the Second World War.

CHAPTER FOURTEEN

HOUSES OF SECRET CHARM AND MYSTERY

Priest-holes, hidden passages, false floors, and such curious features as Bishop Juxon's bulging chimney-stack; these are not the only things that stamp a place with secrecy. The very structure of a building, or its furnishings, may also cause wonderment.

Who erected the Round Towers of Ireland? And for what reason?

Some of these centuries-old towers taper from ground level to a height of ninety feet or more. They have a pyramidal roof and the entrance door—only wide enough to admit one person at a time—is usually twelve to fourteen feet up from the base. On a recent trip to Ireland I photographed one such tower at Bruckless, and another —many days later—at Ardmore, in County Cork.

There are about eighty of them altogether, dotted over the countryside like so many detached steeples. Although achieving a certain fame at Glendalough in County Wicklow and at Antrim, and usually occupying a monastic site, they still constitute a riddle.

From a distance the tall, narrow towers resemble huge, sharpened pencils—yet they have left no definite record of their original purpose. Speculation shuttles between their possible use as watch towers; as places of refuge or imprisonment for monks; belfries; beacons; fire-temples associated with sun-worship; or safe repositories for valuable books. A generous choice!

James White in *Ireland by the Irish* says they were 'probably built for defensive purposes during Viking raids . . . the monks could pull in their ladders during times of oppression and be out of reach of the attackers'. But if safety was indeed the object, surely a less obvious design would have been adopted?

The mystery that still surrounds these finely constructed towers suits the national character very well. Irish folk tend to hug their secrets to themselves. And who can blame them? There are regions of the mind where certainties would leave one cold—almost alien.

I have beside me a copy of the long defunct *Countrygoer* magazine in which various Irish contributors of renown introduce different aspects of their country. To me this particular copy is as good as an armful of books would be, for it contains the very quintessence of Ireland and its ancient lore. Seán O' Fáoláin writes about the Magical Ireland that brims over to this day, making room for such characters as Anastasia and her fairies (see page 2) and an old man in West Cork who knew for sure 'the secrets of Heaven and Hell'. Another writer, Austin Clarke, evokes curious old legends about Croagh Patrick, the holy mountain, and the remarkable Gallarus Oratory, rather like an inverted boat, on the Dingle peninsula. Then, from her home in Connemara, Ethel Mannin scorns those who can only see barrenness in the prevailing 'heaps of stones', which seem to have their own private significance.

So it goes on, this intimate shoulder-rub with the 'land of saints and scholars and poets . . . the last holy place left in this chaotic, materialistic world'. And as if to summarize this fine collection of tales, traditions, and secret knowledge, Norah McGuiness subscribes the cover picture—a lovely landscape of hills and lakes, dominated by that symbol of strength and hidden meaning, a Round Tower, slightly bent over with time.

Ireland also has innumerable souterrains. The word is too subtle, too much out-of-the-ordinary, for my standard English dictionary to tabulate, yet an old Irish fort or castle would be incomplete without some of these curious passages that tunnel beneath the fabric. The *Shell Guide to Ireland* indicates dozens of them. A group of three souterrains are near the route my friends and I took from Bantry to Cork. Not long before, we had seen the island in Bantry Bay where George Bernard Shaw wrote *St Joan*. Here, along the coast road, we were within hailing distance of Castletownshend where Shaw's wife lived before their marriage. I find novelty in the thought that the red-haired Irishman who brought so many hush-hush topics to the light of day, in his provocative plays, should have associations with this particular area, once served by the Knockdrum Fort. If only Shaw's penetrating vision had focused on *archaeological* matters, perhaps we should by now have known more about this ancient fort, including its three souterrains. The very idea savours of heresy, I know, but *John Bull's Other Island* has so many of these souterrains; and they still have the archaeologists guessing.

Seán Jennett says this about these tantalizing features: 'In many instances neatly lined with stone, they are seldom high enough to allow a man to do more than crawl through, and there are often obstructions that make even crawling difficult. These obstructions were designed to compel invaders to come singly and at a disadvantage, so that they could be dealt with easily by those who had taken refuge in the souterrains.' Often 'the passages lead to small chambers: in these dark holes frightened people hid while the tumult of raid or invasion passed over them . . . who these people were and what they hid from is not clear . . .' Mystery again, both as to date and their possible users.

In England, underground passages are highly suspect, often proving to be nothing more than culverts or drains. In Ireland one gets the real thing.

Take Blarney Castle, near Cork. On approaching the fifteenth-century keep I noticed some of the openings to its subterranean passages. Horrid-looking places in which Cromwell's troops, when they besieged the castle, expected to find a hoard of treasure, including cases of Spanish doubloons. What they did find was one old man. Everybody else had fled by an escape tunnel, taking the treasure with them.

Today, of course, it is the famous Blarney Stone that chiefly attracts visitors. This block of limestone about four feet long and one foot wide is built into the battlement of the keep—with a drop of 150 feet for the unwary. During my visit nobody seemed anxious to manœuvre himself into the awkward position necessary if a kiss is to be implanted on the magical stone and the gift of oratory received in exchange.

Why is the Blarney Stone so endowed? It is a well-kept secret. Or perhaps nobody really knows! One either accepts the theory that the stone originated as Jacob's pillow and was brought here from the Holy Land; or that it is the charmed stone revealed to Cormac MacCarthy by a witch out of gratitude for his having saved her from drowning.

The gift of eloquence, or blarney, may be the traditional reward for that precarious kiss, but perhaps there is a choice, for one early nineteenth-century visitor believed that the stone 'possesses the rare virtue of making those very happy who touch it'.

Eloquence or happiness—or just downright relief on recovering one's equilibrium! What does it matter around this farthermost point of Ireland where even Time is a quibble. One of the jarveys at Killarney, only a few miles away, assured me with a knowing smile, 'The One who made Time made plenty of it'.

Time certainly seems of little account at Blarney Castle, for not only is there the keep and its manifold tales to enjoy, but also a fine example of (eighteenth-century) landscape gardening known as Rock Close. This pleasance, with its Druid Circle, its caves, grottoes, and ancient yews, really does evoke the spirit of the witch who so long ago revealed the latent powers of the Blarney Stone.

And then, Dunluce Castle on the Antrim coast. Its haunted appearance has stayed in the credulous part of my mind ever since I first saw the place, more than thirty years ago. One can believe almost anything an Irishman cares to confide about this grey ruin, lapped by the Atlantic.

In this land of such persuasive legend and romance, it is a *sine qua non* that every castle has its *banshee*. Dunluce is no exception. It was the ancient stronghold of the MacQuillins and the MacDonnells. And Mave Roe, their own banshee, is still in residence! She wails bitterly while sweeping out the one surviving chamber every night, hoping for the return of bygone owners. She was evidently resting when my friends and I stopped and listened not long ago.

The castle's gaunt profile must have been much the same in Queen Elizabeth I's day, for one of the Armada vessels mistook the Chimney-pots at Giant's Causeway nearby for the skeleton towers of Dunluce which, it was probably thought, might denote some shelter. It was a costly error of judgement. The *Gerona* foundered on the rocks, and 260 of those reckoned as the flower of Spanish nobility lost their lives. Any treasure the ship may have carried was lost also. As far as I know, the only things yet discovered from the wreckage are a couple of iron chests, and some cannon now at Dunluce. When I next visit the Causeway I shall take my turn at the Wishing Chair, and then delve hopefully among the more remote pools and caves of this fabulous place.

We were setting out to find a few strange buildings that have the secret stamp upon them, when Ireland put us under its spell. Ireland could bemuse us further, with its beehive huts—particularly those on the Dingle peninsula in the far west.

It is somehow comforting in this brusque era of science and technology to find that we know nothing of the people who built these beautifully-made dwellings, walled with unmortared stone.

A delightful folk tale is told about the Saints' Road that runs near the Gallarus Oratory—best of all the beehive buildings—on its way to the summit of Brandon Mountain. One day, on reaching the summit, the leader of a long procession of monks realized he had forgotten his prayer-book. Word was sent down the line, and the last monk, who was just leaving Kilmalkedar, returned to their church, recovered the book, which was then passed up the line, monk by monk, to the waiting leader.

Somewhere along the long line of history, many links have been lost. The pursuit of them is the constant business of the archaeologist and the antiquary, but ordinary folk, entering the same field of enquiry during holidays or week-ends, can have a lot of fun, especially perhaps in Western Ireland.

But other lures await us, in England. There are still so many places about which 'the half has never been told'. Or if told, forgotten by a later generation.

Visitors to Roseland in South Cornwall must have noticed the round houses that are peculiar to the lovely village of Veryan. There are five of them—two athwart each end of the long, straggling street, and one in the village centre, behind the school.

Local guidebooks (and then only the older, more informative ones) simply state that these peculiar houses were built by a Parson Trist, who added a cross to the apex of each to keep the Devil away. The said cleric must have known the tradition that the Devil never ventures into Cornwall lest he should be seized and crammed into a Cornish pasty. But apparently he was not taking any chances, and used his own methods of keeping evil at bay. Everybody once knew that the Devil cannot find any foot-hold in a circular dwelling, but to make doubly sure, a cross was fixed, triumphantly, on each conical roof.

So much for chit-chat. The truth is just as palatable, though it takes some discovering.

Jeremiah (?) Trist had been a missionary in Africa. When he came back and settled in Veryan, about 160 years ago, he was appalled at the high mortality rate in the village. He attributed this to bad housing and therefore had the five round houses built to set a better example. His model for these dwellings—his secret of good health—was the African mud hut! Thatched and white-washed, the houses bear out this story, given to me by one of the present residents.

This man kindly invited my wife and me inside his little citadel—an attractive 'cylinder' of two storeys, linked by a curved stairway and equipped with living-room, kitchenette, bedroom, and bathroom; all within a diameter of twenty-two feet. A wide variety of local sea-shells borders his garden path. These are his individual 'signature', just as a thatched garden wall and other modern additions mark one of the round cottages 'guarding' the far end of the village. But Parson Trist would still recognize them. These five cottages are *his* personal 'signature'—still puzzling, however, unless you know the answer.

The same might be said about the few remaining huers' huts, scattered along the Cornish coast. It is an axiom that some feature perfectly familiar to one generation may completely bewilder those of a succeeding era. What do present-day visitors make of the curious little building on the cliff edge above Fistral Bay at Newquay? It is dwarfed into insignificance by a palatial modern hotel, but clings to its spot like a barnacle.

When I went along one day to photograph the hut a few holiday-makers stopped there also, out of curiosity. Their children asked the inevitable questions, answering them best, no doubt, by referring to some inner world of their own—a world governed by pixies and such-like.

The huer's hut is really a look-out post. It was the huer's job to keep vigil here and warn local fishermen of any approaching shoals of pilchards by bellowing, 'Heva, heva' through his speaking trumpet.

In the example at Newquay the procedure is readily visualized, once the clue is given. The battlemented white hut has irregular stone walls pierced with oddly-shaped windows that light a rather stark and severely cramped interior. On the landward side an external flight of steps took the huer to his observation post in front of the squat chimney-tower.

At one time there was plenty of work for the huers and their colleagues on shore below, pilchards being so plentiful. In recent times, however, pilchards seem to have deserted Cornish waters. The habits of men have changed too, leaving the huers' huts ripe for any legend, fantasy, or gimcrack tale that might be propagated in ignorance.

Another Cornish building likely to suffer in this way, because of changes in usage and social ideas, is the nineteenth-century vicarage at remote Morwenstow. While the Rev. Stephen Hawker, who had the place built, lived here—for forty-one years—within sight and sound of the fierce Atlantic, its oddities had significance. They expressed something of his own colourful make-up.

The vicarage chimneys told a personal story, each chimney-stack being shaped to resemble the tower of a church where Hawker had previously served. The one exception was the kitchen chimney, designed after his mother's tomb. All Hawker need do, to recall old times, was to step outside and see the churches at Stratton, Whitstone, North Tamerton, and two at Oxford 'smoking' their respective memories for him, like a group of cronies. To anybody else, they are just queerly-shaped chimneys and nothing more.

We shall meet this eccentric vicar again, when Morwenstow church receives attention. But the vicarage is a vicarage no more. I heard that it was being sold. It was empty and forlorn during my last visit and the paths were overgrown. Woodland creatures would soon make the place their own. There it stood, deep in its enclosing coombe—a secret-in-the-making for future times, unless somebody has the wit to re-publish Baring Gould's fine study of the man who gave it meaning—*The Vicar of Morwenstow.*

Buildings that are strange, perhaps unique, in some detail still exist in various parts of Britain. Many of these have been investigated by some competent person and his findings published. For want of interest, other places may relapse into a kind of limbo.

At Bury St Edmunds in Suffolk the term Abbey Ruins applies specifically to a block of six houses actually built into the ruined west front of the abbey church. The result is an amazing pastiche. At different times since the Reformation, first one gap in the frontage, then another, has been filled in, giving a medley of architectural styles ranging from Norman and a dash of Early English to Georgian and mid-Victorian. We are not here concerned so much with the hybrid itself, but the crop of queer tales it has engendered and its equally queer passages.

As the whole place has been for some years in the custody of the

Ministry of Public Building and Works the tenants are somewhat fidgety. How long their curious, though beloved, homes might be allowed to stand is anybody's guess. Perhaps for as long as it is taking for the abbey crypt to be opened up, in the adjoining grounds, and for the discovery of the long-lost relics of St Edmund and the abundant treasure that traditionally adorned the saint's shrine. Already, some walls have been uncovered nearby—towering masses of bared flint, weird and nightmarish in profile. The threat to the Abbey Ruins block is (as I write) ever present. If and when the architectural jumble is dismantled, odd things may emerge; but other things will be lost for ever.

I spent several days, therefore, in and around this delightful bit of grotesquery, which my wife has known since her childhood.

Near the centre of the block a passage runs back to one of the house gardens. It once led to the Chapels of St. Denis and St Faith, and of St John the Baptist, now immured somewhere within the massive frontage of rubble and freestone. Today, the passage with its bulging, irregular walls is strangely reminiscent of the catacombs.

The lady tenant of the house at the south end has devised an interior which overlays the monastic framework of the house with Georgian graces. Symmetry is not one of them, however, for the rooms follow the quaint contours of abbey walls and chambers hidden from view almost since the Dissolution. Some walls bulge in a manner that suggest a monastic jamb, arch, or corbel lurking behind the plaster. Romantic-looking recesses—'pockets' of the old abbey—are put to good decorative use. Then there are the passages, now concealed, that run beneath the property.

Future excavations will doubtless reveal the true nature and extent of these passages. Legend has made play with them for centuries, associating them with the ghastly errand of Maude Carew, a nun who was supposed to have poisoned Humphrey, Duke of Gloucester during his incarceration at Bury St Edmunds in 1446.

Not the least of my rewards, while exploring Abbey Ruins, was hearing at first hand how Sister Maude—as the phantom Grey Lady—still haunts the place with her soft presence. Mrs Adams, whose house interior I have described, told me that one day, during a conversation in her lounge, her son suddenly interrupted by exclaiming, '*Did you see that?*' The Grey Lady had just crossed the room, passing through his aunt! Perhaps it was the same phantom that appeared, another day, to the charwoman. The woman refused to describe what she had seen, simply confiding to her mistress, 'Something has happened; I shall never be frightened again!'

I lingered there in the lounge, and in other parts of the house, hoping to be favoured with just one glimpse. But in vain. The 'curtain' did not part for me.

One tangible result of my visit was a Pilgrim's Badge, given me by the Provost of the abbey-cathedral when he heard that I had been probing into Bury's hidden past. A modern copy of those worn in medieval times, the badge represents the martyrdom of St Edmund.

The buildings described above, however curious and secretive, are a welcome change from the anonymous, 'tall box' architecture of today. And what astonishing diversity our forefathers could achieve! What feints and disguises, also, in their household furnishing and decoration! I have space for just a few examples.

In *The Golden Age* Kenneth Grahame has an amusing chapter entitled 'The Secret Drawer'. Reaching back to childhood he recalls a bureau which had a magnetic attraction for him: '. . . I put my hand once more to the obdurate wood, when with a sort of small sigh, almost a sob—as it were—of relief, the secret drawer sprang open.'

Something of Grahame's feeling came over me, a few years back, while being shown around Nappa Hall (now a farmhouse) in Wensleydale. After ascending the taller of two towers—still dimly eloquent of a couple of 'dangerous recusants' who lived here 'obscurely' in penal times—we came to the bedroom once occupied during a brief visit by Mary Queen of Scots. One side of the small room is filled with an old built-in bookcase. I can still see the quaint reflections in its glass doors: Mary's bed, optically twisted in wild disarray; then the powder closet and dressing table—each caricatured in similar fashion.

But there was a further bit of enchantment. 'Inside the bookcase', said the farmer's wife, 'there is a secret drawer.' So I bent down to get the trick of it. Cleverly concealed by a larger drawer, it is partitioned, as though designed to hold jewellery.

Later, when I went back to photograph the bookcase, the carpet in front was strewn with face powder and other cosmetics. The small granddaughter had crept in, unobserved. But there were none of

Kenneth Grahame's 'sighs' or 'sobs' for her. Failing to find the secret drawer, with its imagined finery, she had raided one of the ordinary kind, in the dressing-table. She meant to be queen, if only for a few magic moments.

Another day I went over to Upper Helmsley Hall, near Stamford Bridge, eight miles east of York. I had gone to photograph the portrait of Sir Thomas Herbert (see page 154)—the man who could companion King Charles I at Carisbrooke, and look after his small library there, without once being involved in the secret manœuvres already described. Other members of the illustrious Herbert family also gazed down at me from their gilded frames, but the late George Herbert—who then owned Upper Helmsley Hall—could not say definitely which of them had used the peculiar bureau, then in the sitting-room.

The bureau has imitation drawer-fronts—and is completely *hollow*. It was purposely made to conceal one of the Montgomery branch of the family who had fallen foul of the king. Whenever the searchers drew near, he crept into this empty shell of a bureau and had it pushed up against the wall, with a small space left for the insertion of food.

I tried it for myself and could have sat there, with my knees drawn up, for hours. Not very comfortable, to be sure, but infinitely preferable to one of His Majesty's dungeons!

Almost every old hall I have visited has something *sub rosa*. Priest-holes we have dealt with, ghostly passages, and so on. But the continual urge towards secrecy has also produced obscure forms of decoration—puns and allegories in wood, stone, or plaster. To decipher these one usually needs the help of the owner. For instance, the pair of wings above the entrance door at Norton Conyers, near Ripon, is of little moment unless Sir Richard Graham gives the explanation. The first Sir Richard was Gentleman of the Horse to King James I. He accompanied the Prince of Wales (later Charles I) and Buckingham on that secret mission to Spain which had Charles' marriage to the Infanta as its real objective. When things went awry, Graham took word immediately to James, and such was his speed *en route* that James gave him these wings as a personal emblem.

Even a popular rhyme can hide old meanings. The recent play, *Ring o' Roses*, by Alan Cullen, presents a good illustration. How does the rhyme go? And what does it hide?

Ring-a-ring-o'-roses,
(these signify the red spots appearing on plague victims)
A pocketful of posies,
(these are the fragrant flowers and herbal pomanders once carried as preventives)
Atishoo! Atishoo!
(sneezing, often the first symptom of plague)
All fall down!
(exactly what the victims did, before sudden death).

If this interpretation seems too fanciful one has only to visit Eyam, the Derbyshire plague village, during their annual Well-dressing Week, in September. At various strategic points in the village, different flower-mosaics are set up on large boards, and most of them will bear on the plague that devastated Eyam, and turned it into a self-made prison, in 1665–6.

In 1966, three hundred years later, the children of the village—children who know the inner meaning of the old rhyme—'flowered' Cucklet Delph as their own Well subject. It was in this limestone hollow, just outside Eyam, that the rapidly diminishing population met for worship during that terrible time, when nobody could long conceal his affliction from the rest. 'Atishoo! . . . All fall down.'

It was a childhood game that led us into that digression. Something like child's play can bring us back to our domestic theme. And we shall find it inside a York inn, the Black Swan, overlooking Peasholm Green.

Just who was responsible for its 'Faces' I have never been able to discover. They probably belong to the time when this building was a private house. Sir Martin Bowes, sometime Lord Mayor of London, and Court Jeweller to Queen Elizabeth I, was born here. Then followed the Thompson family, who provided York with one of its mayors. Either family could have introduced this novel form of decoration in the upstairs parlour, though it savours of the eighteenth century—nearer the Thompson period.

The scheme is novel, first, because it is hidden within a camouflage of brown paint. I had been in this room some time when the proprietor popped his head round the door and said, 'Have you seen "them" yet—the Faces?' He then pointed to the wall panelling, and I moved closer. There 'they' were—painted within decorative ovals and rectangles, but only visible from particular slants. Chameleon-like, they take the approximate colour of their background. Once the viewing knack is acquired, however, the little faces begin to peep out as though from some elfin kingdom.

Some are children's faces, two or three inches high and trailing unmistakable clouds of glory. Some portray animals or grotesque creatures such as a child might invent. They are like the creatures of a dream and, like them again, they sometimes merge with others, helping to make a larger and different picture. One panel contains a tiny human face attached to the flowing mass of a woman's tresses. There are celestial heads, each fitted with wings, and then—on a more human scale—several Jewish profiles appear that are just as impossible to account for as the rest of this unique chiaroscuro scheme.

Some people believe that the air around us is full of invisible presences. The Black Swan's parlour seems to illustrate that rather exciting idea. James Barrie would have been perfectly at home in this lonely yet evocative room. . . .

I have just re-read A. G. Gardiner's character sketch of *Peter Pan*'s progenitor. In it the writer says, 'Barrie is not so much a man as a myth, a fable, a fairy tale, a midsummer night's dream, a creation of moonbeams . . .' He goes on, in spirals of delightful prose, trying to lay bare the secret of this elusive little man who disliked to be called whimsical though admitting that his fellow Scotsmen 'are undoubtedly a sentimental people, and it sometimes plays queer games with that other celebrated sense of ours, the practical'.

While preparing this book I knew that I should have to find more than one place for this remarkable man—this master of the world of fantasy and imagination. But where should he appear? In what house, and in whose company? We have already seen him at Thomas Hardy's Dorset cottage. Number Ten, Adelphi Terrace, in the Strand—the house from which the irrepressible half of Barrie threw plum-stones at Bernard Shaw's windows nearby—would naturally have served even better, if only this little corner of London had kept its serenity and charm. My problem was eventually solved—in the Cotswold country.

I had been hunting hereabouts for secret rooms and so forth. One such room used to exist, they told me, in the old Manor at Bourton-on-the-Water. But surely something of the kind still remained behind a few of those golden façades? Even here, persecution and strife must have left a little tell-tale evidence?

Such were my thoughts again on driving, for the first time, into Stanway, near Winchcombe. It is a small village, but there in the centre is Stanway Hall in all its seventeenth-century glory. My hopes began to rise. Here if anywhere . . . But it was not to be. On writing to the owner's family, afterwards, I was told that there are no secret rooms here, no hiding-places, and (worse still) no ghosts.

But one thing did emerge: J. M. Barrie's long association with this beautiful building. People in the neighbourhood used to keep their ears open for any windfalls of gossip from the 'big house' whenever their idol was in residence. In her *Portrait of Barrie,* however, Lady Cynthia Asquith satisfies every yearning in this regard.

We hear about the charades, the plays, and the comic cricket matches in the grounds. *Mary Rose* has to be re-enacted in all its eeriness for every house-party. Barrie invents fresh mysteries for each occasion, fresh games, fresh make-believe. At Stanway the new parlour game, *Murder*, takes on unprecedented dimensions of secrecy and cunning. When Conan Doyle joins the party there is talk of those Yorkshire fairies he has been investigating. When G. K. Chesterton arrives they all become conspirators again, for this genial soul has devised a fresh version of *Murder*. To quote Cynthia Asquith, 'He had drawn, painted, and cut out in cardboard, a wonderful caricature of this [unnamed] "Wicked Nobleman", which he then dismembered, hiding the fragments all over the house. He had also written clues in rhyming couplets. These clues, besides guiding the seekers in the hunt for the dismembered baron, provided curdling sidelights on his personality and public career. A long search, in the course of which limb after severed limb was gradually found, ended in the discovery, in a very difficult place, of the missing head complete with coronet.'

Barrie, Chesterton, Conan Doyle, H. G. Wells, Augustine Birrell, and even the immaculate John Galsworthy—to all of them, and several others, Stanway became a summer-time rendezvous, a place where they could, and did, romp with any available children and re-enter the magic world of make-believe.

But of all this, Stanway House gives no sign today. Through a splendid gateway attributed to Inigo Jones it presents a straight face to passing tourists. Yet, as I have shown, secrets there are—not shameful ones, like so many, even though Murder may have had a hand in them!

The Huer's Hut at Newquay, Cornwall, represents a forgotten way of life

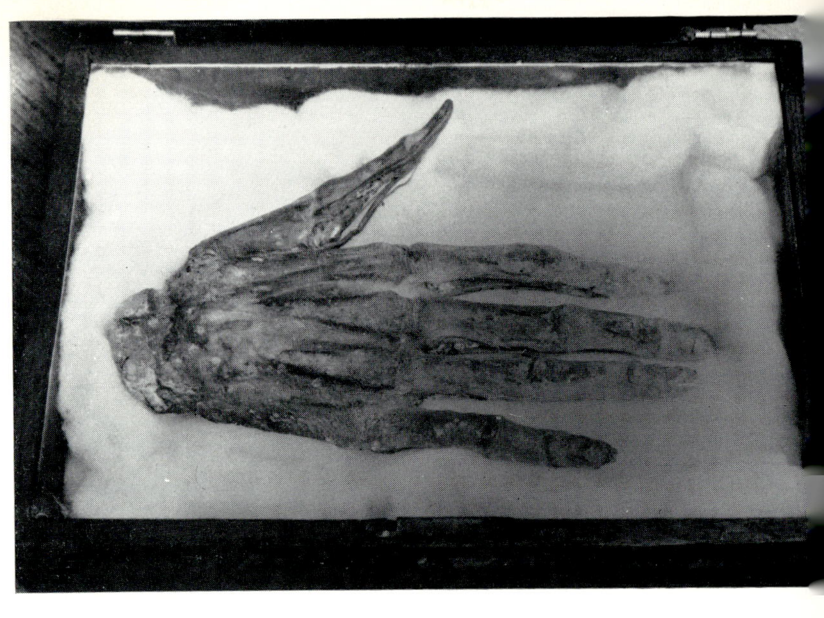

A Hand of Glory, as devi
north-country witches to
unsuspecting household to
Whitby Museum, N.

This wooden doll representing a clergyman was found beneath the floorboards of a north-country cottage

A refuge for lost ecclesiastical property: the strange churchyard mausoleum at Kilmartin, Argyll

This lectern eagle at Southwell Minster, Notts., was dredged from a lake in the grounds of Newstead Abbey, Notts.

'Elijah Fed by the Ravens.' This famous medieval painting, lost after the Reformation, has recently come to light and can now be seen in St David's Cathedral, Pembrokeshire

Paintings hidden for safety during the last war, returning to the Tate Gallery, London, from Sudeley Castle, Glos.

CHAPTER FIFTEEN

WALLS (AND FLOORS) THAT HAVE SPOKEN

Old houses can hoard fascinating things for many years, without anybody's knowledge. Not long ago a friend and neighbour of mine discovered in his roof a complete curved shaft from an eighteenth-century gig. It had presumably been put there to strengthen that part of the house.

One of the most beautiful features at Low Burton Hall, near Masham in Wensleydale, is a five-light Gothic window overlooking the front lawn. Nearly forty years ago the present owner came upon it by chance. In some previous age it had been 'walled up' at the back of the building. Just why, nobody knows. But one can hazard a guess. The window is thought to have belonged to the old domestic chapel of the Wyvil family. In the reign of King James I, Mrs Jane Wyvil was frequently fined for harbouring 'papistical recusants' here. Perhaps the family got tired of paying such fines and decided at length to disguise or even dismantle the chapel so blatantly announced by that lovely, though sacerdotal window.

Who can now plumb the motives of those who hid things away, sometimes in the very structure of their homes? Yet the desire may have been quite straightforward. That carriage-shaft in my friend's roof probably signified many a pleasant ride through our part of Airedale and was therefore preserved—when outmoded—for old time's sake. Did not some foreign baron brick up his first motor-car—a Rolls-Royce—in his castle residence for the same sentimental reason? This car became a family legend, but was found and put on the road again, nearly thirty years later, by the baron's heir.

Changing fashions doubtless caused many worth-while objects to be pushed out of sight. At Clarke Hall, in the Stanley suburb of Wakefield, the late Mr H. C. Haldane used to show visitors, with great pride, the splendid Tudor bread-cupboard recovered last century from the hall moat. In 1546 the cupboard was bequeathed to his son by Brian Bradford of this place, but at some later time somebody threw it out as 'old-fashioned'. Mr Haldane, an antiquary to whom every stick and stone was precious, not only refurbished the cupboard but restored it to what he believed to be its original position—beside the north door in the centre hall, or house-body.

In these days most people simply strip the old paper off the walls when some fresh decoration seems due. In former times the old scheme—quite likely—was buried beneath its successor. To disinter such old forms of decoration is sometimes most rewarding.

One of Yorkshire's best-kept secrets of the kind was at High Sunderland, a fine house near Halifax which was demolished a few years ago. Here was a seventeenth-century wall-painting measuring nine feet by seven feet. When found in 1901 it filled an oak partition—beneath two coats of plaster. Fortunately, one of the Sunderland family had a replica made and this can now be seen, with all its playful imagery and dazzling colour, at Bankfield Museum in Halifax.

Had the fresco been discovered when Emily Brontë modelled her *Wuthering Heights* (in part) on High Sunderland, what descriptive allegories she might have conjured from the golden squirrels, green snakes, pensive frogs, and the hydra-headed monster of this fabulous creation!

I went over to see Woolsthorpe Manor, near Grantham—birthplace in 1642 of Sir Isaac Newton—soon after a Grantham schoolmaster had decided to make it his home, under a tenancy from the National Trust. Remembering young Isaac's penchant for scribbling birds, animals, ships, and such-like on the walls of the lodgings he once occupied in Grantham, the schoolmaster asked the renovators then at work on the manor to keep alert for similar effusions.

Sure enough, as the rotten plaster was removed, several drawings came to light underneath, on the previous wall-covering. They include a rough charcoal sketch of Grantham Parish Church tower, a peacock, geometrical diagrams and calculations, and—on the window-sill of Isaac's birth-room—what seems to be a scratch sundial.

The drawings catch one unawares, in passages as well as rooms, but they invariably occur within a schoolboy's reach of the floor. This circumstance, coupled with the prophetic nature of several drawings, clearly suggest young Isaac as their creator. On a wall just outside one bedroom the workmen uncovered some human figure drawings, but as these are crudely done and unfinished, perhaps Newton early realized that his genius lay elsewhere.

This little 'art gallery' has been attributed to his juvenile years, when he lived here with his widowed mother and any family treasures, including Isaac's 'best Sunday trousers', were kept in a little recess in the birth-room. The drawings have been photographed by the Royal Society. Not always can such scribblings be classed as vandalism!

Graffiti on the old nursery wall at Haworth Parsonage, in West Yorkshire, bring this home of the Brontë family vividly to life. Yet the scribblings were long hidden from view, and of course forgotten. About forty years ago a workman noticed them while stripping off the old wallpaper. He must have had good sight as well as good sense, for the drawings are so minute and of faint outline—tiny, embryonic heads and figures, almost as microscopic as the juvenile bookscript written in this same room by the Brontë children. The books deal with their secret childhood kingdoms, privy to many odd events and ruled over by wholly imaginary monarchs. Among Branwell's contributions to this minuscule 'library' are his *Letters from an Englishman.* The frontispiece to one of them bears a figure of Justice holding her scales. There are other thumb-nail illustrations, too, and curious attempts at colophons and similar devices. Branwell was fourteen years of age when he compiled these books—each about the size of a thin pocket diary. It is tempting to see the nursery drawings as the first tentative efforts which he and his sisters made in this *genre*. Indeed, the drawings on the plaster are now preserved—beneath glass—as the juvenile efforts of the Rev. Patrick Brontë's precocious children.

And then, even more recently, there was another find here. The Parsonage Museum was being re-wired and Harold Mitchell, then Curator, put his hand through an electrician's hole in the floorboards. Luck was with him. He drew out some children's building bricks, a tin trumpet, the wheel of a toy engine, and a silver medallion. Along with the wall pictures, these playthings seem to fill out an important chapter of the immortal story, nurtured among so much childhood secrecy in this fascinating corner of the Pennine country.

Toys, dolls, playing-cards, books—all have been found within house walls, or beneath floors, at different times. Many of them probably enshrine some poignant episode or memory of bygone days. What an immense field for one gifted in psychometry!

Not long ago I held in my hand a crudely made wooden doll resembling a fisherman. It had been found behind some panelling in the Beehive Inn on the south foreshore at Scarborough. Sentiment again, or something deeper? Not very far away a Yorkshire farm cottage was being demolished. From beneath the floorboards came a clergyman, carved in wood and seemingly about to fill a chalice from the flask he also holds. Who was he meant to represent? Could they have seen it, I have little doubt that the Brontë children would have hailed the robed figure as a caricature of one of their father's curates.

When the small secret room in the roof of the Black Swan Inn at York was opened out, the workmen found some old coins, clay pipes —and several *toothpicks*. What story lies there? The only person named as a possible fugitive, in this former private dwelling, is Margaret Clitherow, the Pearl of York—but the toothpicks would hardly belong to her. To make speculation more difficult, the various objects yielded by this tiny room were not preserved. The innkeeper could not even tell me the *period* of the coins.

Things went much better for the antiquary when the supposed birthplace of Guy Fawkes, in Petergate, York, was being altered. This is now the house-shop run by the Misses Pearson. Fortunately they showed interest, not only in the new bakehouse they were having made, but also in the objects this upheaval gradually exposed—an arched doorway into the back courtyard, tree-trunk supports still naïvely complete with bark and lateral branches, and a jack—or leather-bottle. Found behind the fireplace—of all unlikely spots—the jack is now kept among other historic finds, all well worth seeing, at the neighbouring Merchant Adventurers' Hall, in Fossgate.

When visiting some old house a discreet enquiry about anything of interest that may have been hidden there, in walls, floors, or gardens, will often prove fruitful. York is a splendid hunting ground. A few of my own experiences here have been mentioned, but the list is a long one—and still grows. Many another old town, and village, offers similar excitements.

Excitement is not too strong a word to use—not when one has been to a place like Walmgate Bar. This, York's most impressive medieval gateway, incorporates the original barbican and a house added in Tudor times.

Walmgate Bar was manned by Royalists during the Civil War. A Roundhead soldier taken prisoner informed his captors that the Bar had been undermined and was about to be blown up. York citizens in this area did not breathe freely again until the mine was discovered and flooded. But in 1836, while digging near the gateway, some workmen unearthed two of the old shells—and they were still *unexploded*. For nearly two hundred years a succession of tenants had lived here in blissful ignorance.

The Civil Wars left an interesting legacy, also, at Walton Hall, that curious house near Wakefield which still stands on its island within the lake-moat. Latterly the hall has been used as a hospital, but there is some freedom of access to the extensive grounds, laid out early last century by that famous naturalist, Squire Charles Waterton.

The Squire always regretted the passing of the old fortified residence here, and regarded its successor—the present house—as an ugly 'box'. In 1855 he started dredging the narrow part of the lake, near the house and former drawbridge. This bridge had traditionally been burnt and destroyed by Cromwell's men during the siege of Walton Hall. They also made off with all the horses, so that for some time after, Mrs Waterton had to ride about with six of the remaining oxen harnessed to her carriage.

The site of the drawbridge—marked by the surviving Watergate—always had a nostalgic fascination for the Squire. Here he would try to visualize his ancestor's spirited defence (her husband was away on King's business), during which she brought a small swivel gun into action. With this she shot in the leg one of the troopers, just as he was bringing up some ale for their refreshment.

I can hear Waterton chuckling gleefully over this incident, and see him pointing with pride to a small cannon-ball found in the grounds by his father.

Meanwhile, the Squire's dredgers have been at work, and out of the lake sludge has emerged a strange-looking object which proves, after cleaning and examination, to be the family's brave swivel gun which fired those shots and helped to repulse the Roundheads.

Much else came out of the lake, notably some family plate and many coins. They enabled Waterton to confirm yet another tradition. During the Jacobite rising of 1715 this Catholic family expected their home to be raided. A few valuables were therefore hurriedly put together and dropped into the lake from the old bridge. It is hardly surprising that they were not recovered straightway after the rebellion. Silt and mud accumulate rapidly in this narrow neck of the lake. So thick had this deposit become by 1855 that the Squire had to devise a new system of drainage—which conveyed to the neighbouring River

Calder huge quantities of mud and fish, and whatever the mud still retained of the family silver.

Several cottages within the beautiful stretch of Wharfedale that embraces Harewood and Wetherby have links with the old days of witchcraft. A cottage garden at Kearby gave up a yellow bottle containing witchcraft charms—pins and needles for piercing wax effigies, human hair and nail parings, brimstone, and so on. A grey mug containing a mysterious powder, believed to give immunity against the evil eye, was also unearthed. It is tempting to connect these tokens with the times of Jinny Pullen, a local wise-woman of 150 years ago who once demonstrated her skill by crossing the River Wharfe in a cinder-riddle, or sieve.

More recently the owner of Cornborough Manor at Sheriff Hutton, near York, removed a flagstone that formed the kitchen threshold and found herself gazing at a curious assortment of objects—bits of clay pipe, a small piece of glass, and the jawbone of some rodent. Though seemingly unrelated, they had obviously been carefully arranged, fan-wise, in a prepared bed of sand.

Fortunately, expert opinion was sought and this confirmed the idea that the oddments had probably been intended to prevent the evils of witchcraft crossing the threshold. When I called, soon after their discovery, the fragments were being kept in the Library and mischievously shown to visitors as the 'luck of the house'.

The Old Roof Tree Inn at Middleton, near Morecambe, also has an interesting relic—a door-key, found some years ago under the front entrance. It is only too easy to associate this region with omens and spells and incantations. Although attractive to modern tourists, and a good jumping-off place for Sunderland Point and its bird-haunted mud-flats, the very remoteness of Middleton might invite trouble from the most feared quarter of all, in the seventeenth century. Not coastal raiders, now, but one or other of the ubiquitous Lancashire witches. The inn of today was then a farm, and it was well known that a witch could put a blight on your cattle, alienate a wife's affection from her husband, or create other trouble. One almost sure panacea was to deposit a piece of metal, preferably a key, beneath your threshold. At any rate the Salter family of this place were willing to try.

All over rural England, at about the same time, credulous folk were hiding similar 'impediments' about their homes. But one thing completely baffled them—the Hand of Glory. A horrid tale about its use is told, appropriately enough, in connection with one of the wildest and least inhabited areas in the North, namely, Bowes Moor on Stainmore Common.

This is how the incident was described by the Folklore Society:

> One evening, between the years 1790 and 1800, a traveller dressed in woman's clothes arrived at the old Spital Inn on Bowes Moor. The traveller begged to stay all night, but had to go away so early in the morning that if a mouthful of food were set ready for breakfast there was no need the family should be disturbed by her departure. The people of the house, however, arranged that a servant-maid should sit up till the stranger was out of the premises, and then went to bed themselves. The girl lay down for a nap on the long settle by the fire; but before she shut her eyes she took a good look at the traveller, who was sitting on the opposite side of the hearth, and espied a pair of man's trousers peeping out from under the gown.
>
> All inclination for sleep was now gone; however, with great self-command she feigned it, closed her eyes, and even began to snore. On this the traveller got up, pulled out of his pocket a dead man's hand, fitted a candle to it, lighted the candle and passed hand and candle several times before the girl's face, saying as he did so: 'Let those who are asleep be asleep, and let those who are awake be awake.' This done, he placed the light on the table, opened the outer door, went down two or three of the steps which led from the house to the road and began to whistle for his companions. The girl now jumped up, rushed behind the ruffian and pushed him down the steps. She then shut the door, locked it, and ran upstairs to try and wake the family, but without success. Calling, shouting and shaking were all in vain. The poor girl was in despair, for she heard the traveller and his comrades outside the house.
>
> Suddenly she remembered the Hand of Glory, ran downstairs again, seized a bowl of skimmed milk and threw it over the hand and candle, after which she went upstairs again, and woke the sleepers without any difficulty. The landlord's son went to the window and asked the men what they wanted. They answered that if the dead man's hand were but given to them they would go away

quietly and do no harm to anyone. This was refused, and the landlord's son fired among them. The shot must have taken effect, for in the morning stains of blood were traced to a considerable distance.

In these enlightened days the Spital Inn has become a place of friendly welcome, but to get the real impact of that old tale one should try to see a genuine Hand of Glory.

I believe they show one in the Witchcraft Museum at Boscastle, in North Cornwall—the place where local witches were wont to *sell* a good sailing wind to becalmed fishermen. A painting at the museum entrance illustrates this remarkable proceeding. On the harbour pier several witches are showing the promise of wind by the pieces of twine that blow about in their gifted hands, and gullible fisherman come forward with their money. The Hand of Glory was gifted with other powers, as we have noticed.

There is a nasty-looking specimen in the Whitby Museum. Made by a local witch, no doubt, it was found in the roof of a house at Castleton, on the neighbouring moors.

There was a secret recipe for preparing such a fetish. First, the hand must be severed from the arm of a man hanging from a gibbet. It was steeped in a solution of salt, saltpetre and pepper for two weeks, dried in the sun, and then shrivelled up in the smoke of certain carefully chosen herbs. To achieve full efficacy as a burglar's talisman—that is, having the power to put some household under a deep, hypnotic sleep—a special kind of candle had to be placed in the dead man's hand. The candle was made from fat taken from some corpse.

This Hand of Glory at Whitby no longer clutches its candle, but the ancient sorcery seems to hover near, too near for peace of mind. I am told that its supposed powers were last put to the test about 1820.

A Hand of Glory could have other hidden powers, also. According to an old Yorkshire shepherd, 'A family canna' die oot if t' Hand o' Glory's fetched to the hoose.' This fellow also told a caller, many years ago, that the particular Hand of Glory known to him was that of 'a 'ooman burned for a witch'. He continued, as though confiding a close secret, 'It's a safeguard agen devils, smallpox, misfortune and death—but it only acts for the innercent . . .'

In the Whitby area witch posts were favoured to avert evil. A good example—from East End Cottage at Egton—is preserved in Whitby

Museum, but even more evocative, as a relic of the secret power once accredited to the black sisterhood, is the witch post now set up in the Ryedale Folk Museum at Hutton-le-Hole, near Pickering. This specimen, fashioned in mountain ash like all the rest, came from Stang End at Danby, on the North Yorkshire moors. It stood originally, as it stands now, on the left side of the fireplace—a bulwark against any nefarious hanky-panky because of the cross incised at the top, and other incised symbols of which the significance is lost. On the inner face of the post there are extra precautions—a hole just big enough to take a crooked sixpence, and another hole, even smaller, plugged with a bit of sheep's wool. Only when thus protected could the cottager's family enjoy their evening by the glowing turf, or feel safe on going off to bed.

In the garden behind this museum there is a pleasant charm against any such imbroglio. A well has lately been dedicated to the local elf who, as Elphi, received honourable mention for his good deeds on the fly-leaf of somebody's family Bible. This is what one reads—a forgotten echo from the seventeenth century—beside the well:

> Elphi, little chap,
> Thoff Hewer [though he were]
> So small was
> Full o' deeds
> Of kindness.
> Drink tiv him,
> Yan an' all.

There is no telling what an old house may secrete. The salvage drive during the Second World War resulted in several interesting finds; a Stuart chair in fruitwood, a seventeenth-century child's bed fashioned in oak and beech of which only the top posts stuck out of some enveloping rubbish, and so on. A Leeds antiquary built up quite a collection of such items and later exhibited them in a local museum.

The collection was not limited to war-time discoveries, however; its main theme was Childhood Treasures, therefore encompassing a wide variety of charm, romance, and even tragedy.

I recall a toy rocking chair, about three-and-a-half inches high, fitted with a cushion of red Genoese velvet. It was found along with other playthings by some workmen while digging foundations for a new building in London. A handwritten note in the wooden box containing the toys bore the date 1648. As the find-spot was the site of a seventeenth-century plague pit it is assumed that these little treasures were the favourite toys of some child victim, and buried with her, perhaps, by a distraught mother.

There was also on show a toy coach made about 1698 so that a certain boy should have a carriage 'just like father's', exact in every detail, though only twelve inches long. Doubtless used for scores of imaginary journeys, with a coachman summoned from fancy to occupy the little front seat padded with blue velvet, the model gradually slipped into oblivion—to be found, over two hundred years later, when a descendant of its proud young owner was searching the attic for legal papers.

The most amusing find in this particular collection was a birch, recovered from a long-disused well behind a cottage in the York area. It transpires that during the eighteenth century the cottage was a dame school, run by one Bertha Small. In a stained-glass window at York Minster a similar bundle of birch twigs is being soundly applied to the posterior of a naughty schoolboy. It has been suggested that at Bertha Small's little academy some lad due for a thrashing seized the birch and pitched it out of harm's way into the well. Whether the lad really evaded what was coming to him we shall never know.

At the moment of writing it seems probable that a model of the *Gipsy Moth*, the vessel in which Sir Francis Chichester made his lone voyage round the world in 1967, will join other ship models at Arlington Court, the North Devonshire home of one branch of the Chichesters since the fourteenth century. Sir Francis faced many difficult seas on that amazing voyage, but nothing half as baffling as the Sea of Time and Space represented on a painting found fairly recently at Arlington Court.

It is a 'lost' water-colour by William Blake. A preliminary drawing of the subject (now in the Pierpont Morgan Library) was made, but for over a century connoisseurs knew nothing of any finished work—or whether, indeed, Blake had followed his ideas on this subject through to completion.

When Arlington Court was being prepared for its National Trust rôle, in 1949, the painting that seemed never to have reached fruition materialized. It was found along with various documents on top of a store cupboard in Miss Chichester's old photographic room. How odd that in this room where she developed and printed hundreds of her own pictures, the inimitable Blake should wait quietly, year after year, for its own exposure. When found at last, the framed painting—measuring sixteen inches by nineteen-and-a-half inches—was seen to be wrapped in a copy of *The Times* dated 20 January 1820. The picture is signed 'W. Blake, inventor 1821' and must have been acquired, soon afterwards, by Colonel J. T. Chichester.

In the public café here one sees a large framed photograph of Miss Chichester's Natural History Class. The beautiful surrounding park testifies to her love of animals, birds, and fine trees, as the house does to her equal passion for anything to do with the sea—ships, for example, and all the charm and delicacy of sea-shells found on British and foreign shores. I think she would have been glad to know that some of her maritime mementoes now surround the picture found, after her death, in her dark-room.

The picture subject is itself something of a mystery. 'Blake's Vision of the Cycle of the Life of Man' is somebody's tentative title for it, but the attached label reads: 'The subject is thought to represent the Cabbala, a secret belief of the Jews which interested Blake deeply.' Another interpretation of the vision sees the topmost figure as Urizen, the Creator, who 'has fallen asleep in his chariot, while his sceptre touches a nymph who is incarnated as a figure drawn by four horses on the Sea of Time and Space'. The man near the centre, whose soul is on its pilgrim way, seems to be on the point of diving into the troubled sea. There must be many possible interpretations. As an appraiser of this artist once wrote, 'Blake's writing, like his pictures, was as fanciful as the thoughts of an active-minded child, but with truth at the heart of it. He stands alone, a complete original, who can be read with understanding by childhood, but his symbolical meanings sometimes baffle the wisest.' And there we must leave the matter, in a pool of surmise and rippling ideas.

Other pictures by some famous artist may still be in hiding, or be temporarily blotted out by the brushwork of a later, and inferior hand. Art galleries frequently get surprises of this kind. I remember reading about a large picture that once hung in a Lincoln school. For forty years it had been a target for schoolboys' missiles, usually bits of chalk. When the picture was taken down for cleaning, it turned out to be a fine Venetian study of the Madonna and Child.

Similarly, in a Windermere hotel, a Romney of Lady Hamilton remained unrecognized for generations because of its veil of grime.

Sometimes, as with the Blake watercolour, a picture may disappear altogether. For years nobody knows its whereabouts. Theft often accounts for such disappearances, but neglect can be responsible.

In an earlier chapter I mentioned a fine oil painting (artist unknown) of Sir Thomas Herbert, friend of King Charles I. After forming part of the family portrait gallery for many years the large canvas completely vanished, nobody knew how. Sir Thomas, one of the family celebrities, was sorely missed and each succeeding generation heard sadly of the loss. It was easy to describe the painting—from father to son—because Sir Thomas had been portrayed almost life-size, wearing a spectacular outfit—including turban and a tunic of cloth of gold—given to him by the Shah of Persia, and attended by his little black boy.

Herbert's *Travels*, first published in 1634, contain some of his own drawings, showing the 'dodo, cocato, and parrat' and mysterious looking trees, like the 'Palmeto'. The silver watch presented to him by King Charles I became an heirloom. But where had that splendid portrait gone?

Gradually, the family lost all hope of 'Sir Thomas's' return. Then, about 1926, a picture was advertised for sale in some English journal—a picture corresponding in description to the old family account of the lost 'Sir Thomas'. Mr George Herbert told me of the excitement that ran through his household as he went off to identify it. That is how 'Sir Thomas' came back, unharmed. But his adventures during that long absence are still unknown. A lapse of memory could not have blotted out that period more effectively.

But what if the man himself disappears? What if he drops out of life, leaving no trace, no message? This brand of secrecy, perhaps the most poignant of all, is stamped upon several places in Britain.

It was at the Leeds Coliseum that I saw some of the very first 'animated pictures'. One entitled *Caught by the Tide* effectively revealed this new and startling invention, though the hoof-beats of the horse that came to the rescue had to be simulated secretly, as it were, behind the screen. Being a young boy at the time I did not know that some twenty years earlier the 'father of the cinematograph'—Louis Aimé Augustine Le Prince—had conducted his pioneer experiments in a house only a few yards away from the Coliseum. That was in 1885.

The Frenchman settled in Leeds after his marriage to a local lady.

With his new-fangled apparatus he photographed moving objects in his father-in-law's garden at Oakwood Grange, near Roundhay Park. He then gave a demonstration in his Woodhouse Lane residence. The future seemed promising—and then he vanished. Not in Leeds, but while visiting France in connection with his patents. He was never seen again. Even his luggage disappeared. Murder, due to professional jealousy? Accident? Loss of memory? The mystery has never been solved.

In earlier times such disappearances could be engineered differently. Dunster Castle looks glorious in the sunshine. Perched on a hill above the village that is one of the delights of Somerset, it rides above the all-encompassing trees like a stately galleon. There are rooms to match this grandeur, and guides to show you round. But one thing cannot now be shown—the human skeleton found beneath the floor of the old gatehouse during alterations. The skeleton was that of a man over 6 ft. 6 in. high. Who was he? No ordinary prisoner, surely? Did his wondering kinsfolk never trace him to the castle? How futile are such questions today, I thought, when the only tangible things left on view from the episode are the iron fetters that secured the man, even in his enforced 'tomb', by neck, wrist, and ankle!

When I put my questionings to Lt.-Col. Walter Luttrell of Dunster Castle, however, rather more light was thrown on the subject—though still not enough to enable one to do more than *grope*.

After referring to the skeleton found beneath the old floor, Colonel Luttrell writes: 'Under him were, and still are, a pile of human bones which gave rise to the theory that this pit had originally been used as an 'oubliette', possibly at the time of the battles between Matilda (whom the De Mohun of the castle at that time vigorously supported) and Stephen. The castle was the scene of several attempted stormings during an unsuccessful siege and it is thought that the defenders probably followed the usual practice of throwing all the bodies of enemy dead into the oubliette.' (My dictionary describes an oubliette as 'a secret pit in the floor of a dungeon'.)

'The chained skeleton is thought in all probability to have been a foreign mercenary who would have attracted special attention on account of his height.' Colonel Luttrell continues:

> It is a great pity that no record survives (even legendary) of this 'giant'. One might have hoped that the capture of what must in

> those days have been an even greater freak than today would have been the subject of a story which could have filtered down through the ages until committed to some sort of record on paper. This may of course have happened, as when Prynne was imprisoned in the castle and spent his time going through the miscellaneous papers and records which he found at Dunster, he discarded a great number of those which he considered were not strictly business records—and doubtless a great number of interesting historical items vanished in this way.

For opposing the execution of King Charles I, William Prynne was confined in Dunster Castle in 1649. Imprisonment seems too strong a word, for Prynne revelled in his self-appointed task of sorting out the 'confused chaos' of the muniments. But as Colonel Luttrell says, many valuable domestic items were then jettisoned as 'unnecessary paper'. This, perhaps, is why the secret passage leading from the 'four-poster' in the King's Room is still a controversial matter among antiquaries. The same purge has also left everybody guessing about the identity of that shackled giant.

Even more puzzling was the discovery made at Menabilly, in South Cornwall. Daphne Du Maurier, who lives at this fine old house not far from Fowey, has kindly sent me the following particulars. 'The story goes', she writes, 'that about 1820 the owner of the day, a Mr Philip Rashleigh, had certain structural work taking place at the back of the house, near the kitchens. A small concealed room was found and in it a skeleton clothed in seventeenth-century costume, that of a Cavalier, which soon crumbled once the air filled the room. The remains were considered to be those of a member of the Grenville family, who were known to have been in hiding at Menabilly during the Civil War. As Menabilly was untenanted for many years after the Civil War period it was assumed no one knew, then or later, that someone had been concealed in the secret room.' In short, the fugitive had been forgotten and could not set himself free.

So much for the Rashleigh family tradition. Germinating in Daphne Du Maurier's mind, it became the theme for one of her historical novels, *The King's General.* The book's Postscript contains the factual details, as far as they are known, and elaborates them somewhat so that the skeleton becomes that 'of a young man, seated on a stool, a trencher at his feet . . .'

When the young Cavalier was at last found his remains were buried reverently in the churchyard at Tywardreath, near Par Sands. The secret place that had served for so long as his sepulchre was sealed up, or destroyed, for Daphne Du Maurier tells me there is no sign of it today. Adding a little more to the mystery she makes this further comment, 'There is no grave or stone in Tywardreath churchyard extant to mark the spot where the unfortunate man was buried.'

The Rashleighs have their family mausoleum, above Ready Money Cove nearby, and a monument in Fowey Church commemorates John Rashleigh who took out his ship, the *Frances of Fowey*, against the Armada. But for the unknown Cavalier—perishing after being cooped up in worse plight than any medieval anchorite—there seems to be no surviving memorial, except in the thrilling pages of *The King's General*.

Part III
ABBEY AND CHURCH

CHAPTER SIXTEEN

CLERICAL OCCASIONS

When I was commissioned to photograph architecturally important buildings for the national archives during the last war, one comparatively rare feature of some older churches intrigued me. It was the anchorite's cell. Only a few have survived and even those few have become so fragmentary and puzzling to visitors that some mention of them seems justified in our context of secrecy.

An anchorite or anchoress was one who had withdrawn from the world for religious reasons, living exclusively in a tiny cell attached to some church. A book was purposely written for their instruction. Called the *Ancren Riwle*, it was compiled by Richard Poore, builder of Salisbury Cathedral and a native of Tarrant Crawford in Dorset. It was for three nuns of this village that Poore first prepared this set of rules, which others were to follow later.

Imagine Salisbury Cathedral today, with its glorious spire and west front. W. H. Hudson the naturalist was not the only one to watch the doves and jackdaws that nest there, amongst all the saints in their crocketed niches. But grandeur and bird-like freedom were denied to anchoresses. Echoing his own name, Poore charged them to renounce all possessions—and then smiled a knowing smile. 'Ye shall not possess any beast, dear sisters,' he added, 'except only a cat.'

Of all the medieval anchorites perhaps Juliana of Norwich is the only one whose name is familiar today, because of her profound sayings, often quoted in devotional works. But of her cell outside St Julian's Church at Norwich nothing remains save a hole in the ground.

York, however, had several of these retreats and it was part of my photographic mission to seek them out and record them for posterity. A small Gothic window in an unusually low position, just above ground level, is the only surviving clue at St Mary's, Castlegate. At St Cuthbert's on Peasholm Green there is a small crypt partly hidden beneath the raised altar. This crypt may have originated as the cell of the anchorite to whom seven persons, between 1388 and 1416, made bequests for simple food and drink.

A cell at All Saints' Church, North Street, York, was of the kind in which the recluse was actually walled up, with only a small gap left for breathing. Slight remains of this cell can still be seen at the west end of the church. The inmate at one time was Dame Emma Rawghton. People came to her little cell aperture for spiritual advice. It must have seemed like talking with the dead.

Hidden rooms in churches may sound quite incongruous, yet there are a few. Anybody might walk through Selby Abbey in Yorkshire repeatedly, or even worship here among its magnificent Norman arcades for a lifetime, without suspecting the existence of its Dark Chamber. It is above the north porch and can only be reached from a door in the triforium. There is no sign of a window. The space any window might have occupied is covered, on the exterior, with a row of blind arcading, as though part of some conspiracy. The purpose of the room is unknown, but when the base of an old altar was found on the floor, at the east end, about fifty years ago, various explanations were suggested. According to the most tempting one, this small room —sixty feet or more above the nave floor—was a place of banishment for any monk in disgrace. Temporarily deprived of the services below, in the choir, he might still abase himself before that other altar, in the gloom of his obscure prison.

There was to be some mystery, too, within the magnificent abbey which Bishop Oliver King restored at Bath in the fifteenth century. Carved on the great west front are two ladders, with angels ascending and descending, just as the Bishop had seen them in the dream that directed him to this worthy task.

The story is well known, locally, but can anybody say why the abbey chamber in which Oliver King kept his robes was sealed up some years later? Was the Reformation responsible? All memory of the room seemed to have vanished, for there was great surprise when in the eighteenth century somebody stumbled upon the place and opened it up once more. Whatever the reason for its closure, Bishop King had enjoyed uninterrupted privacy, so to speak, for two hundred years. Hanging on the wall of this little sanctum were his copes, alb, and other vestments. But the sudden inrush of air reduced them at once to powder.

The nearest thing to a secret room that many churches possess is a crypt. This word is derived from the Greek *kruptos*, meaning a hidden place. Several good examples come readily to mind for today these underground chambers are often accessible to visitors, stirring a sense of remoteness—in time as well as in space. They are the religious counterpart of some deep cave, particularly when a vaulted roof sends down fluted shafts, almost like stalactites, and white columns rise up to meet them.

The Norman crypt at Canterbury Cathedral is of this kind. After the magnificence of the main building above—the power and the glory, as it were, there comes the still small voice of Ernulf's crypt. On Sundays a dwindling company of French folk thread their way down to the crypt for a special service conducted in their own language. This commemorates the refugees from the Continent who were given the use of this place by Queen Elizabeth I.

York Minster has two crypts—one almost as alluring as Aladdin's Cave when the lights are switched on and the low arches proffer their strange, almost cabalistic carvings; the other crypt leads even further beneath the choir and looks remarkably odd because the original Norman pillars, long dwarfed in size, have withdrawn their support.

Winchester Cathedral goes one better by having three crypts, each leading into the next, like a string of caves, below the giant structure. Under the low, ribbed roof of the crypt at Glastonbury Abbey in Somerset, pilgrims once paid homage to the memory of St Joseph of Arimathea. At Lastingham, in North Yorkshire, other pilgrims honoured St Cedd and St Chad—not in the present church, but in one of England's most exciting crypts, fashioned below ground level. This is an apsidal church in miniature, complete with chancel, nave, and two side aisles. The original entrance is walled up, but the thrill of discovery remains, for a flight of steps leads from above into this sanctuary of Norman times, and all sound is reduced to a whisper.

As Hexham in Northumberland is near the Scottish Border, with its long history of strife, bloodshed and plunder, one can understand why the builders of the priory here felt compelled to provide the place with many underground chambers. Eddi, chaplain to St Wilfrid, recorded the existence of 'many chambers deep down in the earth, built with smoothed stones'. A later chronicler spoke of 'crypts and subterranean oratories, of wonderful carvings upon the walls, of pictures and paintings in great variety and beauty'.

Of this fantastic underworld nothing seems to have survived, except the one Saxon crypt known today. I remember going down there and feeling entirely cut off from my fellow-men. A tourist simply does not know the North Country, at its most palpable, until he has descended that narrow flight of steps at Hexham Priory and entered the furtive little chapel below ground level where the relics of Northumbrian saints were once kept, along with episcopal rings and other valuables.

A similar experience awaits anybody who goes to Ripon Cathedral. It is no straining of words to say that here, as at Hexham, the crypt affords an experiment with Time. I have been down repeatedly, over the years, but never without feeling relieved of current anxieties and aware of a fresh perspective on life. Thirteen centuries slip away and one is back in the days of a simple, fervent Christianity that produced saintly men like Aidan and Cuthbert and Bede.

We shall need to return to the Ripon crypt in our final chapter.

To find anything in the nature of secret practices in church is not easy, except for the smuggling partnerships already described between the occasional parson and his flock. The very purpose of a place of worship makes a mockery of man's devious ways. And yet some people besides the contraband-runners have found a compromise.

There was Ralph Cantrell of Hemingstone in Suffolk. He found himself in a quandary because, being a Roman Catholic, his goods were liable to confiscation unless he attended the local Anglican church on Sundays. His solution can be seen today. It is embodied in the south porch. This has an upper chamber fitted with a peep-hole that gives a token view of the altar. By providing this porch and climbing up to his redoubt, Cantrell kept on the right side of the law—and outside the church proper.

Edward FitzGerald, the poet, did much the same thing, though for different reasons, over at Woodbridge, a few miles away. He too frequented the church porch during divine service, but not in any upper chamber. His private session with his Maker was ensured by just sitting in the porch after the bell had stopped ringing. When the Vicar discovered FitzGerald's secret and requested him to step inside with the others, he plucked his Inverness cape about him and fled. The world remembers him because he translated *Omar Khayaam* from an original Persian manuscript found in the Bodleian Library. But I often think of him deep in reverie as the sound of singing filtered through to him in that quiet porch; or rushing past with a piece of apple pie concealed in one of his notorious hats when off for another sail on his beloved River Deben. He was a law unto himself—full of mysterious impulses and habits that baffled many besides the Vicar of Woodbridge.

Sometimes even a family pew lent itself to private occasions, tinged with subterfuge—especially if it was provided with thick curtains! The curtains were intended to protect the squire and his lady from draughts, but if the sermon was lengthy, or boring, or both, the folds of velvet could be surreptitiously drawn right across the privileged enclave without any fear of the beadle coming over with his tipstaff should a little snoring emerge.

The best curtained family pew known to me is in the lovely old church at Croft Spa in North Yorkshire. It stands at the head of its own grand staircase and was erected in the seventeenth century for the Milbanke family. In Wensley Church, Wensleydale, there is another such pew—one still used by Lord Bolton and his family of neighbouring Bolton Hall. I have taken the liberty of sitting for a few moments in each of these family retreats and can testify to the efficiency of their curtains when closed. One gets a queer, withdrawn feeling, as though in a closed tent.

Fortunately for the sightseer several of these 'country house' pews remain. I have found other good examples at Cartmel Fell and Whalley in Lancashire, Clare and Lavenham in Suffolk, and Selworthy in Somerset. A few even have their own fireplace, and a cupboard or two that could hold much beside the requisite prayer books. Such pews were clearly an attempt to preserve the Squire's dignity and 'apartness'. Even here in church he and his family could foster that degree of seclusion befitting the elect. In Selworthy Church, however, this barrier was apt to be thrust aside by the squire himself. From his elevated pew over the south porch he would sometimes flick the line of his fishing rod upon anybody below who needed correction. This must have been very funny to watch, especially if his lordship had to cast two or three times for his 'trout'.

Persistence will disclose other variations on the theme of secrecy in our older churches. The men who built and decorated them were just as human as the rest of us, sometimes indulging in caricatures that mystify beholders, especially today, centuries after their unwitting 'sitters' have been laid to rest.

Who can now interpret the comic faces carved in stone on the exterior of such buildings as York Minster and Durham Cathedral? Though restored, some of those at York were supposed to poke fun at the town's medieval monks. At Durham, tucked out of normal sight above the Slype, I once found a whole row of faces grinning at me. Obviously a parody, but of whom? Minus these grotesque expressions, the unknown originals would probably walk the streets and river-banks of this beautiful town hundreds of years ago. A merchant or two, perhaps, a tavern-keeper, a toothless old crone, and so on. The carver responsible left no record but this garbled one. His secret is as safe as so many others of like nature.

A church may harbour many hidden meanings. The splendid set of sixteenth-century misericords in the choir of Beverley Minster covers many diverse subjects—a pig playing bagpipes, a cart being placed before the horse, a housewife beating her husband, etc. etc. The gist of each individual subject is fairly clear, but there is supposed to be a *collective* meaning, too. What it is, nobody now knows. A person of Queen Elizabeth I's reign, being accustomed to such conceits, might have figured it out, with patience. Today, all that visitors can do is to enjoy the incidental pleasantries, and pass on.

When the famous writer, Krylov, wanted to voice some criticism of Czarist Russia, and yet keep his head firmly on his shoulders, he resorted to subterfuge, saying what he had to say in the form of his now well-known fables. We have already seen how our own Sidney Smith had to adopt somewhat similar methods, leaving people in the dark as to his real identity. I was once shown a set of cathedral wood-carvings which followed suit, allowing the craftsman responsible to air a grievance and yet avoid rebuke. They are in the choir at Lincoln and decorate the Precentor's stall. In fact, the carvings are said to refer to one particular precentor of old who had the reputation of being bone idle though he turned up promptly on pay day. Dislike of this man was therefore conveyed secretly—through a parable of monkeys.

First, a few monkeys are seen working industriously at their butter churn. One monkey dodges his share of duty and steals a pat of butter from the plate. The miscreant is caught, has a rope slung round his neck, and is hanged without further ado. A misericord nearby gives the sequel. Two monkeys take the corpse away on a bier. With typical medieval allegory, the complaint has been dramatized, rather pointedly, and taken to its logical conclusion! There can be little doubt that many private grudges were worked out of a man's system in this satisfying, though veiled, manner.

Yes, a church can reflect many human foibles, and necessities too. At Ripon Cathedral there is a man's hand, carved in wood, and so cunningly placed that few ever see it. By operating the hand mechanically, from side to side, as required, the organist who made this device could play his instrument and also beat time for the choristers at his back.

The old church of St Petrox at Parracombe, North Devon, shows similar ingenuity. Bygone worshippers here might well have wondered, for a time, how their old bass fiddler was managing to get enough room for his bow during the hymn-singing. His pew was as narrow and boxed in as the rest. The secret was this—he had covertly removed a panel from the pew in front, fairly low down. The accommodating gap is only noticeable if one knows just where to look. Humorous, of course, but no more so than the little device contrived in his stall by a former Rector at Middleton Church in Lancashire. An almost imperceptible piece of wood, perhaps three inches long, slides up the inner face of the pew-end, exposing a tiny cavity. This was the parson's snuff box.

Churches also introduce one to several curious characters. My friends are only too liable to hear about them whenever we drive in the appropriate direction!

There was the shy, dancing parson of Linton-in-Craven, West Yorkshire, whose life was a closed book to all except his valet, and even the valet had to turn his back whenever his master—as often happened—wished to trip a dainty measure. There was the seventeenth-century minister of Aberfoyle, Stirlingshire, whose parishioners must have been startled when he produced a work entitled, *The Secret Commonwealth, or an Essay on the Nature and Actions of the Subterranean (and for the most part) Invisible People*. These creatures, he explained, had hitherto gone 'under the name of Elves, Faunes and Fairis, or the lyke, among the Low Country Scots, as they are described by those who have the Second Sight'. One hopes that the Lowlanders would appreciate the efforts of this man, the Rev. Robert Kirk. In the seventeenth century his was a lone voice, but he is now regarded as a pioneer in psychic research.

Some parsons have steeped themselves in the occult, like a vicar near my own home who promised to return to his flock after his death (about forty years ago) but somehow forgot to keep the tryst. For two further studies in my 'gallery' we must enter Cornwall again.

Something has already been said about the Vicar of Morwenstow's curious home. Here it is the man himself who claims our attention. A lovable if eccentric character, possessed of some secret understanding which made him at all times a delightful companion and guide. He saw hidden meanings in many things, especially in his beautiful church. Over the south porch and again in the north arcade of the nave there is some very fine chevron carving. A friend who was being shown round one day exclaimed, 'What fine zigzag work!' But Stephen Hawker knew better. 'Zigzag, zigzag!' he replied, scornfully. 'Why, those ripples represent the waves on the Sea of Galilee.'

A visitor on looking down the length of the interior will notice that it is slightly askew. Hawker knew the meaning of this. He would say, reverently, 'As Christ upon the Cross, His head inclined, so His sanctuary is built with an inclination to one side.' The oak shingles or tiles that roofed his church were not merely shingles to him, but the type of covering that Noah used for the Ark and therefore well calculated to resist the Atlantic gales that beat upon this Cornish headland. Hawker once used the expression 'carvure' when describing something in the church. His companion declared there was no such word in the English language. 'If no such word,' replied Hawker, undaunted, 'it is time there should be. I invent it.' The said 'carvure' is a strange piece of symbolism on the chancel wall. To read its message one needs Hawker's sublime assurance and insight.

For him everything had its inner significance. But there were clues for the discerning. He lived and worked here from 1834 to 1875, yet the medieval 'doctrine of signatures' must have meant more to him than anything out of contemporary science. Was it some lingering Celtic strain that coloured his outlook? His church is dedicated to St Morwenna, daughter or ward of Breachan and Gladwys, a Celtic king and queen in ninth-century Wales. According to Hawker it was Morwenna who built the first church here, 'in the scenery of my prayer' as she put it—that is, on the wild Cornish cliffs revealed to her. But to know that old story in detail was not enough for the ever-resourceful Vicar of Morwenstow. He who shared the secrets of his parishioners—mostly smugglers and wreckers, whose activities he deplored—had a particularly precious secret of his own. 'I know that

Morwenna lies here,' he once confided; 'I have seen her, and she has told me as much; and at her feet ere long I hope to lay my old bones.'

To meet our other Cornish vicar it is necessary to cross over to Mullion, on the Lizard peninsula. Mullion Church cannot have altered too greatly since the Reverend Thomas Flavel settled here as incumbent in 1634. The chancel screen certainly suffered at the Reformation and later, but Flavel would doubtless enjoy the fine set of carved bench-ends that attract so many visitors today. I wonder how he interpreted some of their designs? A few are clear enough. He would probably smile over those that caricature a few bygone clergy, but one carving might have baffled him as it has baffled others. It is supposed to represent Jonah in the whale's belly—'an intelligent anticipation', says the author of the church handbook, 'of X-ray photography'.

Flavel wins his place here chiefly because he was an extra-sensory of his day, and kept strange company.

Being a staunch Royalist he had known what it meant to go into hiding during the Commonwealth. A contemporary tells us that he vowed 'never to cut off his Beard until the return of His Majesty to his Kingdoms; by which time he had gotten a Very Long One'. I suspect that the long, flowing beard was also part of his disguise. However, when King Charles (the Second) came back to his throne, Flavel returned to his grand old church, free now to serve the faithful —and to follow his secret bent.

Like Dr John Dee, whom we encountered in Manchester, Flavel was on intimate terms with unseen powers. One day, while in church, word came to him that something was amiss at the vicarage. A maid-servant had opened one of his necromantic books and 'a host of spirits sprang up around her'. Flavel stopped the service, dismissed the congregation, and sped home like the wind.

The poor girl was already black and blue with the pinchings and punchings inflicted by the malevolent creatures, when the parson arrived. But he soon had the situation in hand. Seizing the offending book, he read out backwards the magical words that had released the pandemonium, and then swung right and left with his walking-stick. This was too much for the spirits. They had met their match, and vanished. When peace and normality were restored, the girl needed no reprimand for her prying ways. She was cured for once and all.

Flavel's reputation as an exorcist spread throughout the neighbourhood. The Lizard was behind no other district with its supernatural terrors. There were pixies who led unwary people into danger on the terrible rocks. There were ghosts, too, and witches who tried to steal holy water from the church fonts. The Devil himself had set his stamp on several places, as anybody can see today from local maps. So there was much work awaiting Flavel when he cut off that promissory beard.

He was once asked to lay a ghost that haunted a neighbouring churchyard. Flavel, alive to this world as well as the unseen one, demanded five pounds for his services. Two of the petitioners decided that in return for this fantastic fee (for those days) they would keep watch from behind a convenient gravestone at the appointed time. To learn Flavel's secret might justify the expense. They duly heard the parson crack his whip at the haunted spot, and utter a few strange incantations. But their full reward came when, after that first whip-crack, a wild figure peered at them from the opposite tombstone before quitting its earthly prison. The onlookers also fled.

Parson Flavel, who seemed to have the knack of communicating with the nether world, would have been mighty pleased could he have known that almost three hundred years after his time, a Telstar station would be communicating unseen messages to many countries of this world, and doing so from Goonhilly Downs, within three or four miles of his beloved church at Mullion.

There were some who believed that Thomas Flavel reappeared in the parish 150 years after his death, in 1682. The parson of that later day, another exorcist, had to set him at rest. I do not think he has reappeared lately. Perhaps the mysterious powers at work on Goonhilly today—exceeding his own by far—have given him final release.

CHAPTER SEVENTEEN

LOST AND FOUND

'We found the Prior a very honest conformable person, and the house well furnysschide with juellys [jewels] and plate, *whereof some be mete for the King's majestie [h]is use.* 'The said 'house' was Christchurch Priory in Hampshire, and the King, Henry VIII. His commissioners supplied the above report on 2 December 1539. In purpose and greed it echoes dozens of such reports from all over the country, for Henry was polishing off the monasteries—and taking his pickings.

This is no place to examine his motives. What concerns us is the way in which abbots and priors usually tried to outwit the King's minions. The hallowed buildings they could not save (with a few notable exceptions), but the precious contents might be hidden from sacrilegious hands and recovered, perhaps, when the trouble 'blew over'.

And so we get yet another point of focus for our nation-wide survey. Threatened with extinction, the monasteries turned to guile.

At Roche Abbey in South Yorkshire the precious altar vessels were not of silver, but pewter. The Cistercian monks hid them for a time in some natural cavities that can still be seen. The magnesian limestone crags that overhang the abbey ruins are riddled with these vughs. Normally, birds build their nests in them. I wonder where the monks' treasure is now?

One may well wonder the same thing at other abbeys, too. Were the monks' hiding-places effective? Where were those hides, and was the treasure they concealed ever recovered? A thrilling book could be written on that theme alone. Here we shall search as we can, hoping for reward in the shape of stirring tales and traditions.

Of course, the trouble instigated by an avaricious Henry never did 'blow over'. The reformers remained in the saddle and the monks were scattered, taking their secrets with them. Sometimes they took them to their graves. No small part of the archaeologist's task is to tune in to that period, following any clue that might help to unlock the 'back door' of the Reformation.

On visiting some monastic site there is always the chance that one might be standing on or near the hidden cache. When on holiday at Ballycastle, Co. Antrim, many years ago, some friends and I spent the whole of one summer evening trying to light a peat fire on the beach (for some nocturnal frivols), without giving a thought to the ruins of Bonamargy Abbey frowning upon us nearby. Being novices with peat, we did not get the fire aglow. Had we been better informed about other matters, just then, those futile hours might have been turned to good account. For a knowledgeable Irishman will tell you that the Franciscan friars of Bonamargy buried their treasure in the sand, and that it has never been found. *In the sand.* And our little guest-house party was only concerned with potatoes that would not roast!

I suppose the next best thing to finding such treasure oneself is to meet and talk with a witness of some notable discovery. This was my experience not long ago on revisiting Rievaulx Abbey in North Yorkshire. Rievaulx enjoys one of the most beautiful monastic sites in all Britain, and there is still much to admire among the extensive ruins.

When the abbey was surrendered on 3 December 1538 the commissioners placed its annual value at £278 10*s* 2*d*—a large sum for those days. There would be the usual gloating over a fat prize for the King. But several items eluded them—things that only emerged this century, when the Ministry of Works started to renovate the place.

Robert Richardson, a local man, was one of the Ministry's first employees on the site. As a boy he had romped with his playmates over the heaps of debris that had accumulated in the nave and elsewhere. A photograph taken about that time shows what a dump Rievaulx had become. Then, within a few short years, Richardson was on the staff, helping to sift the debris of his old 'playground'. Beneath one rubbish heap, at the west end of the nave, seven pigs of lead were found—each still bearing the seal of King Henry VIII. The lead had been melted from the roofs and stamped in readiness for disposal at the King's pleasure and profit. Somehow those few ingots, representing part of the spoil, were forgotten. There is a notion that they were hidden at first beneath fallen masonry, pushed over deliberately by sympathizers with the dispossessed monks. Time, and the heavy hand of neglect, would effectively complete the secret.

Exciting enough, but Mr Richardson witnessed other discoveries. 'I was present', he said, 'when the silver chalice was found.' We walked with him through the lovely choir arcading and beyond, and then he stopped, beside the shaft of a broken column. 'The chalice was found in this pillar, in a small space that looked as though it could have been specially scooped out for it.' Then he added, 'I remember a gold crucifix turning up in the nave, also. Where are these treasures now? In London, I suppose.'*

To Mr Richardson, who was still a youth at the time, it was the discovery itself that chiefly mattered. And the thrill of it has remained with him—a thrill to recapture for the benefit of any interested visitors in these latter days as he goes around, fondly cherishing the ancient fabric he helped to 'liberate'.

Between 1919 and 1931 Rievaulx yielded many other features, doubtless hidden at the time of the Reformation. Why the monks should wish to preserve an instrument of torture is anybody's guess, but concealed there in the abbey dorter was a bronze scourge, split at one end into four tails terminating in knots. Extremely rare, it throws an esoteric light on the Middle Ages, when erring monks could be chastised in this manner, or even flagellate themselves to gain merit.

A shoe-sole modelled in lead was another of the Ministry's finds. It would be used by some pilgrim as an offering to a medieval shrine—possibly the shrine of Abbot William, found and uncovered here in the 1920s. Also, there were rosary beads in amber, ivory, and jet; various coins, and a roundel or tag probably fixed at one time to the leather case that would hold the Abbot's chalice when he journeyed afar to daughter monasteries. Perhaps the most surprising find was the chessmen, some made of bone, others of jet. If these had turned up in the abbey guest-house, where influential visitors had to be entertained, it would have seemed natural. But the bone king had wandered to the north wall of the nave, and the jet rook to a spot between the frater and the dorter.

The eagle on a fine brass lectern at Southwell Minster, Nottinghamshire, has undergone even stranger adventures. Its first home was Newstead Abbey, a few miles away, where it was a memorial to Prior Savage who had died in 1503. The late Provost of Southwell suggested that the Newstead monks might have used it for collecting Peter's

* R. Gilyard-Beer, Assistant Chief Inspector of Ancient Monuments at the Ministry of Public Building and Works, tells me that the 'silver chalice' must be a rather confused memory of what was actually found, namely, two small leaden caskets, or relic holders, which were claimed by Lord Feversham as owner of the site.

Pence; coins put into the eagle's beak would slide into a box at the end of its tail. At the Dissolution, however, the eagle received something of really prime importance. To outwit Henry VIII's commissioners the monks stuffed their title deeds into the globe on which the eagle is perched, and then flung the whole thing into their fishpond—hoping to recover it later when Henry's wrath had abated.

But the eagle stayed in its unnatural element for two hundred years, being dredged up at last—along with two brass candlesticks—by the fifth Lord Byron (uncle of the poet) who had meanwhile inherited Newstead. Having impoverished the estate, this 'wicked Lord' raised a little ready cash by selling a few things to Sir Richard Kaye. In high glee, Kaye wrote to the Duke of Portland in December 1775: 'I have bought Lord Byron's strong beer for my parish, and his brass Eagle for Southwell, at very good bargains . . . I have also got his Orange and Lemon trees.'

Kaye had made an even better bargain than he knew; the eagle still contained the monastic deeds, which were only discovered while the ornament was being cleaned. The eagle's globular perch had miraculously kept them intact. A treasure of great antiquarian importance, the deeds were, I understand, distributed between Newstead Abbey and the British Museum.

It is fascinating to walk around Newstead today, pondering over the place which, as Byron the poet was to write:

> . . . lies perhaps a little low,
> Because the monks preferred a hill behind,
> To shelter their devotions from the wind.

The abbey's 'low' position gave the estate its beautiful lakes and ponds. Beside the Upper, or Great Lake, the fifth Lord built a few follies; they matched his crazy nature and later won the reputation of being haunted. It seems strange that after his recovery of the brass eagle he paid no further attention to the particular pond that had kept it in secret for so long.

The Eagle Pond was described by Nathaniel Hawthorne as a sheet of water resembling 'an immense looking-glass, of which the terraces form the frame'. Here, within a few yards of the former cloister, a psychic person might sense the past, with monks flitting to and fro. Such paranormal phenomena have been reported several times in recent years at Beaulieu, in Hampshire, and at Fountains Abbey in

West Yorkshire. But the fifth Lord Byron was too impatient to be psychic; too forthright and demanding. Even tangible things could and did escape his grasp.

On returning to Newstead with a party of friends he sent orders ahead that the pond had to be refilled at once. The eagle and the candlesticks had already been salvaged, but two large, heavy-looking chests had also been glimpsed. What might not they contain! But there was no time to probe further. So that Lord Byron and his guests should be spared the sight of a little mud, water was fed into the pond again. The chests receded from view, and have been submerged ever since. Another search last century had to be abandoned as the mud suffocated one of the investigators.

But the Newstead monks still retained another secret. In 1966 a mechanical shovel on a new building site at Fishpool, fairly near the abbey, scooped out of the ground a large hoard of gold coins—one of the largest hoards ever found in Britain. The coins are of English, Scottish, and continental types. There is some contemporary jewellery, too. A report in front of me estimates the total value of the find at about a hundred thousand pounds, though at the time of writing the hoard is still being evaluated by experts.

A picture already conjured in the minds of many is that of a few monks from Newstead burying this wealth here, on the northern fringe of their lands, to save it from the rapacious intruders. Henry VIII certainly enriched his coffers at the expense of the monasteries, but how very much he missed! And the monks of Newstead were not the only ones who proved too clever for him. Like Southwell Minster, the fine old church at Isleham, in Cambridgeshire, treasures an eagle lectern that had been spirited out of sight. It was recovered from the fen dyke towards the end of the nineteenth century. Other churches can play a variation on the same theme.

On travelling through the Mendip country of Somerset, towards the Bristol Channel, there is apparently nothing to turn one's thought, say, to Canterbury Cathedral and the murder there of Thomas à Becket on 29 December 1170. The mysteries of Wookey Hole and the Cheddar caves are far more likely to have people in thrall. And yet this wonderful countryside has or had an arresting link with Becket.

Out there in the Channel, Steep Holme and Flat Holme rear up like huge stepping-stones against the glistening shores of South Wales, far beyond. The 'stepping-stones' which accounted for the arrival of the Becket Cup at Kewstoke Church, near Weston-super-Mare, are dim to the inward vision. But it does nobody any harm, occasionally, to make some leap of the imagination. It is certainly necessary here, to fill out the known story.

Becket's murder needs no re-telling from me. Chaucer's *Canterbury Tales* evoke some of the pilgrims who made their way in springtime to the shrine later set up at Canterbury Cathedral in Becket's honour. The shrine was loaded with gifts, such as the great ruby presented by King Louis VII of France, and a golden rosary from Alderman Brown, a Canterbury plumber.

On all these venerated objects the pilgrims gloated. For three and a half centuries the lovely lanes of Kent brought them cantering along, each pilgrim yearning for a sight of the relics and, perhaps, for a cure of some malady.

And then came the chill wind of the Dissolution. In 1538 the irrepressible Henry swooped on Canterbury Cathedral, destroying Becket's shrine and making off with its accumulated treasures.

But one thing had already gone—the wooden cup which caught Becket's blood when he had fallen to the sword. The cup seems to have been sold to Woodspring Priory, overlooking Bristol Channel near Weston-super-Mare. When the agents of the Dissolution turned their attention in due course to Woodspring, the cup was sent on some fresh travels. But what these were, nobody seems to know. All we hear is that some nameless person brought the cup to Kewstoke and hid it in the church wall, placing a small sculptured figure in front as a kind of guardian. The figure is a guardian no longer. After the cup was found, still 'stained with human blood', according to one account, it joined other treasures in Taunton Museum.

Other secret travels tease the mind when one is shown a very beautiful pre-Reformation cross, some fourteen inches high, at St Oswald's Church in Durham City. The cross was taken out of its cover for me by the vicar, during the last war, as a kind of reward for photographically recording his church in case of bomb damage. It was a happy gesture; appropriate too, for peril of another sort—probably the Dissolution again—would account for this silver processional cross, embodying the figures of Christ, Mary, and St John, being uprooted. But from what monastery or church nobody can tell. Its history is entirely lost. And the mystery deepens on hearing how it turned up, about 1860.

A coach had disgorged its passengers at the Three Tuns Inn nearby. Some unknown person left behind on his seat a curious package. It contained this cross. The owner was never traced, so the innkeeper got rid of the 'bit of popery' by handing it over to St Oswald's. Although the workmanship is probably of the thirteenth century, the simple cross seems a fitting possession for this fine, riverside church dedicated to the royal saint of Saxon times who befriended the poor and carefully explained Aidan's teaching to his thegns.

I have mentioned Becket's shrine at Canterbury and its increasing popularity with pilgrims. Other great religious centres, like York and Beverley, became jealous and earnestly desired a saint who might divert the flow of pilgrims, especially their offerings, to the northern part of the kingdom. This rivalry is well known to students of history, but one would hardly expect somebody's need for a garage, in twentieth-century York, to supplement the old story.

While digging out the garage foundations, in the Hungate area of the city, about ten years ago, workmen unearthed a strange heap of slabs. They were alabaster tablets, five of them, all facing downwards in a shallow depression as though to protect their decorative side. The different parts of an old reredos, it would seem, and deliberately buried, most likely at the Reformation when such ornaments could jeopardize any church because they smacked of Popery.

What are the designs? In vivid manner they illustrate various episodes concerning the life and cult of William Fitzherbert—York's riposte to Becket. The first tablet represents the birth of William, with his uncle, King Stephen, standing beside the bed. A nurse fondles the babe while a posset is being prepared nearby for the prostrate mother.

In the second tablet William is about to perform one of his miracles, near Ouse Bridge. So many people had assembled there to greet him that the bridge collapsed, precipitating most of the crowd including several horses into the water. The alabaster shows Ouse Bridge disintegrating in very truth, owing to its prolonged burial in a damp place.

Two further miracles appear on the fourth tablet. William—although long departed to his fathers—was credited with the rescue of King Edward I when he fell from a great height on a Welsh mountain. In this alabaster the King is shown in the act of falling, and one may suppose the queenly figure standing by in supplication is his affrighted Eleanor. With typical naïveté and economic use of the available space, the alabasterer turned the bottom of the Welsh hill into a vignette of the River Ouse at York, where a fisherboy is drowned and then restored to life.

Eventually, William's remains were translated from his tomb in the nave of York Minster to a specially prepared shrine behind the High Altar. The ceremony this entailed animates another alabaster panel, leaving the fifth of the series for a portrayal of Christ.

This fine little picture gallery, now displayed in the Yorkshire Museum at York, may have been made originally for St William's College, near the Minster. But nobody can be sure. A four-hundred-year-old secret does not peel off all its layers straight away—if ever.

At the Reformation many such alabasters were taken down and sold abroad, some to be recovered in better times, when people could safely give them house or church room without incurring anybody's wrath or a government penalty. But others were buried, as at York. It is fitting that Nottingham, which fostered England's most important school of alabasterers in medieval times should now have the finest collection of its own bygone products in this *genre*. They are displayed in Nottingham Castle.

If any visitor will spend an hour or so among these curious little passports to the medieval period, with all its mysticism and broad humour, he will be enriched. If, also, he reads the available handbook, by Francis Cheetham, the more secretive aspect of the subject will emerge, for several of the alabasters shown here, and others mentioned by the author, were long hidden away.

In the Nottingham Castle collection three notable figures represent the Virgin suckling her child, St Peter, and an unnamed Bishop—possibly St Wilfrid of York. All were carved about 1400 and—to save them from Henry VIII's image-breakers—all were ignominiously entombed beneath the floor of Flawford Church, near Nottingham. Some workmen found them in 1779.

Breadsall Church in Derbyshire kept its secret for another century; then, in 1877, an alabaster showing what would be called Our Lady of Pity in the Middle Ages, reappeared from beneath the church floor. At Ripon Cathedral a fine rendering of John the Baptist's head being served up on the charger had been buried among the dead in the churchyard. Worshippers at St Peter's Church, on the Isle of Thanet in Kent, came and went for generations without suspecting that beneath their feet was an unfinished work of art. Another alabaster, this, yet still in the embryonic form indicated by a few incised lines. The craftsman evidently had to hide it hurriedly, in view of the general interdict against 'images of stone, timber, alabaster', etc. Had he lingered over his tablet it might have been too late. The penalty for having custody of such 'idolatrous' stuff was a heavy fine or 'imprisonment at the King's will . . .'

Apart from the Flawford examples it is not known which, if any, of the alabasters in the Nottingham collection were hidden at or about that time. Some, however, have clearly undergone adventures. The Entry Into Jerusalem, for example, has a bad break right across the feet of Christ's donkey. A fracture also appears on another fine alabaster, one depicting St Eloy shoeing a horse—but this fracture is part of the episode. As the horse was uneasy, Eloy somehow removed the leg to be shod, restoring it to the surprised animal later.

Stories of a miraculous nature were part of an alabasterer's stock-in-trade. Perhaps that was an added cause for the interdict, which continued through several reigns. Yet there were always a few people willing to run the risk of saving some cherished altarpiece or image. I am permitted to quote the following passage from Francis Cheetham's splendid handbook:

> . . . during the reign of Queen Elizabeth the ecclesiastical commission for the province of York recorded on the 25th of October [1567] a case of the wilful concealment of an alabaster alterpiece at Ripon, against Thomas Blackburn, Richard Terry, Ninian Atkinson, and two others, all of whom were Vicars of Ripon Minster: 'The said Vicars took the keys of the church from . . . the sacristan there and that night all the images and other trumpery were conveyed forth . . . and bestowed by the said Vicars where it is not known . . . In addition to this there is a house within a vault of the said church yet remaining reserved 6 great tables of alabasters full of images and 49 books, etc.'

Mr Cheetham concludes, 'It seems likely from their survival until 1567 that the images, books and alabaster altarpiece . . . were hidden away in the reign of Edward VI, brought out again during the reign of the Catholic Queen Mary, and were hidden again after the accession of Queen Elizabeth.'

At one church I know, the search for missing alabasters has lately been resumed. This is the fine, fifteenth-century church of St Michael the Archangel at Kirkby Malhamdale—a West Yorkshire parish which includes many of Britain's more important limestone wonders. Zealots have been digging and probing hereabouts for many a long year, but a few have now started excavating near this church, with the vicar's encouragement.

He was digging too, that cold, dank November afternoon when we called. After a swift change into his cassock, he then led us across to the church.

The building has several remarkable features, notably a series of niches cut in the nave pillars. There are six of them (and a seventh on the south wall)—but all empty! Quite clearly they were meant to contain figures, which would be about eighteen inches high. A crown and monogram carved above one niche indicates that its missing figure was that of Christ. 'Other niches', said the Vicar, 'are known to have accommodated the Virgin Mary, St Syth, St Nicholas, and St Dominic.' The carved surrounds are all different, ranging from crosses and flowers to comic little heads.

When did Our Lord and his retinue depart from these lovingly prepared niches? It is a moot point. The figures may have been buried, like so many others, at the Reformation, but the Vicar propounded another theory.

In 1655 Oliver Cromwell came to stay with his friend, General Lambert, at Calton Hall in the same parish. As evidence of this visit we were shown Cromwell's supposed signatures, three of them, in the marriage register covering that year. 'Somebody could have taken the register over to Calton for the great man to sign,' the Vicar suggested, 'for then, as now, people loved being buttered up.' A newly married couple would bask in the prestige value of Cromwell's signature against their own. But there was a snag. Cromwell abhorred statues! Even if he never set foot in this church, there was a danger that he might hear of the alabaster figures through one of the soldiers who then garrisoned the place. So, the theory continues, the 'offending' images could have been carefully removed from their niches, one dark night, and given interment somewhere until Cromwell should leave the district. There is no sign that the figures were torn down, ruthlessly, as elsewhere. But if devoted hands removed them, as suggested, why did memory fail when it was safe to reinstate them?

It is still an open question. Perhaps, after all, the Reformation offers the better solution. Meanwhile, the niches are still bare and forlorn; and the digging goes on, in the vicarage garden.

When trying to assess the range of the British heritage, due place must be found for secrecy in all its manifold forms. That heritage flowers gloriously in our ancient cathedrals and in many of our town and village churches, but, as already indicated, its story sometimes falters on the brink of mystery or the unknown. Two further examples must suffice here, though dozens could be cited from many parts of the country.

I remember once sailing up Ranworth Broad in Norfolk to see the impressive fifteenth-century church at its head. Of several lovely things that stirred my admiration, easily the best was an illuminated manuscript called the Sarum Antiphoner. Its 285 pages are actually pieces of sheepskin and on some of them the monks of neighbouring Langley Abbey painted a great variety of colourful pictures to illustrate the text. That was in the year 1400. Then, 152 years later, the book was 'shut', by order of King Edward VI, and went perforce into hiding. But as to *where* it went, there is no known record.

Queen Victoria had been on the throne fourteen years before it was heard of again. An art collector had somehow acquired the treasure. But it was a London bookseller—after the collector's death—who traced the manuscript back to Ranworth. And a few months later, for the sum of five hundred pounds, Ranworth recovered the lost 'picture book'. It had been swallowed up as effectively as Jonah by the whale—one of the incidents so curiously portrayed in the Antiphoner. The monastic limner must have been very conscious of the surrounding countryside, for surely this particular scene is modelled on one of the reed-fringed Broads! A homely venue for Jonah's strange exile and eventual return.

As Jonah disappeared into his 'great fish' so did Elijah into his cave—when Queen Jezebel was making things too hot for him. The monks of Olney Abbey, Buckinghamshire, treasured a fourteenth-century painting of this biblical subject, which included the friendly ravens that fed him. Then called the 'Elijah of Olney', it was one of the most widely known religious pictures of the Middle Ages. At the Dissolution it vanished. Olney was among the first and richest of Henry VIII's spoils, but the Old Testament prophet escaped him, as in the Bible story he escaped Ahab and Jezebel. He went into some wilderness, and the manner of it all long remained unknown. When Frank Kendon came to write his masterly book, *Mural Paintings in English Churches during the Middle Ages*, he could only record, sadly, 'Elijah fed by Ravens was painted on a panel of the screen at Olney, but no longer exists . . .'

Happily, he was mistaken. 'Elijah's' travels after leaving Olney so hurriedly only came to light, later, though few, if any, seemed to realize where he had set out from. At the Dissolution the painting was surreptitiously sent for safe keeping to the Abbot of Talley Abbey in Carmarthenshire—until 'that tyranny was overpast'. But the same tyranny spread and soon overtook Talley. Elijah was hastily despatched once more, this time to Dolaucothi, the 'big house' of its neighbourhood, away there in the Welsh hills.

But there was still no fixed abiding place for poor Elijah. One of the Johnes family of Hafod, near Devil's Bridge in Cardiganshire, borrowed the painting; when this mansion was burnt down it was assumed that Elijah had perished also. But he turned up once more, quite unscathed, and ready for another journey—now to Clumber, the Nottinghamshire home of the Duke of Newcastle. In more recent years the painting was bought, at Christie's, by Mr Herbert Lloyd-Johnes and restored to its Welsh setting at Dolaucothi.

Yet another transfer awaited Elijah and his ravens. When Dolaucothi was acquired by the National Trust, in 1941–3, the prophet left this region which the Romans had mined for gold, and settled at St David's Cathedral. There he can now be seen, in the south transept, watching from the cave mouth as the ravens drop food into his little hanging basket. Judging by an inset at the top left corner he is thinking back to his triumph over the priests of Baal on Mount Carmel . . .

From leafy Buckinghamshire to the rocky headland of St David's in South Wales, with several hazards *en route*, and more than a dash of secrecy; all this makes one of the most exciting itineraries sponsored, however unwittingly, by the rapacious Henry.

Of course, Henry VIII and his anti-Catholic offspring cannot be blamed for every mysterious disappearance from monastery or church. Other agencies have sometimes been at work. But the charge against King Henry is certainly heavy.

For the last four hundred years or so visitors to Winchester Cathedral have hoped to see the final resting-place of that old-time weather prophet, St Swithun, who was bishop of this diocese from A.D. 852 to 862. Not only was Swithun's shrine destroyed by Henry's commissioners in 1538, however, but the very site was left unmarked. It was just too bad. Evidently the Friends of Winchester Cathedral thought the same, and decided to act. This they did, in 1962, by providing a new shrine, on or near the proper site, in the present retrochoir. Nobody can overlook the shrine, for it is suitably embellished and on festal days a canopy is slung over—a velvet canopy with ruchings to simulate heavy clouds and pear-shaped pendants of glass for raindrops.

But the old doubts have since returned. Current excavations lead those responsible to say that even now nobody really knows where Swithun's body rests.

Traditionally, Swithun had requested a humble burial, in the open, 'where the faithful going in to prayer would walk upon his body, and the drops of rain from the roof would fall on his grave'. It sounds as though Swithun longed for obscurity as much as any medieval anchorite. According to the same tradition, his wishes were countermanded, in the year 971, when the authorities translated his remains to the interior of the cathedral. Swithun's annoyance at this betrayal seems to have shown itself in the deluge that fell and continued to fall for the next forty days; all because his secret slumbers had been disturbed.

But if the present investigators are able to prove their theory that from the very outset Swithun enjoyed a good, comfortable, well-recognized place for his bones *inside* the old minster, yet another hoary tradition will be banished to the realm of fairy tale.

If modern methods of enquiry should explode several ancient ideas, there is often some compensation. Romance may take on a new guise. Occasionally, of course, it is the archaeologists who produce the rabbit out of the hat. And it is they who propound newer puzzles.

I am thinking in particular of the work even now going forward at York Minster. Extensive repairs to the huge fabric are presenting archaeologists with a unique opportunity, for the very foundations of the building are under scrutiny.

In the process even Walter de Gray, the master builder at York, who died in 1255, has given up a secret or two. At some time his tomb in the south transept was evidently made into a kind of refuse dump. In it have been found these strange objects—a few clay pipes, several shards of pottery, a George III halfpenny, and part of a wig-curler. Walter de Gray must have been surprised when they dropped in beside him, through a gap in the stonework. But who pushed them through?

This is where imagination comes into play. Obviously, the oddments are of the eighteenth century. 'The source of these objects is a matter of speculation', says the archaeologist in charge. 'One possibility is that they came from the kitchen of the Dean of York of the period. The pottery is good quality and evidently belonged to a person of some wealth and distinction. The Dean's house is not far from the Minster and I imagine it would have been fairly easy for some serving maid to have carted some refuse across to the Minster, where it could be used for filling in a hole.'

A queer sort of votive offering. I wonder if the Dean knew, or approved?

Much better things than the above items have sometimes been discarded. A too thorough spring-clean was the probable cause of some fine woodwork, several monuments, and other decorations disappearing from the cathedral church of St Nicholas, Newcastle upon Tyne, in 1784–7. Some of the monuments were actually used to strengthen the foundations of Mosley Street, one of the town's eighteenth-century thoroughfares. These monuments are beyond recall, but in 1881 a beautifully carved chest inscribed 'Saynte Nycholas Newcastell, 1604' turned up 'from nowhere' at a local auction room. The purchaser kindly gave it back to the church, and it now stands in the south transept, near Nicholas Stone's fine monument to Henry Maddison, who had originally given the chest in 1604.

Oddly enough, another piece of furniture presented to the same church by Maddison and his wife, in 1604, returned not long ago. It is a credence table bearing their names, and probably disappeared with the chest in that eighteenth-century purge. Eventually, this table found a home at Carnfield Hall at Alfreton, in Derbyshire. How it got there is not known, but since the Friends of Newcastle Cathedral bought and returned the table, the inscriptions carved upon it—such as 'Doo this in remembrance of Mee'—have regained their significance. It is once more being used at Eucharist. The lost has been found and welcomed home.

To conclude this chapter we must turn once again to Scotland, for in Argyll there is an archaeological puzzle which lends itself to much scratching of pates. It is in the churchyard at Kilmartin.

With our usual exploratory friend, my wife and I had driven along the full length of Loch Awe, stopping every mile or so to feast on its almost ethereal beauty. Then we came quite suddenly upon a different kind of enchantment—a group of ancient carved stones. Little sign-posts in Kilmartin churchyard directed us to them, but as to their origin and meaning—silence. No explanatory leaflet was available in the church. Nobody in the village could do more than acknowledge their existence. The locals were apparently as much 'at sea' as we three Sassenachs.

Some of the stones speak for themselves, being clear, if mutilated representations of Christ and a few saints. The puzzle really began with a stone shelter and what it contains.

Looking within I got the impression of a medieval knight taking some sort of posthumous comfort from his proximity to several carved sacred emblems, including vine scrolls and other plant motifs. Although the shelter is open to the sky there is a strange peace about the place. Yet it is a precinct of something just beyond ordinary understanding, for why should that Crusader have Mactavish inscribed across his chest, and one of the carved emblems be overlaid with the unlikely name of John Lammo(?)t? What curious influence has been at work here?

I put this conundrum later to Miss Marion Campbell of Kilberry, who had already told me about the Torran Hoard. For answer to my query she introduced me to some strange byways of Scottish history.

The shelter I have mentioned is apparently the family grave of Neil Campbell, the last episcopalian Bishop of Argyll. His knightly companion owes his Mactavish label to those who gave him sanctuary here last century. Perhaps the knight came originally from Eilean Righ, an island in Loch Craignish which had belonged to this clan. A peculiar if traditional feature of the effigy is the awkward placing of the hands, with a sharp outward turn of the wrist. On this point Miss Campbell says, 'The only explanation I have ever heard is . . . that it symbolizes the knight laying his sword aside only in the hour of death.' The fifteenth-century stone to his left was perhaps a coffin lid, much admired for its vine pattern by somebody in the seventeenth or eighteenth century and therefore re-used on behalf of the said John Lammo(?)t.

Miss Campbell plunges deeper into the unknown when she says, of this same rugged shelter, 'I can't help wondering if the little building itself is possibly the earliest church [here] re-used and "fossilised" by being done up for the Bishop's grave'. In other words, some time last century, the shelter seems to have become a refuge for lost ecclesiastical property. The good people of Argyll might well be reticent about the Kilmartin stones. These are still on the secret list—waifs and strays from various sacred sites.

POSTSCRIPT

CHAPTER EIGHTEEN

WAR-TIME 'HIDES' (1939-45)

Few of the younger generation today can have any idea of the hide-outs that were used during the Second World War to protect the nation's art treasures. We have seen how man, from the earliest times, has repeatedly needed to conceal his prized belongings as assiduously as any squirrel with its nuts. That need was intensified a million-fold when the bombs started dropping over Britain in 1940.

Rarely, if ever, had there been so much secret coming and going throughout the country. One might see lorries hastening from our art galleries and museums to some unknown destination with carefully disguised loads. If anybody guessed what was happening they kept quiet. It was not wise to know too much just then. And hiding a nation's priceless art treasures represented only one phase of the general hush-hush system that modern war was so tragically bringing nigh to perfection. . . .

When the need for secrecy began to recede, towards the close of 1945, I undertook a survey for *Country Life* which disclosed many of the hide-outs that had been devised by museum and art gallery directors, librarians, church authorities, and other bodies. It was astonishing—and grimly amusing—to find how many of the old refuges, such as caves, quarries and cellars, had been requisitioned for this war-time purpose. The old primitive instinct had gained the ascendancy once more. True, there were refinements of the old hides, as we shall see, and many country houses in 'safe' areas gave harbourage—not to recusants or Royalists this time, but to fugitive Old Masters and sculptures and other threatened works of art.

By the outbreak of war the National Gallery had already dispersed two thousand pictures, mainly in country houses and provincial centres, including the National Library of Wales at Aberystwyth, and the University of Wales, Bangor. In 1941 the Treasury was asked to provide a safer repository, with the result that the Manod Slate Quarry, near Blaenau Festiniog in North Wales—reputed to be the deepest slate quarry in the world—was transformed into a series of strongrooms. Within quarry chambers cut three hundred feet deep into the mountainside, the Ministry of Works constructed five brick galleries for the reception of paintings by Titian, Rubens, El Greco, Michelangelo, etc., and for Hogarth's famous series, *The Rake's Progress* from Soane's Museum in Lincoln's Inn Fields. The pictures were fed into the quarry by a specially constructed light railway. To regulate the temperature and humidity, air-conditioning plant was installed. Alarm signals were also provided; steel doors closed upon the rock-chambers, which were guarded day and night by picked attendants.

The Tate Gallery collection was at first spread among three sanctuaries—Muncaster Castle high above Ravenglass in Cumberland; Hellens at Much Marcle in Herefordshire; and Eastington Hall, Worcestershire. Later, Sudeley Castle in Gloucestershire and a house not far away at Stow-on-the-Wold became secret outposts for the Tate. Other valuable exhibits stayed in London throughout the blitz, for the Tate housed a number of pictures in a disused section of the Underground—the Piccadilly tube—sharing this with the London Museum, Westminster Abbey—which placed its renowned wax effigies down there—and the Royal Academy.

Looking back it is curious to visualize all those studies from the National Portrait Gallery—Holbein's Henry VIII, Mary Queen of Scots, the Chandos Shakespeare, Sir Christopher Wren, Dr Samuel Johnson and so many more—finding asylum at Lord Rosebery's Buckinghamshire house, Mentmore, along with the statues of saints, apostles and philosophers from Westminster Abbey. It is strange also to think of Lord Hertford's treasures from the Wallace Collection—so many of which he bought from the French aristocracy who survived the Revolution—figuring again as emigrés, this time at Hall Barn, Beaconsfield and West Wycombe Park, Buckinghamshire.

Montacute House—that majestic National Trust property near Yeovil, Somerset—early became a 'foster parent' for the Victoria and Albert Museum, but the greater part of the V. and A. Collections went underground, later, in a limestone quarry near Bradford-on-Avon in Wiltshire. In this Bath Stone area, therefore, were kept such famous treasures as the Ardabil Carpet, the Constable paintings, the Gloucestershire Candlestick, Queen Elizabeth's virginal—probably the very instrument on which she beguiled her courtiers and ambassadors—and, not least, the 'idea notebooks' of Leonardo da Vinci.

Here again additional precautions were necessary. The air was mechanically filtered and cooled. Placed in the quarry at intervals were devices to indicate any change in humidity. Across the quarry chambers rays were directed which, if intercepted, would operate an alarm.

Wales, being a less vulnerable area, was able to put on public display several masterpieces from the great London collections. A selection of the historic armour from the Tower of London was sent to the National Museum of Wales, at Cardiff. King Henry VIII—founder of the Armouries collection—was appropriately represented by a mounted figure wearing the engraved suit of mail given to him by the Emperor Maximilian. At the Fall of France, however, Henry and his armoured companions left Cardiff for the greater security of Caernarvon Castle. What an ignominious retreat it must have seemed!

The country house plan accounted for several piquant situations. Haigh Hall, near Wigan, Lancashire, opened its cellars to some drawings by Flaxman, Chantrey, Robert Adam, and others, all from Soane's Museum. I think old John Soane, who chose his own London cellar for that alabaster coffin of Pharaoh Seti I, would have applauded the site. The prison at Shepton Mallet, Somerset, took into temporary custody many things from the Public Record Office, notably Domesday Book, the ancient royal seals, and some bygone treaties with France, Spain, Portugal, etc. Documents revealing the Gunpowder Plot; various Jacobite items including 'A Chart Wherein are mark'd all the different Routs of P. Edward in Great Britain . . .'; Charles James Fox's application for £3,800 secret service money, in 1783; correspondence relating to the poet Shelley's activities in writing seditious papers at Lynmouth, North Devon, and despatching them across the Bristol Channel in bottles—these and many other fascinating records—their 'sting' long removed—were distributed among places like Belvoir Castle in Leicestershire, Haddon Hall in Derbyshire, Clandon Park in Surrey, Grittleton House in Wiltshire, and Culham College, Oxfordshire.

Yet further country seats turned themselves into safe repositories at the nation's behest—Tattershall Castle peacefully mirrored in its moat in Lincolnshire; Wray Castle beside Windermere; and so many more. Tattershall and Wray were entrusted with specimens from the Natural History Museum, but its important type specimens, preserved in spirit, found refuge—quite fittingly—in the Carthouse Quarry at Godstone, in Surrey.

All these places have therefore an added appeal today for tourists. No longer can anybody say that such houses speak entirely of a bygone way of life. To me, Skipton Castle in West Yorkshire is not only the place from which some hostages once escaped by a hidden passage during the Wars of the Roses; and a rampart against the raiding Scots—but the destination of several of those war-time lorries from harassed, twentieth-century London. The British Museum had annexed part of Lady Anne Clifford's old home. Similarly, Temple Sowerby Manor—tucked away there almost at the foot of Cross Fell in Cumberland—had its long history revitalized by secreting a load of precious things from Manchester Art Gallery. Alnwick Castle, that imposing stronghold of the Percys, in Northumberland, is another of the places that befriended Manchester in its time of need. At Alnwick Castle the Manchester treasures would rub against such family heirlooms as Edward VI's gloves and Oliver Cromwell's nightcap!

Various items from our churches also found some strange bedfellows. But there were other adventures, too, all the more exciting because so very few people, then or since, were aware of them.

Think of St Paul's Cathedral. Protective work here was carried out by the Dean and Chapter, assisted by the Ministry of Works. Jean Tijou's wrought-iron grilles at the entrance to the choir aisles and Jesus Chapel, and his unique ironwork at the foot of the Geometrical Staircase, were taken down. Then they disappeared, along with the Grinling Gibbons carvings, Sir Christopher Wren's model of St Paul's, and other features. Some of them were stored throughout the war in the cathedral crypt; others left for certain country houses in Hertfordshire and Lancashire. Many of the cathedral monuments were entombed in brick casings. One exception was the well-known effigy of John Donne, the poet and a former Dean, which had survived the Great Fire of 1666. This was transferred to the crypt, where, during the desperate nights of 1940–1, it lay side by side with the current Dean of St Paul's, when this gentleman was off fire-guard duty.

Forgotten chapters in ecclesiastical history came to light through different storage schemes devised by some of the provincial cathedrals. At Lincoln, wooden cases containing the old stained glass, such as the Bishop's Eye and the Dean's Eye, were relegated to an underground chamber—part of some workings where, it is now thought, Remigius might have obtained the stone for the cathedral he began here nine hundred years ago. With thirty feet of solid oolite overhead, this chamber was excavated from a passage found by accident some years before the war. Mr Godfrey, then cathedral Clerk of Works at Lincoln, had made the initial discovery. As he told me the story I realized that what had intrigued him most was not the human skulls and the bison remains found down there, but the draughts of fresh air that greeted him and his men. The air came through gaps in the stone beds and served, very conveniently, to give natural ventilation to the war-time treasure chamber.

Oscar G. Farmer has left an interesting account of how the famous stained-glass windows at Fairford Church, in the lovely Cotswold countryside, were saved. At his suggestion these fifteenth-century scriptural windows were taken out in 1939 and buried in some stone vaults beneath the large house in Fairford Park. 'When all was complete the cases were lowered down into the vaults on rollers running upon a long wooden ramp, and the opening was walled up.' That is where Eve, Moses, Gideon, Solomon, and all the rest of this colourful company were imprisoned for the next six years. All the pageantry had gone out of the church.

In September 1945 Mr Farmer went along to release them. He wrote: 'I broke down the wall into the vaults and I raised the glass to floor level. It was all removed from vaults to church within the day.' Almost two years elapsed, however, before the restoration was complete and Fairford became its lovely self again. While doing repairs, bygone glaziers had made mistakes, in some instances reducing the clear message of the windows to something obscure and doubtful. Such enigmas had to be clarified before Fairford could again speak to the people through its priceless glass.

A similar story could be told about York Minster and its stained glass. Here, no fewer than eighty windows were removed, mostly to the cellars of various country houses that seemed to live in a dream. I was present when much of this glass returned, after the war, and it was my pleasure, later, to look on while the Minster glaziers rectified bygone errors that had rendered many of the windows quite meaningless. Short of shattering the glass, Cromwell's iconoclasts could hardly have destroyed their original significance more effectively. The windows had become gigantic jig-saw puzzles; it took several postwar years to unravel them.

One other treasure house of York must be mentioned—All Saints'

Church in North Street. Its windows spent three years in the basement of Thorganby Hall, in the East Riding. The subject of one especially famous fourteenth-century window still seems apt in this newer age with its threatened Armageddon. The window's vividly portrayed scenes are based on a contemporary poem, *The Pricke of Conscience*—some unknown person's startling vision of the Last Fifteen Days of the World.

We see the overthrow of towns, with buildings crashing in ruin; fire spreading everywhere, so that even the sea-serpents rise up in protest; men and their families hiding from the general holocaust in wayside caves; then—on the fifteenth day—the chaotic end of all things. The Great Secret behind the universe is reserved for the tracery lights. Heaven is at one side, with Peter giving a hearty welcome to the good folk. But Hell, on the opposite side, seems to be much busier!

At Durham Cathedral valuables that included the remarkable Cuthbert relics and accoutrements—found when the saint's tomb was opened in 1827, were removed to a vaulted stone chamber which had long served only for lumber. Few visitors knew of its existence, though it once went by the name of the Spendiment. Situated on the west side of the cloister, it was the treasure chamber of monastic times, where not only the monks but noble families hid their precious belongings when raiders were abroad. But two of the Cuthbert vestments, known today as the Horseman and Byzantine Textiles, in which the saint's remains were robed, were on loan to the Victoria and Albert Museum at the outbreak of war in 1939. So, for once in their long history which dated back to Saxon times, the vestments were parted from the other Cuthbert relics, and went with the museum's own treasures into that quarry near Bradford-on-Avon.

The Central Council for the Care of Churches was instrumental in saving many church fittings. These were collected from St Paul's, Southwark, Exeter, Salisbury, Portsmouth and Lichfield cathedrals, and from many parish churches, and stored 'somewhere in the west of England'. The cellar of a large house on Exmoor—the Lorna Doone country—was used for valuable church plate. Other treasures were deposited in the huge, stone-vaulted crypt of a church rebuilt just over a century ago. Conveniently, this crypt had been subdivided for interments which never took place—until the said church fittings arrived.

As already observed, some of the older crypts were also pressed into service, becoming secretive places once again. At Gloucester Cathedral the crypt preserved the fourteenth-century east window which commemorates the men of Gloucestershire who fell at Crécy; also the Coronation Chair from Westminster Abbey. But my final word must be about the Saxon crypt, mentioned earlier, at Ripon Cathedral.

It is a miracle that Ripon's older crypt should have survived all the vicissitudes of thirteen centuries, for the superstructure was several times destroyed. Of this district Domesday simply records *Wasta*—a terse reference to William the Conqueror's scorched earth policy. The same crypt was practically all that remained of subsequent buildings overhead after various Scottish invasions. It seemed indestructible.

The crypt is reached through a trapdoor in the floor of the nave choir, though many visitors are completely unaware of its existence. A verger leads the way through the connecting underground passage and switches on a light that sends the shadows scuttling towards St Wilfrid's Needle—an aperture in the far wall of the crypt. I cannot decide which is the more eerie—the narrow cul-de-sac corridor leading round to the back of the Needle, or the main crypt chamber with its low, vaulted roof. A dozen people would fill the available space.

This was the place of reception chosen by the British Museum authorities, during the last war, for some of its smaller treasures. To keep them company there were nine cases of books from the British and Foreign Bible Society. Among those books was a manuscript translation of the Bible into the Tibetan language.

The story of this translation on behalf of the Land of Mystery, for so long closed to outsiders, is an epic in itself. The Ripon crypt represents just one of its many adventures.

Yoseb Gergan, the Tibetan scholar who made the translation, could have no conception of this Saxon centre of culture, or that the Bible he had toiled over for many years would at length become a 'refugee' like his father who first taught the language of the forbidden country to some missionaries. Neither would Gergan envisage the post-war perils—loss of the first printed proofs among the Himalayas, the constant threat of floods and obliterating snowstorms, encounters with Pakistani troops, etc. Eventually, faith and perseverance were rewarded. Printed Bibles have now reached a few Tibetan monasteries. Their priests—and a few Chinese troops also—have unhindered access to the words of Scripture concealed for six long years in that strange little crypt at Ripon.

That episode was kept a tight secret during the war. Most, if not all the clergy then at Ripon Cathedral have died. When I mentioned the matter to Canon Bartlett, a former cathedral librarian who is well into his nineties, he could only profess surprise and say, 'It must have been before my time as librarian.'

But for a brief sentence I happened to notice in an old, dog-eared Bible Society leaflet, Ripon's pivotal part in that epic might well have drifted into oblivion.

APPENDIX

(N.T.—National Trust)	*(Times of opening, subject to change)*
Arlington Court, 7 miles N.E. of Barnstaple, N. Devon *N.T.*	April to September; daily except Saturday; Bank Holidays
Athelhampton, near Dorchester, Dorset	Easter to September; Wednesday and Thursday, 2–6 p.m., and Bank Holidays
Blarney Castle, near Cork, Eire	Daily
Blickling Hall, 15 miles W. of Norwich *N.T.*	May to September; Wednesday, Thursday, Sunday, Bank Holiday, and Easter Monday afternoon
Bolton Castle, Wensleydale, N. Yorks	Daily
Bramham Park, 6 miles S. of Wetherby, W. Yorks	Easter to September; Sunday and Monday afternoon, and each Bank Holiday Tuesday
Brighton Pavilion, Brighton, Sussex	Daily
Burton Agnes Hall, near Driffield, E. Yorks	May to October; daily except Saturday
Burton Constable Hall, Sproatley, near Hull, E. Yorks	Easter Saturday to mid-October; Sunday, Tuesday, Wednesday, Thursday, Friday, and Bank Holiday Monday
Capheaton, 10 miles S.W. of Morpeth, Northumberland	To be opened eventually
Cliveden, near Maidenhead, Bucks *N.T.*	April to September; Wednesday afternoon; daily from mid-August to mid-September
Crantock Manor, near Newquay, Cornwall	Guest House
Culzean Castle, near Kirkoswald, Ayrshire *N.T.Scotland*	March to October; daily
Dunluce Castle, near Portrush, Co. Antrim	Frequently
Dunster Castle, near Minehead, Somerset	Regularly, but see local announcements
Epworth Rectory, Epworth, Lincs	Frequently
Gretna Hall, Dumfriesshire	Daily
Haddon Hall, near Buxton, Derbyshire	Regularly, but see local announcements
Hall-i'-th'-Wood, Bolton, Lancs	Frequently
Thomas Hardy's Cottage, Higher Bockhampton, near Dorchester, Dorset *N.T.*	Wednesday, Thursday, Sunday; 2–6 p.m.
Haworth Parsonage (Museum), Haworth, near Keighley, W. Yorks	Daily

Hodge Hill, Cartmel Fell, near Grange-over-Sands, Lancs	Guest House, etc.
Izaak Walton's Cottage, Swallowford, near Stafford	Daily
Levens Hall, near Kendal, Westmorland	See local announcements
Little Moreton Hall, near Congleton, Cheshire *N.T.*	March to October; daily except Friday
Lyme Park, Disley, Cheshire *N.T.*	March to November; daily
Margaret Clitherow's House, Shambles, York	Daily
Merchant Adventurers' Hall, Fossgate, York	Daily
Montacute, near Yeovil, Somerset *N.T.*	February to December; daily except Tuesday; Bank Holidays
Newburgh Priory, Coxwold, N. Yorks	Occasionally; see local announcements
Newstead Abbey, near Nottingham	Daily
Nostell Priory, 6 miles S.E. of Wakefield, W. Yorks *N.T.*	Easter to mid-October; Wednesday, Saturday, Sunday, Bank Holidays
Penfound Manor, Poundstock, Cornwall	Frequently
Plas Mawr, Conway, North Wales	Daily
Ripley Castle, near Harrogate, W. Yorks	May to September; Sunday, Monday, and August Bank Holiday Monday
Rufford Old Hall, near Ormskirk, Lancs *N.T.*	Weekdays except Monday; Bank Holiday Monday; Sunday 1 p.m.
Sawston, Cambridgeshire	See local announcements
Skipton Castle, Skipton, W. Yorks	Daily
Speke Hall, near Liverpool, Lancs *N.T.*	Throughout year, weekdays and Bank Holidays; Sunday 2 p.m.
Sudeley Castle, Winchcombe, Glos	April to September; Wednesday, Thursday, Sunday, and Bank Holidays
Tattershall Castle, near Woodhall Spa, Lincs *N.T.*	Daily
Temple Newsam House (Art Gallery), Leeds	Daily
Towneley Hall, Burnley, Lancs	Daily
Wallington, near Morpeth, Northumberland *N.T.*	Easter to end of September; Wednesday, Saturday, Sunday and Bank Holidays
Woolsthorpe Manor, near Grantham, Lincs *N.T.*	Monday, Wednesday, Saturday, 11 a.m. to 1 p.m.; 2.30 to 6 p.m.

INDEX